Praise fo
REPRODUC
RITES

T0277015

"*Reproductive Rites* is not only a fascinating and engaging read but, in our current post-Roe climate, a necessary one. From the time of the pharaohs to Donald Trump, Sophie Saint Thomas details society's conflicted relationship with reproductive rights. This volume offers readers exacting research into everyone from ancient midwives to modern day anti-choicers. The facts will help every reader understand how we came to find ourselves in our current position. And it's all presented with wit, humor, and verve that make it an unputdownable read for every feminist."

—Jennifer Wright, author of *Madame Restell: The Life, Death, and Resurrection of Old New York's Most Fabulous, Fearless, and Infamous Abortionist*

"An exciting, racy, angry, and well-informed survey, which ranges across a wide span of history in order to make points of tremendous relevance to the present."

—Ronald Hutton, author of *The Witch: A History of Fear, from Ancient Times to the Present*

"Through a cross-cultural lens, Saint Thomas offers us a fascinating exploration into the sociopsychological dynamics that underscore the practice of witch persecution and the ongoing oppression of women's reproductive rights. Her work is an incisive critique of human prejudice and its historical consequences."

—Alan Kilpatrick, author of *The Night Has a Naked Soul: Witchcraft and Sorcery among the Western Cherokee*

REPRODUCTIVE
RITES

THE
REAL-LIFE
WITCHES &
WITCH HUNTS
IN THE CENTURIES-LONG
FIGHT FOR
ABORTION

SOPHIE SAINT THOMAS

RUNNING PRESS
PHILADELPHIA

Running Press
Hachette Book Group
1290 Avenue of the Americas, New York, NY 10104
www.runningpress.com
@Running_Press

First Edition: October 2024

Published by Running Press, an imprint of Hachette Book Group, Inc.
The Running Press name and logo are trademarks of Hachette Book Group, Inc.

The Hachette Speakers Bureau provides a wide range of authors for speaking events. To find out more, go to www.hachettespeakersbureau.com or email HachetteSpeakers@hbgusa.com.

Running Press books may be purchased in bulk for business, educational, or promotional use. For more information, please contact your local bookseller or the Hachette Book Group Special Markets Department at Special.Markets@hbgusa.com.

The publisher is not responsible for websites (or their content) that are not owned by the publisher.

Cover illustration by Tanvi Baghele
Print book cover and interior design by Amanda Richmond

Library of Congress Control Number: 2024942015

ISBNs: 978-0-7624-8529-1 (paperback), 978-0-7624-8530-7 (ebook)

Printed in the United States of America

LSC-C

Printing 1, 2024

*This book is dedicated to
Major Tom Cat, my familiar who,
along with the lights of New York City,
kept me company during the many sleepless
yet productive nights over the year
this book was written.*

*And to my parents.
I'm glad that you're okay with an
orange tabby named after
David Bowie as your grandchild.*

CONTENTS

INTRODUCTION

I f you're searching for a nice book on reproductive rights, this one isn't for you. Put it down before Ron DeSantis sees, seriously. From the use of crocodile-dung suppositories to obtain an abortion in antiquity to Donald Trump's golden toilet, the imagery and themes present in the cultural history of pregnancy and political witch hunts reek of hypocrisy (and sometimes just reek), and this book isn't afraid to go there.

Reproductive Rites will seek to astonish you by presenting the unvarnished truth behind the thousands of years of history that led us to our current climate when it comes to abortion, birth control, and reproductive justice, as well as revealing the witches and witch hunts along the way. Whether you're uncovering reproductive trailblazers like Madame Restell, the "murderess" of Fifth Avenue in nineteenth-century New York, or contemporary activism through hexing anti-choice politicians, brace yourself for startling revelations.

We'll begin by exploring the landscape of reproductive justice and health care before the time of Jesus Christ. This era for the ancients was marked by a yearly calendar aligned with the three cycles of the Nile. (Fitting, given a modern reader might have other trimesters on their mind.) As you delve into the abortion practices and intimate lives of the elite from antiquity, it's easy to forget the era you're reading about. The echoing of these dynamics is all too familiar, whether it involves a politician (be it a president or a pharaoh) wanting to bang their own daughter, a government promoting reproduction during times of war, or, as seen quite literally in the case of alleged hysterectomies in US Immigration and Customs Enforcement (ICE) detention centers, a regime stripping away the health-care rights of those deemed inconvenient. If it feels as though little has evolved over the span of four thousand years, it's because, in many aspects, it truly hasn't.

Reproductive Rites is ripe with juicy legends, from the role of rape in the formation of Rome; to the historical burying (and ultimate #witchesofIG reclamation) of Lilith, Adam's alleged first wife, cast out for wanting to get on top during sex; to the infamous QAnon-propelled rumor that Hillary Clinton was partying with Lady Gaga by drinking babies' blood and eating pizza in a Washington, DC, party wilder than any I've ever been invited to.

During the COVID-19 pandemic, when the #witchesofIG hashtag might have included images of QAnon-believing, antivax wellness influencers, death enveloped the nation. Conservatives, commendably organized, capitalized on the prevalent fear, medical apprehension, and societal turmoil to push anti-abortion stances and other right-wing measures, including the criminalization of teaching children about trans-inclusive reproductive health care and outlawing drag queens in public. Looking on history, transitioning from ancient times to the Middle Ages, this 2020s scenario recalls events such as the animosity toward Asian people when merchant ships from Asia arrived in Sicily in October 1347 bearing deceased sailors and survivors riddled with pus-filled boils. Pandemics create ideal conditions for using collective crises as a pretense to reinforce social hierarchies, so it's no surprise that the Black Death stands as a grim milestone in the narratives of both reproductive rights *and* witch hunts, which peaked in what historians commonly term the "Great Hunt" between 1550 and 1650.

Together, we'll delve into some of these sensationalized witch hunts, like what happened in Salem in 1692, juxtaposing them against the authentic ones that had much greater human costs but are missing from the zeitgeist. Often, these genuine witch hunts are overlooked by the same contemporary witches who deny the influence of oppressive cultures on their own practices, the cultures that subjected Native peoples to brutality, enslaved Black people, and launched attacks on trans women far more lethal than the Salem trials. While the modern witchcraft movement may pride itself on inclusivity, those same white supremacist and colonialist influences continue to propel white women to the forefront while stifling the marginalized cultures the practice draws from.

Of all historical witch hunts, the Inquisition (the medieval Inquisition's bloodiest dates spanned from the 1250s through the mid-fifteenth century) remains noteworthy for its genuine belief in witches, amplified by real violence and persecution. This period was not just marked by bloodshed but also distinguished by the way accusations and their consequences emerged as a source of entertainment, with periodicals of the era brimming with more gossip than present-day celebrity Instagram accounts like @deuxmoi. Here we'll uncover the tale of Béatrice de Planisoles, a figure in the *Fournier Register*, an epic set of historical records kept by a cruel man named Jacques Fournier documenting the life of medieval peasants. Although Fournier originated as a peasant himself, his relentless witch-hunting propelled him to prominence, eventually earning him the title of Pope Benedict XII of Avignon in 1334. Incarcerated on charges of witchcraft, Béatrice's actual transgression was her audacity to relish sex postmenopause (though the menstrual blood in her possession might have fascinated a New Orleans Voodoo enthusiast).

Amid the havoc wrought by the Black Death and the Inquisition, the Middle Ages saw witches being increasingly associated with the devil. If the devil proposed a financial incentive in exchange for one's soul, especially when one was being evicted from their home due to escalating private land enclosures, who wouldn't be tempted to negotiate? Once upon a time, science and the divine weren't considered warring enemies. This era unfortunately severed the bond between magic and medicine, increasingly linking midwives to diabolical entities. It's true; some families, in desperation and absence of reliable birth control or abortion, abandoned infants in forests, perhaps convincing themselves they had struck a pact with the devil and he would take the child, or maybe hallucinating due to the psychedelic of yesteryear: ergot fungi consumption. (And if you thought QAnon pioneered the idea that the elite engage in Satanic rituals using babies' blood to achieve a radiance superior to Botox, think again.)

In the late sixteenth century, many Puritans—as depicted in the 2015 film *The Witch* (or *VVitch*), starring Anya Taylor-Joy and (spoiler alert) featuring a witch procuring baby's blood in the New England woods—relocated to the New World seeking freedom from the Church of England, which was far too liberal for their tastes. Even as they made the journey in large numbers, others, like Sir Matthew Hale, remained. Hale is infamous for burning witches, disbelieving in rape within marriage, and enjoying a posthumous comeback four hundred years later when Supreme Court justice Samuel Alito cited his work in the 2022 *Dobbs v. Jackson Women's Health Organization* case that overturned the constitutional right to abortion in the United States.

As we reach the nineteenth century, I'll introduce you to Madame Restell. Her story is a captivating rags-to-riches tale of a Manhattan immigrant, originally from an English town, enamored with the pagan god Pan, the same deity admired by the English occultist Aleister Crowley. As a midwife, she performed abortions and earned the notorious reputation of being hell's representative on earth. Her shocking death is not the most surprising detail about her.

In the early twentieth century, Crowley, the "most wicked man in the world," took us back to Egypt after persuading a guard to let him spend a night in the King's Chamber of the Great Pyramid with his new wife (the latest incarnation of the Scarlet Woman, his version of the Whore of Babylon). His infamous rituals involved "sacrificing" himself—code for bottoming—in the name of Pan, an ancient Greek god of sex, drugs, and rock and roll. Ozzy Osbourne howls about Crowley in metal songs, and many self-identified witches today have his books, such as *The Book of the Law*, on their shelves. The guy's often credited with inventing sex magic. Crowley founded the religion Thelema, whose members included L. Ron Hubbard, the infamous founder of Scientology. Oh, did you think being obsessed with sex would make him supportive of reproductive rights? Nope. Crowley wrote against abortion. But he allegedly approved of spiritual eugenics, the belief that through selective (read: racist) breeding, one could create a superhuman, a man-god, a pharaoh, if you will. Yes, just like in *Dune*.

But, of course, eugenics wasn't limited to those who invoked the left-handed path, which means a life dedicated to Satan. Until Hitler's Final Solution, well, *finally* gave eugenics a bad rap, the most respected scientists in America believed that some (nondisabled attractive white) people should have as many babies as possible, while Black people were involuntarily given hysterectomies. Or castrated—they didn't limit this evil to women. And even Margaret Sanger, the founder of the organization that would become Planned Parenthood, got in on the eugenics trend in the period after World War I (mainly because it offered an avenue to promote birth control after any early attempts at sex positivity failed).

Moving closer to the present day, we'll have probably too much fun during the 1980s. We'll delve into the Reagans' decision to consult an astrologer to advise them on significant political choices, while at the same time they propagated an occult-inspired Satanic Panic, aiming to bolster anti-choice conservatism. Interestingly, these Hollywood elites—according to their daughter—didn't even entirely subscribe to anti-choice beliefs themselves. In a twist of irony, the era's actual Satanists (including the notorious Anton LaVey, the Church of Satan founder who upheld the theatrical

Satanic tradition), like Crowley, actually wrote against abortion. Then there's the McMartin preschool trial. Recognized as the costliest criminal trial in American history, it's akin to a modern-day Salem Witch Trial in which children were manipulated into claiming that Satan (one actually said it was Chuck Norris), invoked by their *gasp* unmarried teacher and his older grandmother, raped them. This was instigated by adults desperately seeking to reinforce a potent political narrative. We'll also delve into the Reagan administration's handling—using the term loosely—of the AIDS crisis and the complex interplay between queer and reproductive rights.

Finally, you'll encounter contemporary occultists like Dakota Bracciale, who organized the "Ritual to Hex Brett Kavanaugh," and Jex Blackmore, a prominent figure on the left-handed path and abortion activist known for taking the abortion pill live on FOX. Also in the present day, it may surprise you to discover a burgeoning pro-life movement that isn't solely composed of conservative Christians. This movement boasts its own #ACAB icons and represents an emerging anticapitalist, socially conscious, punk music–inspired stance against abortion.

Armed with this history, we must recognize that the original *Roe* decision establishing the constitutional right to abortion might not have been comprehensive enough. We should consider starting anew, drawing inspiration from the fervor of those conservatives who painstakingly reversed it. We need to build a foundation for abortion rights more solid than a single reversible court ruling. And as we seek to reestablish our rights, our approach should be underpinned by a genuine respect for human life, devoid of the pro-life movement's violence, like the organized attacks on abortion clinics. Something good that Christianity, and all major religions, do is teach that one can find value even in rough times, and the grace of the end of *Roe* is that we have an opportunity to build something better.

If I've done my job well, this book, like the reproductive justice movement itself, will cater to all: those who have or plan to have children, are unsure, or are resolutely opposed; the agnostic, the devoted Satanist, the witch, or the Christian in search of a compelling history lesson; and people of all genders and sexes—because while cisgender men have caused harm, so have their wives, and we can't make real progress if we exclude men from the discussions, or if witches continue egregiously branding coven meetings as moon circles and continue to ostracize trans women.

The overturning of *Roe* is a reality. The tide seems to be turning against the pro-choice movement, even if a majority of Americans still support abortion rights. And the far-flung oppressors you'll meet in these pages didn't just kill witches; they erased them from history and credited men with their achievements. It's time to reverse *that* decision.

So can you handle the truth, witch?

A NOTE ON LANGUAGE

"Reproductive justice," coined in 1994 by Black women including feminist activist Loretta Ross, reaches far beyond reproductive rights, weaving reproductive health with social justice. This concept underscores the intersection of reproductive rights and systemic inequalities. It addresses not only the legal right to abortion and birth control but also the rights to have children, parent in safe environments, and maintain overall health and well-being. This comprehensive viewpoint highlights the challenges that marginalized communities, especially women of color, face in accessing reproductive health care and securing those rights.

"Reproductive rights," which gained prominence in the 1960s and 1970s through activists like Margaret Sanger and Betty Friedan as well as organizations such as Planned Parenthood, pertain to the freedoms and legal rights related to reproduction and reproductive health with an emphasis on abortion. These rights ensure individuals can make autonomous decisions about when to have kids, access birth control, and obtain safe, legal abortions. While reproductive justice provides a wider framework, reproductive rights focus on the legal and policy dimensions of reproductive health and autonomy. Its critics say it leaves people out (true) and doesn't ask for enough (also true). At this point, it's also just outdated as a term on its own.

Finally, "reproductive health care" refers to medical services, education, and information related to reproductive health. It includes prenatal and postnatal care, contraception, safe abortion services, testing and treatments for sexually transmitted infections (STIs), reproductive cancer screenings, fertility treatments, and sexual education.

This book champions reproductive justice, though it also employs other terms depending on the time frame and context.

Reproductive Rites and its author intend to advance the narrative rather than rehash existing ones. The book is pro–trans rights and anti-TERF (trans-exclusionary radical feminist). Given the vast historical scope covered, there are instances where reproductive health is discussed in terms of "women" and "mothers," which vary based on time and context.

It should be evident that both the book and its author are pro-choice, often referring to those opposing these rights as "anti-choice" instead of "pro-life." While writing, I noticed much of my early research was from liberal pro-choice sources. To ensure balanced journalism, I also explored works by the "pro-life" faction, which led to surprising discoveries like Joan Andrews, a.k.a. "Saint Joan," an anti-abortion activist who allegedly once yanked out her fake eye to chuck at a prison guard who just kindly gave it back, in addition to winning over Mother Freaking Teresa. Such discoveries acted as a reminder that the pro-choice crowd is doing itself no favors by ignoring and underestimating the other side. There are moments when the term "pro-life" is used, depending on the time and context.

Covering four thousand years of history, I may not have used period-accurate terminology at all times, but I did my best based on available resources, and I hope for your understanding regarding any minute language mishaps. Throughout, I have endeavored to be as accurate, inclusive, and thorough as possible.

CHAPTER 1

ABORTION, ALLIGATOR DUNG, AND THE BEAUTIFULLY ADORNED ANCIENTS

1

An arid wind scorches your face. It's sometime around 1800 BCE, "before the Common Era." It will be another two millennia until Jesus Christ is born, but when people reflect on this time in the distant future, his birth will be the marker. Not yet, though. Now, your yearly calendar is based on the three cycles of the Nile: Akhet (flooding season), Peret (growing season), and Shemu (harvest season).

You don't care what trimester it is right now. You have others on your mind. What you want—what you *need*—is a steaming pile of crocodile dung. With green and brown hues similar to those of bird excretions, crocodile poop contains both feces and urine as they are discharged together, one and the same. You need the shit because someone is pregnant and can't be.

It rarely rains in ancient Egypt. Water is life; the Nile is the life force and, therefore, holy. It's also where crocodiles hang out. Much like the reproductive justice movement that will emerge nearly four thousand years from now, the Nile welcomes anyone interested in family planning—whether you're there to have a baby, prevent pregnancy, or have an abortion. Today, you're at the Nile to make a pessary—an old-fashioned word for a suppository and a term that will become crucial to our understanding of the modern battle for reproductive justice thanks to Hippocrates—that is thought to have the power to end pregnancy.

You're not a pharaoh, a.k.a. the "god-king," or one of their many wives or consorts. You're a farmer, or perhaps in the military, and while your bloodline may one day fight for Ramses the Great, right now you cannot afford another child, which is why you're on a hunt for the poop. When Rome eventually conquers Egypt in 30 BCE, laws will pass to encourage people to marry and have children—after all, they need soldiers. But we're not at that part of the story yet.

Ancient Egyptians threw female fertility figures, delicious cakes, sacrificial animals, stunning jewelry, and other offerings into the Nile in rituals to encourage—or prevent—conception. One such necklace just tossed into the river may very well have been adorned with crocodile heads, which were commonly depicted on ancient Egyptian uterine amulets. From the crocodile-faced god Sobek to the mummified reptile bodies found in the tombs of the rich and famous, crocodiles were a big deal.

In this culture, abortion was another part of family planning, just one of the complexities of life. Which, of course, is all it ever should be. No one would try to ruin your life for using jewelry to prevent pregnancy. (In the modern world, by contrast, there *will* be witch hunts related to jewelry used in abortive rituals. In 2019, New Yorker Ursula Wing, a single mother, sold medical abortion kits online, which she shipped hidden inside the packaging of handmade jewelry to avoid getting caught. She was discovered anyway and indicted on one count of "conspiracy to defraud various US governmental agencies," fined $10,000, and put on two years' probation. More than $60,000 worth of sales were seized.)

Back in ancient Egypt, adornment is expected rather than punished, even if the jewelry relates to birth control. The gods are delightfully vain, in contrast to future deities who will frown upon looking pretty. If you're a commoner, you likely have beads around your neck; higher classes get gold. Everyone wears makeup, regardless of gender or status. The gods love it, you love it, your partner thinks it's hot, and the delight of black kohl around the eye is enjoyed by all. The gods would be offended if you showed up in the afterlife smelly and looking like a scrub. A far cry from warning you of the evils of vanity and a good-enough reason to keep ornamentation of all kinds trending.

Pharaoh Ramses II, also known as Ramses the Great, has an entire glam squad dedicated to his wigs, perfumes, and makeup. And that makeup gets its sparkle from ground rubies and emeralds, thank you, not polyester like many of the cosmetics peddled today. That gorgeous Ramses the Great is said to have fathered more than one hundred children. Easy for a guy who can wear semiprecious eye shadow.

Ancient Egypt was far from perfect. Obviously, it is not recommended or effective today to induce abortion using crocodile shit. But perhaps all genders wearing makeup was less scandalous during a time when everyone believed in magic—without being called a witch. We know that menstrual blood was treated as a source of strong magic, even if the biological understandings of menses hadn't been wholly sorted out yet. Fertility was understood to be related to the moon's phases, for example, and women's periods were believed to be a defense mechanism against insect plagues. One account recommends sending women to the fields during their periods to strut through the crops because beetles and other pests would perish from the power of their magic.

In this ancient time, it's normal, too, to worship Heka, a "cannibal pharaoh" who devoured other gods until he turned into one himself. Heka is also the god of medicine and is often depicted with at least one serpent. (The National Institutes of Health says that the snake figure we now see in modern medical symbols is associated with Asclepios, the ancient Greek god of medicine. But there was so much battling and merging of gods that Heka deserves some credit for starting the snake trend, too.) According to Heka, magic and medicine, far from foes, are one and the same. After graduating from god-eater to god, Heka took it a step further and became a word for a force contained in all gods, synonymous with all Egyptian magic. Such a fame whore.

This "Heka" is a pleasure-encouraging primordial energy that is here for summoning without judgment. According to Egyptologist Ogden Goelet: "*Heka* magic is many things, but, above all, it has a close association with speech and the power of the word. In the realm of Egyptian magic, actions did not necessarily speak louder than words—they were often one and the same thing. Thought, deed, image, and power are theoretically united in the concept of *Heka*."

Another selling point for Heka: Under this power, you can spill the tea. No coded messages to your friends, no secret exchanges necessary. Abortion and birth control are as much a part of daily life as bread with Heka magic. You can just invite your friends over to hold a ritual for finding the ingredients, following the recipe, and keeping everyone who doesn't want a baby unimpregnated. No secrets, no shame.

And about that recipe: you're using crocodile dung for birth control because that's what Prescription Number 21, "Recipe Not to Become Pregnant," from the Kahun Papyrus—Egypt's oldest medical text and perhaps the earliest mention of birth control on record, written sometime circa 1825 BCE—calls for. Prescription Number 21 is likely linked to Sobek, among the oldest deities name-dropped in the Pyramid Texts. The origin of the name Sobek, *Sbk*, means "to impregnate" in ancient Egyptian. As a result, in addition to potentially inspiring contraceptives, Sobek was a god of fertility and is sometimes credited with creating the Nile (casual).

Sobek was famously revered by the first female pharaoh, Sobekneferu, whose name means "beauty of Sobek." Sobekneferu reigned from 1806 to 1802 BCE (remember, we count time backward in BCE) and may have been married to her brother. Unfortunately, records of her are scarce, but if that's true, try not to kink shame. The arrangement likely wasn't her decision, and incest was the norm back then for the ruling class. The famed King Tutankhamen, a.k.a. Tut, was born of a marriage likely between siblings (although more recent research suggests they were cousins)—a tradition that continued much longer than using crocodile dung to prevent pregnancy.

Birth control recipes are found globally in every era, including in ancient Vedic texts, Chinese works, and Indigenous cultures. But in this book, we're mostly following the Christians who will one day lead us to *Dobbs v. Jackson Women's Health Organization*—the overturning of *Roe v. Wade*. We began our journey here because records of reproductive care in ancient Egypt before the Roman takeover contain some crucial gems that are at least worth discussing, even if you can't turn them into eye shadow.

The second significant mention of birth control in ancient Egypt comes from the Ebers Papyrus, written between 1550 and 1500 BCE. The Ebers Papyrus discusses a pessary containing acacia fruit, dates, and honey. While it's not been studied on humans, there is some modern animal evidence that acacia could prevent pregnancy. One study suggests that rats fed *Acacia koa* twice a day over a five-day period had fewer litters, reduced by up to 88 to 100 percent. And when they ate the *A. koa* seeds, they ceased getting pregnant altogether.

The Ebers Papyrus also covers depression. After meticulously reviewing more than fifty years of research, in 2022, the American Psychological Association reported that while having an abortion is not linked to mental health struggles, "restricting access to safe, legal abortions can cause harm." Those denied abortions, traditionally poorer and Black communities, have worse physical and psychological health, not to mention economic outcomes, compared to those who can easily access such care. Cheers to the Egyptians for finding a link first, even if theirs were more romanticized: The Ebers manuscript poetically relates mental health conditions to dysfunctions in the heart, which is "the center of the blood supply with vessels attached for every member of the body." Speaking of both the literal and what we now know as the metaphorical heart, the Ebers Papyrus contains quotations such as *"When his heart is afflicted and has tasted sadness, behold his heart is closed in and darkness is in his body because of anger which is eating up his heart."*

And, in antiquity, hearts indeed tasted sadness, made all the more complicated by that royal tradition of incest I mentioned, an example of enforced family planning that caused all sorts of problems for 1 percenters. Typically, pharaohs had many wives, but one was usually more in charge than the others. This honor goes to the queen consort, or "king's great wife." When the pharaoh was succeeded by one of his children, the new pharaoh's mother became the "king's mother." Ideally, the queen consort was a relative from the royal family, like a sister or a half sister. Occasionally, marriages occurred between fathers and their own daughters. While we can't be fully certain of the figures, most research suggests that only one of these resulted in a child: a daughter from Ramses the Great and *his* daughter Bintanath. (Remember, this guy had at least one hundred kids.) Whether it's as the result of a slight, simply a loss of records, or both, their child's name is lost to history. Ramses the Great's first wife who *wasn't* his daughter, Nefertari, was his true love and the coveted "great" wife. She was honored with all of the statues.

Remember, pharaohs were not just kings; they were god-kings. But as mythological gods tended to be better at listening than their royal earthly counterparts, especially to those who were of a lower class, folks tended to call upon gods and their magic to help them obtain an abortion.

2

The goddess Isis is one of the rare deities clearly tied to abortion. Isis, often invoked in healing rituals, is believed to help one enter the afterlife. She appears in a prayer from the Roman poet Ovid (43 BCE–17 CE) who called upon Isis to heal his lover, Corinna, after she had an abortion. Ovid was a member of the Roman knightly class, meaning he was in between the commoners and members of the Senate (or *senatus*, which, by the way, literally means a "gathering of old men"). His writing was inspired by the sensual pleasure-seeking society of the time, and, just like so many poets to come after him, his muse was love.

According to an inscription on the Temple of Philae—which, if it wasn't already beautiful enough, is on a goddamn island surrounded by the waters of the Nile—Isis is said to "love the joy of fresh myrrh," according to Sam Wise in *Sacred Choice: Paganism, Witchcraft, and Reproductive Justice*. Myrrh is also one of three items famously gifted to Jesus by three wise men. It got its name from the Greek myth, in which a beautiful Myrrha, a mortal, was tricked into having sex with her father and got pregnant, just like Bintanath. But as Myrrha's legend tells it, she, too, also asked the gods for help, so they hid her soul in a plant. She gives birth while in her tree form, and the sap becomes her tragic tears. In addition to this sap being desired in perfumery (perhaps Ramses the Great had a stash), it was also recognized in the ancient world as an abortive drug.

Other plant remedies revered by the ancients for reproductive health with divine connections include the tart pomegranate. The use of pomegranate invokes the story of Persephone's misadventure into the underworld and the barren winter Demeter cast over the earth in protest. Because of the association with coming back to life, the pomegranate is often used in fertility work, in addition to being an aphrodisiac. Persephone, whom people worshipped back to 1400 BCE, was abducted to the underworld by Hades while she was picking narcissus flowers with her nymph friends. Her mother, Demeter, the ancient Greek goddess of the harvest, reached out for help to Hecate (yes, like *Heka*), the goddess of magic, to try to get her daughter back. Persephone is finally able to leave, but only after Hades forces her to eat pomegranate seeds. These might make a tasty treat, but as a result of eating the fruit, Persephone has to spend a third of every year in the underworld with her new husband. Taking on his legacy, Persephone will go on to be known as the Greek goddess of the underworld.

Her worried mother, Demeter, a goddess of fertility and agriculture, is associated with the chaste tree. This is an herbal form of birth control that could regulate hormones and was used in ancient Greece to induce menstruation. It likely got its name from the word we know as "chastity."

Aside from a few limited animal studies, we don't know if any of these methods worked or what the side effects might have been, and at any rate, there are *much better* current options. However, there is one ancient herb that absolutely no pregnant person today could test out if they tried: the now-extinct silphium. Silphium is an unidentified plant, probably of the fennel family, with heart-shaped leaves. Ancient Greeks and Romans likely used it as a contraceptive, but we know very little because it no longer exists. The most exciting possible explanation is that people loved and used silphium so much, it went extinct from overharvesting for abortions. However, it could also have been due to environmental changes or a combination of the two. In addition to its abortive and contraceptive properties, silphium was used in classical antiquity as everything from a seasoning for food to an aphrodisiac and medicine.

According to mythology, silphium was associated with the ancient Greek god Apollo. Apollo was a handsome deity with a fresh-shaved face, carrying a bow and quiver of arrows, connected to queer men due to his own love of sex with guys. From ancient times, he was called upon for gay unions. Today he is often invoked by modern witchy queer couples who wish to end a pregnancy. Apollo is the god of music, dance, prophecy, healing and diseases, and poetry. It's said that Apollo invented string music in addition to archery. These gods are such overachievers.

About a hundred years after Rome successfully expands its empire, doctors will agree with Apollo and suggest the use of silphium for contraceptives. Soranus of Ephesus (101–200 CE) was a Greek physician who made a name for himself in both pediatrics and midwifery. In addition to noting that oral contraceptives worked better than pessaries, Soranus suggested a chickpea-size amount of silphium, with water, once a month, both as birth control and to terminate an existing pregnancy. He is most famous for writing *On Midwifery and the Diseases of Women*, which influenced medical opinion about women's health, including pregnancy, and child care for nearly fifteen hundred years. His works also include what's considered the oldest biography of Hippocrates.

3

Hippocrates (460–375 BCE) was an ancient Greek physician regarded as the father of medicine, known for his common sense and logic. In particular, we know him for his ethical standards, professed in the Hippocratic oath, which doctors still refer to today. There is a lot of debate over whether the original text of the Hippocratic oath prohibits doctors from performing an abortion. It translates to: "I will not give to a woman a pessary in order to induce an abortion." While there are many mentions of pessary in writings from antiquity, most birth control was taken orally in ancient times, so this advice would make sense—Hippocrates advising prescribing the most effective version of birth control. There is also evidence that he didn't want to prescribe pessaries because they could have caused vaginal ulcers. Maybe the guy just didn't want people shoving crocodile shit into their vaginas. However, the oath was changed in a later translation, probably during the Roman Empire, to prohibit giving a woman an abortion by any method, which is the translation American conservative lawmakers still hold on to.

Despite biased translations of his oath, we know that Hippocrates at least advised the use of birth control. According to Sam Wise in *Sacred Choice: Paganism, Witchcraft, and Reproductive Justice*, Hippocrates's go-to birth control method was the beloved pomegranate. And in Hippocrates's medical treatise *Nature of the Child*, he wrote of a dancing girl thought to be six days pregnant. She was told to get rid of the fetus by jumping up and down so high that her heels touched her butt, like a flapper rebelliously dancing in a short dress during Prohibition in the 1920s.

While it's tempting to turn Hippocrates into a pro-choice icon, wrongly translated for millennia and leveraged for control by conservative powers that be, the real question is: Why are we still looking to this guy for abortion laws and medical care? He was influenced by a Pythagorean theory stating that nature consists of four elements: water, earth, wind, and fire—"elements" that are a common thread in pagan practices even today, such as astrology, which, while wonderfully witchy, does not align with modern science. If you're looking to use horoscopes to decide how to deal with a pregnancy, any sane astrologer will agree that such questions are above their pay grade. Hippocratic texts also states that "When a woman has intercourse, if she is not going to conceive, then it is her practice to expel the sperm produced by both partners whenever she wishes to do so." Anyone up to write an updated oath?

4

The Hippocratic oath will be used for thousands of years to strip away the rights of women, and considering that the mythology around Rome's beginnings—the origin story of the birthplace of colonialism—is rooted in rape, misogyny, and population control, this should come as no surprise.

Around the time Hippocrates was alive, the legend of the founding of Rome starring the twin brothers Romulus and Remus took hold, permeating society so thoroughly that you might already know at least some of it—likely the "family-friendly" version featuring a pair of babies who narrowly escaped death by court-ordered drowning. While the story of Rome's founding events is often viewed as mythology, recently archaeologists discovered remains from the eighth century BCE of a cave, what could be boundary walls, and a palace that looked like the Rome of myth, showing how blurry the line is between history and legend. And this is a juicy legend.

Romulus and Remus are the sons of Rhea Silvia, who, according to folklore, was raped by Mars, the god of fucking and fighting. Rhea wasn't supposed to have kids. To ensure she had no heirs, she was ordered by her uncle, Amulius, to become one of the Vestal Virgins. Vestal Virgins were the state cult of Vesta, the goddess of the hearth. Vestal Virgins were expected to kill themselves if they broke their chastity vow. And before you judge the ancients for placing such high stakes on virginity, know that if you're American, you paid taxes to "A Silver Ring Thing," a purity-ball organization, throughout George W. Bush's presidency and under Obama until 2010.

Amulius was not happy about the birth of these twin babies with the formidable god of war as their father. So he went to drown them both in the Tiber River. In antiquity, abortion happened all the time—but so did infanticide. Christian Greeks and Romans even went so far as to judge other religions like Judaism that did not include the practice. They thought infanticide was rational, as you couldn't tell the sex of the child until it was born. Indeed, throughout history, killing female babies seemed morally preferable to electing to have an abortion that could eliminate the possibility of a male heir. But Amulius was trying to do just the opposite: to get rid of a pair of heirs. It didn't work. Rather than drown, the twins just floated down the river in a trough until they arrived at a site known as the *Ficus ruminalis*, which would become Rome.

Mars, expecting his kids' divine arrival, had a wolf and a woodpecker waiting for them. He's a god, after all; he can convince a few animals to act as wet nurses. This odd couple fed Romulus and Remus, who were often depicted suckling at the wolf's teats, and raised them until the herdsman Faustulus found and adopted the twins. They were naughty but effective teenagers, sort of like frat boys, if we want to call a spade a spade.

By young adulthood, having won over locals with their charisma and now aware of their assumed birthright to leadership, it was time to assume power and establish a city, but the twins had to find a way to share. Rather than talk about it, or seek the advice of others, they opted for augury, a form of ancient divination involving reading bird patterns, to decide. But they couldn't agree on what the birds meant. So, naturally, Romulus killed his brother and took over, creating his city, Rome.

At the time of Rome's founding, Romulus invited anyone and everyone to move there. Party's over here! With those pesky family members gone, he needed people to fill his city. As a result, a lot of men with criminal histories came to Rome, which also meant the population was seriously skewed male. After Romulus tried and failed to get women to move to Rome consensually, he came up with a scheme to kidnap a bunch of them from the Sabines, a central area of the Apennine Mountains. He lured them in with what seemed like a thoughtful party invitation: a festival to honor their god, Neptune. (Today, when the planet Neptune comes up in your horoscope, it's associated with dreams, intuition, and psychic power. Neptune is the god of the sea, and water is always associated with emotion.) The party was bullshit, and regardless of the invocation of wise Neptune, the poor lasses didn't know what they were in for (again, not unlike going to a frat party).

During what would become known as Neptunalia, the Sabine women were abducted, while their guy friends were killed or forced to retreat. What was billed as a thoughtful festival for a sea god came to be known as "The Rape of the Sabine Women." The story goes that Romulus ordered the women to stay in town after the event for the sake of the "common children," writes Eric Brown in *Ancient History: A Concise Overview of Ancient Egypt, Ancient Greece, and Ancient Rome*, acknowledging that some women got pregnant during their rape—which meant that their future children would be property of the Roman military. It's also been speculated that "The Rape of the Sabine Women" is an entirely made-up legend. You see, the Romans had a bit of consensual-nonconsensual roleplay in their nuptials, where the future husband pretended to kidnap his "virginal" bride-to-be from her mother. The legend of a mass capture of nonconsenting women for the purpose of breeding a state army is not exactly rom-com material to modern ears, but it could have been compelling at the time.

Despite the Sabine women's bloody arrival under the guise of a sea-themed party and forced motherhood, all evidence does suggest that Romans practiced birth control. From looking at records, historians now know that ancient times of economic growth positively correlated with population decline. Christian historians will sometimes purport that this is just because people stopped having sex, but as John M. Riddle writes in *Eve's Herbs: A History of Contraception and Abortion in the West*, "Those who have studied the classical literature of the ancient Greeks and Romans know that sexual restraint was not a quality about which the ancients could boast or lament."

The sex life of Romans makes the sex-positive poly-dens of modern-day Brooklyn seem like nunneries. There were epic orgies and legal sex work. Gay sex, especially between men, was so normal that there was no word to differentiate it from straight sex. Putting Park Avenue dominatrix dungeons to shame, some ancient Roman eunuchs even self-castrated as part of their role in the fertility cult for the goddess Cybele.

At the risk of killing anyone's sensual view of the ancients, remember that decadence was reserved for the wealthy, not unlike a bougie *Eyes Wide Shut*–inspired sex party today. Enslaved folks made up 10 to 15 percent of the Roman Empire; for enslaved people, avoiding unwanted pregnancies was more important than for upper-class citizens. In addition to herbs and pessaries, women were advised to drink something cold before sex. Afterward, the trick suggested was to hold their breath, pull away, and squat and sneeze while wiping the vulva to avoid getting pregnant. This practice hints at an understanding of what we call the pull-out method.

Having a healthy supply of legal sex workers seems way less fun when you realize that, for many of ancient Rome's *scorta*, or lower-class "women who earn," their profession was not a choice, nor were they paid. Not only were wealthy Romans allowed to enslave people, but such folks were also considered private property in Roman law and could also be abused by their owners or sold off for sex in what we'd now consider sex trafficking—regardless of age or gender. It was only a matter of time before there would be a revolt, which is exactly what happened during the Servile Wars of ancient Rome. And the first one, which took place in modern Sicily, was led by an enslaved man with supernatural powers named Eunus.

5

Eunus was an enslaved Roman originally from Syria. He was an oracle who received divine visions from the goddess Atargatis, a Syrian fertility goddess, who is, quite awesomely, often depicted as a mermaid. At the time of the Servile Wars, the Romans were seriously exploiting enslaved people. That's a redundant sentence because of course all enslavement is exploitative to a horrific degree, but even within that framework, the Romans really did some damage. Thousands of enslaved people were worked or starved to death. So, in 135 BCE, a group of them decided to revolt against Damophilus, the landowner who enslaved them and thus their sworn enemy. Thousands turned to the mermaid-blessed Eunus as their leader, stormed into the city of Enna, and captured, tortured, and killed Damophilus. While his daughter was allowed to flee, his complicit wife was also killed. The revolt's success spread across the Sicilian territories, and as the formerly enslaved forces prevailed, they minted coins printed with a portrait of Eunus, who was eventually crowned King Antiochus of Syria. It is believed that between ten and seventy thousand—and by some accounts as many as two hundred thousand—joined the fight. They burned bridges, battled, and brandished weapons, taking quite a bit of territory, but ultimately the revolt ended around 132 BCE in favor of the Romans. Many revolutionaries were tortured and then thrown off a cliff. Twenty thousand prisoners were crucified.

As for Eunus, he was captured and died in prison of disease while awaiting punishment, avoiding a death as bloody as his comrades. In all, the revolt lasted from 135 until 132 BCE. Importantly, it was the first of three pivotal uprisings against the Roman Republic by enslaved people. Karl Marx's beloved Spartacus famously led the final campaign. While the records are too hazy to determine the extent of social and political change caused by these wars, historians believe that the end of the Servile Wars does coincide with the Romans adopting "better" attitudes toward slavery, as in enslaving fewer people. However, the practice of slavery continued the world over, and mapping its history is crucial to understanding the path to today's reproductive justice efforts.

In antiquity, speaking out against slavery could get you killed, and, as society moved away from worshipping Heka, so could witchcraft. The "filthy sorceress" Theoris of Lemnos (that's a direct quote from her trial) was tried and executed around 323 BCE for practicing incantations and distributing "illegal drugs," language that sounds like it came from the witch hunt that was the US War on Drugs some two thousand years later. Considering she was also accused of "committing many misdeeds and teaching the slaves to deceive," we can safely assume she was a badass at minimum.

Theoris was a folk healer who worked in Athens and was openly a witch. Keep in mind that the term "witch" changes with each chapter in history. The Instagram-famous witches of the current era with their rose-quartz face rollers are very different from the witches put to death for their practice in eras past. Words and their meanings have power, whether you call yourself a witch or not.

Theoris is described as a *pharmakis*, a term that translates to "a provider of drugs and potions" and could also mean a witch or sorceress. For this, she was executed—ironically, along with her children, as there's a chance that some of her "crimes" included aiding women in procuring miscarriages. The drugs she used may have been ancient herbal abortive remedies such as sage, juniper, and figs. In Athens at the time, it wasn't illegal to use magic. And in ancient Athens, while abortion wasn't legally banned, the decision wasn't in the woman's hands but rather depended on the father of the unborn child. The mother needed permission, highlighting a lack of personal sovereignty over her body. But killing someone with potions *was* a crime—one that would later be carried out against Socrates.

6

Socrates (470–399 BCE), a Greek philosopher from Athens, is one of history's biggest influencers—he's credited with founding pretty much all of Western philosophy. But he never actually wrote anything (honestly, much like many influencers today). However, plenty of people have written *about* him. This includes honorable texts by Plato, and far too many by others giving the guy a hard time about his appearance. We think Instagram delivers mean comments, but the fact is, humans have always had, and likely will always have, the capacity to be total dicks. We're going to be good people and look at what he did for reproductive justice and women. In *Charmides*, Plato, quoting Socrates (remember, people wrote about him, but he didn't write himself), says that charms and incantations work for the soul, while drugs heal the body. So he was down with a little woo-woo, but totally weird, and continuously bullied for his looks. So much so that he's frequently described as looking more like a satyr (which is a friendly nature demon type with ears and the tail of a horse—as well as a constant, massive erection, so I guess hung like a horse as well; props, Socrates) than a man. Allegedly, he had wide-set eyes, popping out of his head, that moved erratically, helping him keep watch in all directions like a crab. He let his hair grow, walked around barefoot, and, like any other hippie, didn't bathe much. Allegedly, he was immune to the effects of alcohol—the guy couldn't get drunk. Despite having access to political power in Athens, he opted for a life of poverty. Such a philosophy carries far past Plato and finds its way into contemporary Christian guidance within sects that value the simple, unselfish, and, frankly, less sexy life.

Socrates was known for his ability to drag anyone who made fun of him, always outwitting his critics. Perhaps it was that Big-Dick Energy. But beyond being odorous and scathing, Socrates's biggest eccentricity was what has been historically described by the *Stanford Encyclopedia of Philosophy* as his "higher opinion" of women. It likely helped that his mother, Phaenarete, was a midwife. We know very little about her, unfortunately, and we know even less about her midwife activities. But Plato wrote that "midwives, by means of drugs and incantations ... cause abortions at an early stage if they think them desirable." Socrates often described himself as a kind of midwife for ideas, or a midwife for the soul.

Despite gaining a reputation for logic, the man famous for stating that the unexamined life is not worth living experienced an *X-Files* moment of his own that would lead to his downfall. By his own accounts, Socrates experienced a *daimonion*, or internal voice, a sort of literal inner demon. This made him sound not only weird to those around him but perhaps also supernatural, or, even more dangerous, semidivine. His strange behavior, known now to be well-documented neurological symptoms, caused speculation about his potential divinity at the time. At least one modern retrospective study of the historical Socrates suggests he may have had temporal lobe epilepsy. When Socrates was seventy, he went to trial on a charge of impiety. His punishment was death by forced suicide. The method was poisoning, likely by the toxic plant hemlock.

Not long after the death of the father of Western philosophy came the Hellenistic period of ancient Greek history (323–31 BCE), which began with the death of Alexander the Great, a glamorous man known for his love of fragrance and vast colonization campaign. It was during this time that the Septuagint was written, which is the earliest known Greek translation of the Hebrew Old Testament, penned in its original language of Hebrew. This translation features Lilith, the much-ignored (by Christians) and much-embraced (by witches) disobedient first wife of Adam. Lilith became far more famous in the Jewish mysticism of the Middle Ages, described in the Zohar Leviticus (crucial literature of Kabbalah) as "a hot fiery female who first cohabited with man." Legend states that Lilith was banished from the Garden of Eden for not obeying her husband. (The *real* tea is that she wanted to get on top during sex with Adam, which emasculated the poor guy.)

The Hellenistic period ended with the rise of austere Augustus in Rome in 31 BCE. But you should know that Augustus didn't always go by this name.

7

Cleopatra VII Philopator (70/69–30 BCE), known posthumously simply as Cleopatra, is an icon of wealth, beauty, the power of female sexuality, and witchcraft. She was the final active ruler of Egypt. Roman propaganda painted her as a power-obsessed witch who used her infamous sexuality to her advantage. And you know what? They weren't wrong. While Cleopatra's story ended in tragic death, just like that of Theoris of Lemnos, her legacy as a witch is much more alluring and offers an insight into the sex lives of the ancient rich and famous.

The Battle of Actium (31 BCE) was a bloody naval battle that went down off the western coast of Greece and a pivotal moment in Rome's takeover. After the assassination of the Roman dictator Julius Caesar in 44 BCE, Rome erupted into civil war. Three of the most powerful and well-connected belligerents created a coalition called the Second Triumvirate to end the chaos and cultivate peace. This band included Octavian, who was Caesar's great-nephew and chosen heir (and he firmly asserted himself as such); Roman statesman Lepidus; and Mark Antony, an authoritative military general who called himself the new Dionysus. He even dressed like Dionysus, the Greek god of wine, parties, and ritual madness, when marching in military campaigns. They divided the empire in three ways. If you're not familiar with Lepidus, don't worry about it. Few people are. In Shakespeare's depiction of Lepidus in the tragedy *Julius Caesar*, Antony describes him as "a slight, unmeritable man, meant to be sent on errands."

For some background, the iconic Queen Cleopatra, the ruler of Egypt beginning in 51 BCE, and Julius Caesar used to be a thing. With the support and riches of multiple kingdoms, not to mention enslaved people, they had a son. Cleopatra named him Caesarion, which means "little Caesar." As future foes would correctly assume, Caesarion was born to rule and redeem his father.

Antony was given an area known as the eastern provinces in Asia Minor (modern-day Turkey). Once there, he summoned Queen Cleopatra (the 1-percenter antiquity version of sliding into someone's DMs), only to accuse her of aiding his enemies. Then, in a brilliant and baller move, Cleopatra batted her original cat eyes, likely paired with blue or green eye shadow, and seduced Antony, just as she had Caesar before him. Miss Cleo knew she was a bad bitch and had a thing for powerful men. She was undeniably hot, apparently mostly for her allure rather than for perfectly symmetric features. The biographer Plutarch writes in his 75 CE text, *Life of Antony*, "Her actual beauty . . . was not so remarkable that none could be compared with her, or that no one could see her without being struck by it, but the contact of her presence . . . was irresistible. . . . The character that attended all she said or did was something bewitching."

She rolled up to Antony on an opulent river barge, dressed as the Egyptian goddess Isis (other accounts say Venus, which was basically the Roman version of the goddess of love). Cleopatra often made a point to connect herself with Isis throughout her reign. The holy roleplay worked on the man who himself enjoyed dressing as a god, and he fell for her. So Antony returned with her to Alexandria, where they spent the winter engulfed in a passionate affair. However, Antony still had politics and business to attend to. Despite his love and lust for Cleopatra, in 40 BCE, Antony returned to Rome and married his rival Octavian's sister, Octavia, to try to cool his heated relationship with Octavian; back in the day, banging someone's sister was the way to peace and power.

The triumvirate's downward spiral continued, demonstrating their attempt at shared power would soon erupt more violently than the events that led to its formation. Antony needed help, so he went back to Cleopatra, who, by the way, had had his twins while he was gone. So, in 37 BCE, Antony separated from Octavia and arranged for Cleopatra to join him in Syria. They married, which broke a major law: Romans could not marry non-Romans.

Antony went on to carry out several ill-fated military campaigns. There were many wars, deaths, and orgasms for the royals, but despite the power couple of Antony and Cleopatra's best efforts, on September 2, 31 BCE, their fleets had a showdown at Actium in Greece. Cleopatra thought "fuck this," left the battle, and headed back to Egypt with sixty of her ships. Antony followed his woman. The abandoned remaining soldiers surrendered to Octavian, who ultimately won and took power. On January 16, 27 BCE, the Senate granted Octavian the title of Augustus, which derives from the Latin word *augere* (meaning to increase) and *principles* (the first in order). In addition to a name change, it was a title of authoritative religious power.

Then the infamous tragedy unfolded.

Cleopatra hid from the world in a gorgeous mausoleum. Antony was told she was dead, so he stabbed himself using his sword. A messenger arrived saying that this was not true, that his queen lived, but he was too wounded and died from his self-inflicted injuries after saying Cleopatra should make a peace deal with Octavian.

So, naturally, Cleopatra tried to seduce Octavian.

It didn't work. Strict Octavian did say he would let Cleopatra live—on the condition that she accepted him as her ruler. Rather than fall under his power, Cleopatra chose to die by suicide through the fatal bite of the asp, a poisonous Egyptian serpent that represented divine royalty, also associated with Sobek, thus completing another life-and-death circle.

If we wanted to be petty, we could trace Octavian and Cleopatra's beef back to Julius Caesar. You see, Caesar actually adopted Octavian, who was once a student of his. However, if we are to believe Antony and the rumors of the time, the two men were also sleeping together. Cleopatra and Octavian may have once pined for the same man. Sleeping with your adopted son? Totally cool. Marrying a non-Roman? Death.

And as for Little Caesar? Octavian had Caesarion executed. Octavian then ruled under the name Augustus, whom some call the most successful Roman emperor due to a rise in abundance during his reign, not to mention a massive expansion of the Roman Empire. (If we judged modern rulers by the same standards, Ronald Reagan might be considered America's "most successful" president given his hypocritical morality laws.)

Augustus enacted a series of stringent social laws that mandated marriage for citizens, regulated marital unions across class lines, and imposed severe penalties for infidelity. Adulterers faced exile, with each party isolated on separate islands. Men held the right to execute unfaithful wives, while women caught in adultery had to be divorced by their husbands. Additionally, fathers could opt for the execution of their daughters caught in the act. This extended to Augustus himself, who had to sentence his own daughter to exile for her extramarital affairs, sparing her from the capital punishment allowed under his laws.

While these rules were extreme, to say the least, Augustus didn't bother adding a ban on abortion. Abortion was not technically

illegal in ancient Rome at the time, but the state strongly disapproved of it. In the first several centuries of Christianity's existence, teachings weren't unified enough, or widespread enough,
to enact social change on abortion or birth control. Christianity
addressed family planning for the first time at the Synod of Elvira,
a convention of Christian leaders who gathered to agree on official
doctrine in 305 or 306 CE. In addition to deciding burning candles
in a cemetery in the daytime was an offense punishable by denial of
Communion, the Synod of Elvira also deemed abortion a sin so terrible that it was "beyond forgiveness," as Sam Wise writes in *Sacred
Choice: Paganism, Witchcraft, and Reproductive Justice.*

8

Enter scene: Emperor Constantine, the first Roman emperor to
convert to Christianity. Before we get to the bad stuff, you should
know that under his rule, most of Augustus's morality and marriage laws were overturned. Also known as Constantine the Great,
he reigned from 306 to 337 CE. He gave orders for a feudal system
(read: slave system) during the process of creating a Roman Catholic Church. The *coloni* were a class of people who gained property-
ownership rights by cultivating previously wild lands. They're the
reason we have the word "colonialism." According to some historians, Christianity did not spread naturally, but was forced upon
on citizens by the people in charge. What we do definitively know
is that during this time, most folks knew only what the ruling class
of the Roman Empire wanted them to know. Christianity may be
taken from previous traditions, but that's okay, as long as it gives
people comfort. Unfortunately, many have picked and selected
text to suit their needs, in particular the desire to control. The
literacy rate was 10 to 15 percent at best, perhaps closer to 5 to 6
percent, so the number of citizens who could get through the Bible
indeed may have been limited to ruling classes.

And these ancient celebrities had thoughts on where and how people with penises should ejaculate. The pull-out method, likely used throughout all of human history, gained airtime thanks to the Bible passage in the story of Onan in the Torah (Gen. 38:8–10). Onan's dad, Judah, commanded him to have sex with Onan's widowed sister-in-law, as part of an ancient tradition in which brothers married the wives of their deceased siblings. Onan had no issue with porking his dead brother Er's wife, but he was offended by the idea that the resulting heir might still be considered more his brother's than his. At the time, economically, the resulting sons would still receive Er's inheritance. So he infamously spilled his seed, and that was interpreted as bad. Obviously, eventually, even most Bible thumpers accepted the pull-out method, coitus interruptus, which works about 78 percent of the time overall, according to Planned Parenthood. When pro-lifers joined hands in the fight against abortion, they had to let go of their disapproval of the pull-out method, cycle tracking, and breast-feeding, all forms of contraception as old as humans, if they wanted a shot at successfully banning clinical methods.

In *Creating Christianity: A Weapon of Ancient Rome*, historian Henry Davis asserts that the creation of the Bible as we understand it today can be traced back to the Roman-Jewish family of Calpurnius Pisos, an elite Roman senator in the first century, who also happened to star in the Pisonian conspiracy of AD 65, the most infamous plot against the throne of Emperor Nero.

Constantine officially legalized Christianity in 313 CE. Apparently, in order to get numbers up, the first churches were also brothels. Bishops ushered attendees into sex rooms where they could worship with a "helper" who was really just a sex worker pretending to be a virgin to please patrons.

In his youth, Constantine actually worshipped a pagan sun god, and he converted to Christianity only later—some speculate he was as old as forty—finding a new, perhaps repackaged, sun god in Jesus. Constantine never directly outlawed paganism, agreeing it was okay if they practiced their *superstitio*, "the rites of an outmoded illusion," as long as they didn't force Christians to join in. He was, however, enough of a party-pooper to outlaw blood sacrifices and ritual sex work. He also ordered the execution of the eunuch priests.

Constantine's extremism and nonsensical sexual standards proved impossible to satisfy, as other leaders' will on a timeless loop throughout history. Constantine paid personally for his strict moral code when his son Crispus was executed after being accused of adultery. Even juicier, rumor has it that Constantine's second wife, Fausta, is the one who made the accusations against her stepson—because she was in love with him. Fausta also died due to the drama; some say by execution, and others insist it was suicide. Constantine regretted his actions for the rest of his life.

Constantine's nephew Flavius Claudius Julianus, or Julian, was appointed to power in 361 by Constantine's (surviving) son, Constantius II. Like so many relatives of strict Christians, Julian rebelled and converted to mystical paganism. However, he was far from an idol. While he rebuilt the Jewish Temple destroyed in Jerusalem, he did so more to piss off Christians than to help the Jews. He had a violent streak and enjoyed torturing and killing Christians. Rather than cheering him on, other pagans found him pretty ridiculous, especially for his claims of harnessing some kind of magical power through his bushy beard.

Julian was the final ruler of the Roman Empire who adhered to a non-Christian faith, but not the last pagan.

9

Hypatia of Alexandria (350/370–415 CE) was one of the first women to research and teach the subjects math, philosophy, and astronomy. She was also a pagan. Those who feared her accused her of enchanting the Roman imperial prefect Orestes with witchcraft—though she likely just gave him political advice on how to find religious peace between the Christians and pagans—and of being "devoted at all times to magic, astrolabes and instruments of music" and "beguil[ing] many people through her Satanic wiles." Magic, music, and Satan? Where's the sign-up sheet? Perhaps much of the fear Hypatia induced was actually rooted in the fact that she refused to marry.

In March 415, a mob of Christian extremists seized Hypatia as she rode her carriage, then dragged her violently into a church, stripped her, and beat her with roofing tiles. As she fought back, they carved out her eyeballs using oyster shells and then ripped her apart limb from limb. Hypatia's remains were set on fire.

Five years after Hypatia's murder, misogynistic gender roles continued to be strictly reinforced, leading to further witch hunts by Augustine of Hippo (354–430 CE), who was the author of the doctrine of original sin. His teachings focused on the Garden of Eden. Lilith was not present, but Adam and his wife, the less slutty but still troublesome and inherently subordinate Eve, crafted from Adam himself, were, and they got kicked out for eating from the tree of knowledge. Here's a fun fact: in *Seventy-Eight Degrees of Wisdom: A Book of Tarot* by Rachel Pollack, when discussing the Lovers card, she notes, citing Joseph Campbell, that the ancient goddess-centric religion of Palestine also contained a myth of a garden, apple, and snake, but in that version, eating the apple got you *into* paradise rather than kicked out.

Now may be the time to share a fact for those who don't know: the word "occult" means "knowledge of something hidden." Writing about the occult is, well, a rather un-occult thing to do.

Augustine of Hippo, who would become Saint Augustine, was a bishop and one of the most influential men in the history of Christianity. In Roman Catholicism, he's formally recognized as a doctor of the church and a saint. He's also mostly known for his repressive views on sexuality, despite having an interesting personal life prior to finding Christ (tale as old as time): He had a son with a lover from a lower class. Some say he was gay, others offer proof of his relationships with women and argue he was straight, but I think he most likely was bisexual. Saint Augustine famously wrote: "Grant me chastity and continence, but not yet." (That was before he found Jesus.)

After he entered his Christian era, Augustine's hot new take on original sin, a phrase he was the first to record in writing, was that it resulted from pride, of putting oneself before God. (Many scholars now see his position on the idea as evidence of him working to reconcile his past sexual experiences with his newly adopted holy life.) Augustine hotly condemned abortion, and although he disapproved of abortion during any stage of pregnancy, he distinguished between early and later abortions, saying there was a difference between "formed" and "unformed" fetuses. He called infanticide a "cruel lust," but also wrote that abortion wasn't homicide, "for it could not be said that there was a living soul in that body, for it lacks all sense."

Augustine thought that pleasure was okay, as long as it was for procreation to increase the ranks of soldiers and saints. Today people often suggest that part of the reason the Right wants to criminalize abortion is to ensure more people for the working class. While there's truth to this, it's also important to remember that criminalizing abortion has dire economic consequences for individuals. As Stanford economist Luigi Pistaferri said in an interview with Melissa De Witte for *Stanford News*: "If we accept the premise that access to abortion (as well as broad availability of birth control methods) allows women better agency over fertility choices leading to greater labor force participation, investment in education, etc., it is clear that women who happen to live in states that make abortion illegal (or severely restrict it) will experience worse economic outcomes than those living in states where abortion is still legal."

As for saints, one can become one only after death, but you can never have enough candidates. Perhaps this was part of Augustine's living campaign to secure the honor for himself one day.

When the Roman Empire fell, Paulus Orosius, Augustine's protégé, insisted that pagan practices were at fault—not Christianity. Orosius was a Christian theologian and historian famous for his *Seven Books of History Against the Pagans*, which he wrote with Augustine's encouragement. The text argues that the 410 CE Sack of Rome had simply nothing to do with the Romans adopting Christianity, as pagans claim. This three-day routing by Visigoths, prominent Christians from eastern Europe, signified a critical moment in the fall of the western Roman Empire. It was the first time Rome had been ambushed and looted in eight hundred years and signifies the end of antiquity and the beginning of the Middle Ages. Some pagans asserted that this happened because people were pushing out paganism, so their gods were revoking their protection of the city of Rome. With the rise of the Christian faith, the resulting repression of pagan gods forced them to take their religion underground. Repression never puts an end to anything—it only makes it a secret. The whole point of Orosius's book was to counterargue and begin a long tradition of finger-pointing. According to Orosius, if anyone was to blame for the violence, it was the pagans who refused to accept Christ into their hearts and thus brought it upon themselves.

—∿—

The tea on the most famous names of antiquity—from the voices heard by Socrates, son of a midwife, to the glamour witch Cleopatra's legacy of breaking hearts—is riveting, and at times harrowing. For instance, due to literacy rates among the different classes at the time, the Bible may have been able to be put on paper only by the rich and famous, and the Hippocratic oath may actually be dissuading the use of a pessary (perhaps one made with crocodile poop). And while reading about some ancient methods of birth control (yes, such as reptile excrement) may seem a bit unhinged, even more fascinating than the sex lives of the ancients is the fact that some of these methods, such as the acacia mentioned in the Ebers Papyrus, may have actually worked. Such a text, which covers mental health conditions in addition to the logistics of family planning, seems more modern than outdated, given how far, as you'll learn in the chapters to come, society deviated from such wisdom in the millennia to follow.

And of course, things were far from perfect. Many modern critics of anti-abortion laws suggest that such ideology may be rooted more in the desire for a loyal workforce than actual religious beliefs, which isn't too different from pharaohs wanting the working classes to keep creating soldiers. But just like the reproductive justice movement today, which honors the rights both to have children and to not have them, the Nile welcomed anyone interested in family planning. And Heka, much like the enslaved people who brought their conjuring practices to North America, was understanding enough to get that both spirituality and reproductive desires are vast and varied, rather than existing on binaries.

As the founding of modern societies moves into the Middle Ages, you'll learn once again that the more that changes, the more that stays the same, whether it's controlling powers weaponizing plagues to dial back reproductive health access and wage racist propaganda campaigns or the demonization, and even incarceration, of women who dared enjoy hot sex with younger men in their postmenopausal years.

CHAPTER 2

DOUBLE, DOUBLE, BOILS, AND TROUBLE IN EUROPE: WITCHES BURN AND INQUISITORS BABBLE

1

I t's October 1347, and you're shopping at the market with your family in the arrestingly picturesque Sicilian port of Messina for cabbage to make a stew. (You raise your own chickens at home.) The smells of exotic (and out-of-budget) spices such as turmeric and cloves fill the salty air, which is not sharp enough to be biting, but cool enough to call for fur. As you're from a middle-class family, you're wearing fox over your embroidered clothing—all the rage, even for commoners. Nobles wear imported furs of cheetahs and leopards, while peasants, bringing to mind a very *Game of Thrones*–esque aesthetic, wear wolf hides. You're carrying a basket in one hand and holding your youngest daughter's hand in the other. The outdated ages of antiquity are long over, and the ruthlessness of the Middle Ages is falling out of favor as the integrity of the Renaissance takes hold.

You dodge a rat that scurries across the small cobbled market road fanning out to the port as your daughter yanks your hand and points at the ocean. Twelve trade ships are on the horizon. Thanks to the little critter that just crossed your path and the pretty incoming boats, you have little time to concern yourself with politics. Soon, both you and your daughter, along with nearly fifty million people, much of Europe, will be dead from the bubonic plague.

But on the bright side, at least you won't be burned alive at the stake for suspected witchcraft during the Inquisition.

At the time, the Black Death was just called "the pestilence" or "the epidemic," but as years passed, history came to name the plague for its distinctive dark-colored boils. The plague began in Asia and was brought back to Europe first through these twelve trade ships, which rolled up to Sicily filled with dead sailors. The few survivors still piloting the boats had skin covered in boils oozing blood and pus. Soon, starting in Venice, such ships would be turned away in a medieval attempt at a lockdown. Those allowed to enter would be mandated to enter a forty-day quarantine; the word "quarantine" translates from the Italian word "quarantena," or forty days.

But the damage would be done.

Death by the plague, which attacked the lymphatic system, began with an apple-size bump, often around the groin or armpit. These bumps would seep blood and pus and eventually turn black; meanwhile, the hosts experienced cruel aches and pains, diarrhea and vomiting, and fever and chills, and they were often dead by the next day. It spread incredibly easily, through even a simple brush of clothing, and the only reason it didn't kill more than its estimated nearly fifty million body count is because, as with modern-day virulent diseases like Ebola, infected people often died before they could pass it on.

The Black Death marks a terrible turning point in the story of reproductive rights and witch hunts, culminating in what historians often call the "Great Hunt," which took place between 1550 and 1650, kicking off shortly after the famous Protestant Reformer John Calvin wrote a letter describing what he saw as a conspiracy to spread the plague through sorcery.

It certainly wasn't just the Catholics who tortured and executed witches. Protestants got into the witch-hunting game basically as soon as the Reformation began. During this movement, they thought killing witches was God's command, citing Exodus 22:18, which in the King James version, the translation states, "You shall not allow a witch to live." While the word "pharmakis" is based on what we call drugs, it's often translated to mean "sorcerer," as interpreted by Martin Luther. In the Bible, "pharmakis" therefore basically became translated to mean "witch." Marty was certain that the Bible detested female witches who might poison anyone—especially babies. Martin Luther did not discuss abortion in his writings but saw motherhood as women's "highest vocation" and even wrote, "Let them bear children to death. . . . They are created for that."

Some historians even speculate that the Great Hunt may have been orchestrated so Catholics and Protestants could compete against one another for followers—whoever could kill the most witches would win. The most extensive witch trial in Geneva occurred in 1571, which marked the climax of the witch hunt in question, as it was the biggest and most lethal bout. Twenty-nine people were killed, and many more were banished just to satisfy the need to blame someone for the plague, which was so horrible it seemed to make it tricky for some people to believe in a loving God. Shifting the blame to witches and women offered an easy target to unload an emotional response on.

As European societies continued to look for scapegoats to blame for the ravishes of the plague, which were still being felt two hundred years later, they zeroed in on both witches and natural healers like midwives. Witchcraft and midwifery became inextricably linked in the eyes of the prosecutors. Such lay healers had failed to cure their patients of the plague, and now they were accused of making pacts with the devil and intentionally letting people die. This also led to stricter regulations about who could practice medicine. While there are arguments to be made that this brought about medical breakthroughs and safer science, it also supported gatekeeping of the medical establishment in an effort to keep decent health care in the hands of the wealthy. According to Barbara Ehrenreich and Deidre English in 1973's *Witches, Midwives & Nurses: A History of Women Healers*, "Witch hunts did not eliminate the lower-class woman healer, but they branded her forever as superstitious and possibly malevolent."

Catholics and Protestants also blamed Jewish people for the disease. Historians speculate that this was because, in addition to regular ole anti-Semitism, Jewish people in this time may have been culturally accustomed to using common wells less frequently than Christians, and, as a result, they would have gotten sick less. There were several barbaric mass attacks on Jews during this period, and there is evidence that some were tortured into false confessions to uphold narratives that they had poisoned the wells. And, of course, Asia, where the illness originated, was also blamed. We saw some of the exact same shit during the COVID-19 pandemic: distrust of healers, a resurgence of hate and xenophobia, and a boom in conservative thinking that ultimately led to the overturning of *Roe v. Wade*.

In those postplague years, arising from what we can safely assume was Continent-wide grief and a nasty case of PTSD alongside the growing distrust of folk medicine, came a desire to repopulate, which led to much stricter laws and opinions regarding birth control and abortion. According to *The Criminalization of Abortion in the West: Its Origins in Medieval Law* by historian Wolfgang P. Müller, one can trace a direct line between the population loss resulting from the plague and changing attitudes toward abortion, essentially making birth control into the enemy of baby-making rather than a crucial tool for safely regulating it, as it had been for so much of history. As a result, two concepts that had previously been largely unconnected—the targeting of those who use (or endorse) birth control and witch-hunting—met up in the center of the Venn diagram of persecution.

While the Black Death made witch-hunting mania widespread, the inquisitors of the time had a solid basis to build on. It's time to meet a woman you won't find in your history books.

2

Béatrice de Planisoles was born around 1274 and died sometime after 1322, before the plague landed in Europe, but not before she found herself testifying in front of the Inquisition. While this word will become synonymous with some of the most brutal witch hunts in history, technically, the Inquisition refers to an office set up within the Catholic Church to infiltrate communities and root out heretics. Beginning in the twelfth century, the whole thing was a hot mess of an affair that mainly killed Muslims and Jews (and, of course, witches). Inquisitors were like traveling salesmen, and, like so many to come, they dealt in Bibles and blood.

Béatrice de Planisoles was from the mountains of the South of France, the Comté de Foix, an independent fief not far from the shorelines that would one day host villas for the parties of the ill-fated, and very public, twenty-first-century tabloid-fodder love affair between Angelina Jolie and Brad Pitt. But in the 1320s, everyone read the tabloids written by inquisitors, and their focus was on Béatrice's love life.

Christianity had spread following the era of Cleopatra (shout-out to Charlemagne the Great, the Father of Europe, known for uniting western Europe and then some under what would become the Catholic Church). But five hundred years after Charlemagne, Béatrice's family still hadn't made the switch, and her life would be more difficult for that. She was a minor noble and a Cathar, or a frowned-upon brand of Christian that, at the time, was going out of fashion and into flames—literally, on the stake. (A pretty juicy tid-bit about Cathars, and the root of their name, is that they allegedly worshipped the devil, who took the shape of a cat.)

According to some of Béatrice's friends, she personally leaned Catholic, but the damage was already kind of done thanks to her bloodline. You know what they say about labels: once they are stuck on, they can be tricky to peel off.

At age twenty, she married Bérenger de Roquefort, a knight and chatelain, or castle keeper. Like so many interesting women, Béatrice, regardless of what she may have been passionate about, is remembered simply for her passions in love. When she was eventually called before the Inquisition, she had to answer questions about lovers from *decades* before. Despite all the slut-shaming in history from all over the world, from Cleopatra to Béatrice, sexually liberated women *will* make the history books—even if they usually do end up dead or tossed aside.

Béatrice didn't love her first husband, Bérenger de Roquefort, even if he came with a castle. But don't feel bad for her; that's just how marriages worked for most of history. No matter how much Americans may turn their nose up at arranged marriages in cultures that continue the tradition today, romantic marriages weren't the norm in the Western world until the eighteenth century. Marriage was a thing your parents arranged for utilitarian reasons, like obtaining land and securing power through family alliances. Accounts paint Béatrice as a Princess Diana–type figure, someone who related most to peasants despite living in a fortress high above them. Plus, Bérenger was not a bad guy—and she would have to deal with plenty of those.

One of the first was Raimond Roussel, the steward of her estate. According to Béatrice's testimony, Roussel's preferred form of flirtation seemed to be giving Bérenger shit about God, Béatrice's body, and her nasty cat-worshipping roots. After she repeatedly declined his offers to leave her family behind—never mind the fact that she was pregnant again with her husband's child—to live with Roussel and the "good" Christians, one night, by Béatrice's account:

> He entered secretly into my bedroom and hid himself under my bed. I put the house in order and lay down to sleep and when all was quiet and everyone asleep and I myself was sleeping, Raimond came out from under my bed, placed himself next to me and began to act as if he wished to know me carnally. I said "What is this?" He said to be quiet. I replied "What, churl, remain quiet!" and began to cry and call my servants who slept near me in the chamber, saying to them that there was a man in my bed. Hearing this, he left both bed and chamber. The next morning, he said to me that he had done badly to hide himself close to me. I told him "I see now that all your invitations to go to the good Christians are only intended to possess me and sleep with me. If I did not fear that my husband would not believe that I have done nothing dishonest with you, I would send you immediately to the tower dungeon."

She still stealthily managed to have him fired, even if she spared him the dungeon, and didn't feel bad about that at all. In fact, it made Béatrice feel so powerful that she bragged about it and asserted that no man would ever cross her again. Sadly for Béatrice, this would come back to bite her.

In 1302, her loveless marriage came to a natural close when Bérenger died. Unfortunately, her mourning attire (required by law), a black dress complete with a veil, did the opposite of deterring her next unwanted pursuer: the villager Pathau Clergue. And, apparently, he either hadn't heard or didn't care (or didn't take Béatrice's power seriously now that her husband was dead) about what happened to those who came on to her. This one succeeded in raping her. But Béatrice didn't let him steal her sunshine.

She found happiness and consensual love (or at least lust) with Pathau's cousin Pierre Clergue, a Cathar priest and a very famous guy in their village. The Clergue family were considered wealthy peasants, and while Pierre was actually born a Catholic, he had inverted the Inquisition's desired path and converted to Catharism.

By all accounts, Pierre Clergue was that rebellious bad boy— the kind you just can't help but fall for, even though *everyone* talks about what a dirtbag he is. He was known for being a scoundrel. He exploited a lovely moral loophole that he created for himself: because everything that's good is a sin, one might as well sin; and if all sins are equal, why not get your dick wet? In his own words: "One woman's just like another. The sin is the same, whether she is married or not." He'd probably be easier to hate if he didn't end up dead in prison for being a Christian priest of the wrong brand, despite many attempts to bribe and charm his captors. Béatrice's story has a happier ending than his.

After her love affair with Pierre ended, she remarried another minor noble, named Otho de Lagleize, who died just a few years later. In her postmenopausal years, rather than tuck away into her bedchamber to hide out until death, as was expected, she married a third time. Her third husband was a younger priest, Catholic this time, named Barthélemy Amilhac. Béatrice's hot young husband was concerned that his wife's Cathar roots would land both of them in front of the Inquisition, and he was absolutely correct. In the dog days of summer, after being caught with witchy objects in her purse (but let's be real, more likely for daring to be a hot grandma with a libido), she and Barthélemy both appeared before the infamous bishop Jacques Fournier on charges of blasphemy, witchcraft, and heresy.

Béatrice's testimony was transcribed in the *Fournier Register*, the text regarded as one of the most detailed records of medieval peasants' lives. Fournier was born a peasant himself, but his ruthless measures catapulted him to power, ultimately earning him the elected title of Pope Benedict XII of Avignon in 1334. While he used most of his power for evil, he did strongly oppose and try to root out nepotism within the Catholic Church due to his peasant past. So while he was vile, at least he wasn't also a nepo baby.

Fournier conducted interrogations with hundreds of individuals and ensured transcripts were made for each session. Before he came around, authorities were pretty much letting Cathars live and worship in peace. But Fournier was champing at the bit for a hunt, and Béatrice, with her cursed libido, easily met the medieval definition of a witch.

You see, she didn't just *like* having sex; she was responsible about it. Béatrice practiced birth control—and, depending on which source is telling her story, perhaps even abortion—even if she didn't know how it worked, thanks to the charismatic but problematic Pierre. Before the plague, and far before the Scientific Revolution, Béatrice lived in a time when the line between birth control and abortion was blissfully blurry. Despite the lack of antibiotics and low-dose hormonal birth control pills, the folks of the Middle Ages had some cards to play that would not fly today. Think about how many advantages a pregnant person who wanted to hide the details of their pregnancy (or its end) had before stethoscopes existed, let alone ultrasound machines or pee-on-the-strip pregnancy tests. For most of history, people found out about a pregnancy only when someone wanted them to, or when it was far too late to conceal, at which point performing a safe and effective abortion was likely out of the question anyway.

Abortion was already frowned upon by the church, even though it would be another five hundred years after Béatrice's time before the 1869 publication of the papal bull, or apostolic constitution, *Apostolicae Sedis*, in which Pope Pius IX screamed that an abortion at any stage of pregnancy resulted in the penalty of excommunication. Up to then, even the Catholic teachings—those preached by the very folks out for her blood—held that no killing was involved if abortion took place before the fetus was infused with a soul, the point known as "ensoulment." But fearmongering persisted nonetheless. There is a record of a Scottish mother-daughter duo stating that the daughter was, apparently, pregnant with cats and thus needed an abortion. They testified that they thought if she ate food stepped over by a male cat, it would make her pregnant with kittens. As bonkers as this seems today, we can assume this superstition was likely used as an excuse to secure an abortion during a time wrought with paranoia about the practice.

For this combination of reasons, for better and for worse, people had more time on their side to consider options when faced with pregnancy in Béatrice's day. But don't get it twisted. That doesn't mean it was all smiling covens and happy midwives.

Whether you identify with Béatrice in this story or (no judgment) the more problematic Pierre, you can feel good about the fact that the two talked openly about birth control in a conversation that was recorded and lives today in the Vatican's library, which contains more than one million books.

We know this because she had to tell the whole court in front of the inquisitor, her friends, and her current husband that Béatrice responsibly asked before having sex with Pierre, "What shall I do if I am pregnant by you?" Pierre reassured her that he had an herb that prevented pregnancies. He kept the name of that herb to himself. Pierre gave her choice through birth control, but he did not give her knowledge. It was seen as far too dangerous to let those who can get pregnant hold the knowledge of how to control their own bodies. Or maybe, on a pettier note, Pierre just didn't want his lover using his birth control methods with his rapist cousin (or anyone other than himself).

It didn't matter that Béatrice didn't actually have knowledge of abortive herbs, though, or even those used for birth control, for that matter. Her reputation as a wild woman was enough. She was charged with witchcraft based on what was found in her purse, which included "objects strongly suggestive of having been used by her to cast evil spells."

These may not have been abortive agents, but they *were* witchy—and not just a nice piece of rose quartz to sweeten her third marriage. She had spell ingredients that would impress Tik-Tok's most intimidating Satanic witch today.

Béatrice's purse contained the two umbilical cords of her grandsons, which she carried to win victory in any lawsuit. (Sadly, the outcome of her story shows us this is not a reliable spell.) She began carrying them after being advised to by a Jewish woman, who was likely a midwife and friend, which didn't win her any points with Fournier, either. The term "midwife" technically wasn't even used yet—in France, the word describing such women was often "sage-femme," referencing both wisdom and the friendly, aptly named herb used for everything from abortive properties to clearance spells.

Béatrice also carried cloth soaked with her daughter's first period blood, as the same friend said that if the daughter's husband drinks it, she will maintain his love and loyalty. Ask any self-proclaimed witch today: *that* spell is legit. In the Voodoo-influenced city of New Orleans (which we'll visit in Chapter 3), from the time of Marie Laveau to the present, smart men know to avoid drinking coffee served by someone crushing on them, as love and obsession spells are commonly cast by adding brick red period blood to dark beverages such as coffee.

Béatrice must have had a big bag, because her purse also contained frankincense, often used to treat headaches. She also had a mirror; a knife wrapped in linen; a bundle of muslin containing "the seed of the herb ive," which she claimed was a medicine for her grandson's epilepsy; and many notes (described as "written formulas"), not unlike your lost grocery lists crumpled in the bottom of your bag.

She *also* carried arugula—yes, like the salad, a.k.a. *Eruca sativa*—a popular Middle Ages supplement for enhanced sperm-quality sex drive in men. Given that she was postmenopausal at the time, she was likely carrying it for the latter, making her a fucking icon for investing in her sex life without shame.

Béatrice claimed none of the items were for use in "black" magic, or the kinds of magic that might cause trouble or illness for someone else. But to no end, and it's no surprise. Throughout history—and often with racist undertones—the powers that be have tried desperately to distinguish between "white" and "black" magic, that is, acceptable forms of practice and unacceptable witchery. But the two go hand in hand. As a woman's testimony before the Inquisition in Modena in 1499 stated, "Who knows how to heal knows how to destroy."

Apparently, the only thing that Fournier officially classified as evil was the bread, which was believed to be consecrated in the Cathar faith, thus making her a heretic. Béatrice, along with her hot younger husband, Barthélemy, spent a year in prison. Both were released on July 4, 1322, an independence day of sorts fully 454 years before the United States would claim the date as their own in 1776. At the time, the American colonies were but a twinkle in their European fathers' eyes. Béatrice, now officially stamped a witch, was sentenced to wear a yellow cross forever on her embroidered clothing as punishment, signifying her Cathar shame; Barthélemy, a Catholic (and, not for nothing, a man), was considered rinsed of his sins after his stint in prison.

So what was the forbidden fruit from the tree of knowledge that could prevent pregnancy? Well, while Pierre kept that info to himself and the records don't identify it by name, some historians speculate that it could have been a fig, which has a history of use in reproductive rights. Béatrice told the court that "when he wished to ravish me, he carried with him the herb wrapped in linen cloth." While this seems to indicate a suppository—those controversial pessaries from the previous chapter—there's a chance that this magic cure-all was actually an amulet, not unlike those imprinted with the head of Sobek, the Egyptian crocodile deity, and exactly as witchy as Catholics continue to be today with their "blood"-drinking rituals.

Béatrice describes the contraceptive in question in her testimony: "It was about an inch wide or long, or about the size of the first joint of my middle finger with a long string that he put around my neck and it descended between my breasts. He always placed it like this when he wanted to make love to me and it remained around my neck until he got up." A necklace, or a (reusable?) pessary on a string, like a tampon? We may never know. We do know that individualists like Béatrice provided the tabloids of the time with the image that would become synonymous with witches: an older woman (perhaps a cat owner) who doesn't fit in with society— and maybe even gets around on a broom. The earliest recorded depiction of witches riding brooms comes from illustrations in the French poet Martin Le Franc's 1451 manuscript *Le Champion des Dames* (Champion of Women). Both women depicted in the drawings are Waldensians, another non-Catholic Christian sect that, like Cathars, was hunted down during the Inquisition, primarily because they allowed women to become priests. But while *Le Champion des Dames* depicted witches, it wasn't a diss. This manuscript stands out, because, in a time of witch-hunting, as the name suggests, it was a defense of women. While the women of the Middle Ages were spared from the stress of social media trolls, you won't be surprised to learn that the *Fournier Register* was far from the most misogynistic text of the Middle Ages.

3

Malleus Maleficarum (The Witch Hammer) is a 1486 "witch-hunting handbook" or, more accurately, a book written by a guy who blamed witches for his unsatiated sexual desires and then attributed that opinion to the Catholic Church to lend it authority. It was penned by the German Catholic clergyman Heinrich Kramer, a guy who became an inquisitor with the intent of "bringing witches to justice." Sounds like a Trump tweet, doesn't it?

Before the 1400s, no one was really tried and executed for being a witch, because, well, a lot of people just didn't believe in witchcraft. Kramer's book argued that not only did witches absolutely exist, but they were also certainly evil sex-crazed maniacs responsible for his own pervy impulses who should be tried for heresy. While it's an undeniably evil text, at the risk of playing the devil's advocate, here's one note regarding the fear of sexuality at the time: syphilis was a big deal, so fear of that factored in, somewhat mirroring the later sexual revolution of the 1960s and the conservative backlash that would unite Protestants and Catholics in the fight against abortion. While the long effects of untreated syphilis include death, deformity, and insanity, and those are valid concerns, the church's fear of female sexuality is still not, and their methods were cruel, tortuous, and beyond ethically questionable.

Two years before his book dropped, Kramer made one of the first stabs at prosecuting alleged witches and, as a result, was unceremoniously kicked out of the city of Innsbruck and written off by the local bishop as "senile and crazy." *Malleus Maleficarum* was his revenge—and it worked. Not only did he get people to take witches seriously, but it's Kramer's book that cemented the idea that witches are usually women. Not only did Kramer fuck up the lives of women for centuries, but he's also the reason men feel silly enjoying witchcraft today. As British historian Christina Larner put it, "Witch-hunting *is* woman hunting."

Kramer wrote *Malleus Maleficarum* while riding high on the support of Pope Innocent VIII. Kramer was still stung after his first attempt to kill a bunch of witches failed, and, even worse, he was laughed at for his effort, so he lapped up the pope's enthusiastic endorsement. Innocent VIII wrote an official papal bull that gave Kramer formal permission to go after witches, in addition to offering other information on the subject.

According to the 1484 treatise, the seven things witches did were as follows, per John M. Riddle in *Eve's Herbs: A History of Contraception and Abortion in the West*:

1. practice fornication and adultery
2. obstruct the generative act by rendering men impotent
3. perform castration and sterilization
4. engage in bestiality and homosexuality
5. destroy the generative force in women
6. procure abortions
7. offer children to devils

These fall in line with the main accusations witches faced during the Inquisition: having sexual power against men, simply having a sexual nature at all, being organized, and having magical powers, which included medical ones (especially ob-gyn skills). Witchcraft, birth control, and midwifery were now officially and inextricably intertwined.

Some modern relationship therapists will have you do a simple exercise by asking what makes you jealous. They say your answer— women, money, men, power, sex—is your weak spot. If we look at the most common modern accusations against women this way, it seems the current US Senate—or, generically, the old men in charge in our society—is most threatened by sexuality, or, to be more direct, a woman's ability to use sexuality to take power away from men.

Witches were accused and persecuted for having any knowledge of female sexuality and were often charged for possessing medical and ob-gyn skills. *Malleus Maleficarum* proclaims, "No one does more harm to the Catholic Church than midwives," and "All witchcraft comes from carnal lust, which in women is insatiable." This book also stated that "the judgment of doctors" could tell the difference between a natural illness and one caused by witchcraft, demonstrating that only men should make medical decisions.

To save you from the trouble of reading the tedious *Fournier Register* or the maniacal *Malleus Maleficarum*, I'll say that one thing that sticks out when reviewing Inquisition testimony is the blurred lines between magic and medicine and how those formerly braided ropes were turned into competing and opposing forces, two lines coming together to form a giant *X*. During this time period, in part thanks to the Black Death, physicians *were* taken seriously—as long as they were men of the right faith.

But long before the twelve death ships entered the Sicilian port of Messina, the medieval text *Decretum*, written by a Roman bishop in the eleventh century, referred to the "fetus being expelled from the uterus by maleficia and by herbs," associating herbal birth control, formerly nothing more than an accessible remedy, with black magic, too. (*Decretum* also helped start the Christian trend of moralizing abortion and decreeing that some reasons for an abortion were more valid than others. "It makes a big difference if a poor little woman does it on account of the difficulty of feeding, or whether a fornicator does it to conceal her crime," the text states.)

By the time *Malleus Maleficarum* came around, the word "maleficia" had gone from meaning evil, to witches, to specifically witches with herbal knowledge. This was cemented with Pope Sixtus V's 1588 papal bull, *Effraenatum*, which censured contraceptives and abortions "by means of magical deeds (*maleficiis*) and by cursed medicines (*malefuciis medicamentis*)," declaring that abortion at any stage was murder.

While witches were being burned for the crime of knowing the right remedies, "scientists" in the Middle Ages used astrology, a future tenet of witchcraft, when describing fetal development. It was during this time that *The Secrets of Women (De Secretis Mulierum)* was published. It is thought that the work was penned by Albertus Magnus, born around 1200 and deceased on November 15, 1280. He was a German member of the Dominican Order and wore many hats as a philosopher, scientist, and bishop. His contributions led to his sainthood as Saint Albert the Great and recognition as an official doctor of the church. Some argue that he didn't write it at all but that it was penned, at least partially, by his students. *The Secrets of Women* also states that the planets affect the fetus with their corresponding powers. For instance, it asserts that Saturn, the taskmaster of the zodiac, provides reason in the first month, while Venus, the planet of love, creates the sex organs.

Whether it was by Magnus or one of his groupies, *The Secrets of Women* sure wasn't written by women. Among its secrets is that women with high sex drives must have weak fetuses, and those who abstain will have stronger children. It also says that women pee and menstruate through the same hole. Its thirteen chapter titles contain everything from "Concerning Monsters in Nature" to "On the Exit of the Fetus from the Uterus." Interestingly, despite its rampant misogyny, it advises that drinking sage, cooked for three days, will prevent a woman from conceiving for one year, showing that even the real dickheads of the time weren't *staunchly* against family planning. And forget about nagging your boyfriend to get a vasectomy. According to *The Secrets of Women*, if you eat a bee, you'll never conceive.

A proponent of Christian humility, Magnus refused to ride horses, finding it too fancy, so went everywhere on foot. However, a nice sparkly gem wasn't too pretty for his liking. He was an early advocate for crystals, declaring that certain stones held occult powers. An early hipster of sorts, Magnus loved writing about the local music scene, so he's best imagined as a hipster with an MFA and a loose freelance arrangement with the Middle Ages equivalent of *Pitchfork*.

While texts such as *The Secrets of Women* would ultimately pave the way to the Renaissance, which was viewed as a gilded time of knowledge, in the Middle Ages, people still acted like they knew what they were talking about even if they didn't. It was quite an odd time: Italian doctors and surgeons were *actually* learning about the body, as demonstrated in the great illustrated anatomical treatise of Andreas Vesalius in 1543. But centuries before Vesalius taught us the organization of the skeleton, women physicians were writing about medical breakthroughs in history—even if their work was passed off as a man's.

Trota of Salerno lived in southern Italy around the early twelfth century as the doctoress of Salerno. She is considered the first gynecologist in the world, which is an epic brag to say the least. Trota was apparently very beautiful, but other than what she wrote in her medical texts, not much else was known about her. Trota didn't explicitly mention abortion in her work, but she did write about "menstruation stimulators," advising women to drink artemisia in wine and take a bath (which sounds glam), and if that didn't work to take it with other herbs, such as the tried-and-true sage, to bring on their periods.

Trota, with help from her students, is often credited with writing the *Trotula*, a collection of three important medical texts of the era. As a professor, she taught her expertise as a gynecologist to her students, spreading valuable knowledge and making life healthier for women. Her works were influenced by African and Arabic medical, herbal, and general insight into wellness.

Of all the texts, *Practica secundum Trotam* (Practical Medicine According to Trota) is the most comprehensive, covering everything from infertility and menstruation pains or problems to snakebites (RIP Cleopatra) and cosmetics—which Cleopatra would already have known about. But what made Trota most infamous during her time was that she expressed the radical idea that if conception failed, either the man or the woman could be responsible. The thought until then was that it simply *must* be the woman's fault.

People tried to discredit Trota for her gender. Georg Kraut—a German man with no other Googeable legacy than what follows—got his hands on *Trotula* in 1544 and rearranged the three components into one to appear as though a single person authored it, in a move best understood to make the text look older than it was by slicing away any mention of common names. So when Casper Wolf edited the newly bastardized *Trotula* in 1566, he switched the name from *Trotula* to *Eros* (which is a male name). As a result, they passed the book off as an ancient text written by a man, erasing women's contributions to science during the Middle Ages. Trota had to wait posthumously, to say the least, to enjoy recognition for her work in 1985 when John F. Benton, a historian at the California Institute of Technology, realized the change, corrected it, and made sure she was properly credited.

4

In an era in which women were burned, tried as witches, and even the most accomplished erased from history, it's not surprising it was during the Middle Ages that witches became directly correlated with the devil. While the ancients had lords of the underworlds and concepts of either chaos or paradise in the afterlife, it was during this dark and transitional era that the devil became a bargaining tool and even an excuse to get away with everything from infanticide to having hot, stoned sex with tall, dark, and handsome men. In his *Examen of Witches*, compiled in the late sixteenth century by a chief justice who served as France's inquisitor and was known for his ruthless nature, Henry Boguet wrote: "Those midwives and wise women who are witches are in the habit of offering to Satan the little children which they deliver, and then of killing them. . . . They do even worse; for they kill them while they are yet in their mothers' wombs. This practice is common to all witches." You know how people say that if their partner unfairly accuses them of cheating, it makes them want to go ahead and do it because they're already getting blamed for it? It was kind of the same thing for accused witches and devil worship. *Yes! The devil* did *make me do it.* Much like a male version of Lilith, this Lucifer character, the incubus to her succubus, began appearing in Inquisition testimonies.

As any modern-day real Satanist will get on a soapbox and tell you, for practicing nontheistic Satanists, such as the Satanic Temple or Brooklyn's League of Rebel Eve (LORE), Lucifer is not seen as a vile and seductively evil demon who will come and have wild sex with you in the middle of the night. Not in modern Satanism, anyway (even if he may be portrayed that way in certain TV series). Rather, Lucifer represents the fallen angel, he who turns away from tradition and church to embrace a delicious life of individuality.

Granted, that's not how Lucifer was discussed in the medieval courts. The accused parties there were often all too quick to blame the man himself for their sinful behaviors. But can you blame them? They were facing down an *Inquisition*, for fuck's sake. As Paris Hilton once told *Vogue*, "I'm not a dumb blonde. I'm just really good at pretending to be one." If pretending to be in cahoots with the devil was the safest bet to a longer life span, women were going to take it.

Here's an example. Once upon a time, a servant woman named Appolonia Mayr wanted to get married. However, she was dealing with a pregnancy that would have hindered her socially and economically and prevented her from getting hitched. Apparently unaware of Pierre's magic necklace, and alive in a time before Planned Parenthood, she turned to the tried-and-true method of infanticide and killed her newborn by leaving the baby out in a field. People did leave newborns out in the woods to die of exposure when left with no options; films like *The Witch* have more basis in reality than one would expect. Appolonia confessed. But rather than take the blame for infanticide, she blamed it on the devil, who she testified was disguised as a midwife.

It didn't work. Appolonia was burned for being a witch in 1686.

The details of the accusations of the devil's interference offer insight into the poverty of many women at the time. They testified that he offered them clothes, food, and cash, not to mention debt payment. A deal with the devil at the time could also be interpreted as a euphemism for sex work, which, despite the ever-present demand, was seriously frowned upon due to an unfortunate rise in conservative thinking.

Some of the "witches" may only have been outsiders who refused to go quietly, as it was around this time in Europe when communal spaces began to die as private land thrived, thus displacing the tired, the old, the hungry, and the rebellious, argues modern-day

feminist activist and historian Silvia Federici. Agrarian capitalism and English enclosures began in the late fifteenth century in
Europe, and both played an undeniable role in the witch hunts of
that time, as getting rid of communitarian societies demonizes
those who need them most, namely, older, poorer women without
the social currency of a husband and menstrual cycle.

But real baby-sacrificing, nonmetaphorical witchcraft absolutely took place in Europe during the Middle Ages and the Renaissance that followed. Another woman, Anne-Marie de Georgel of
Toulouse, France, confessed in 1335 under torture that "a tall, dark
man with fiery eyes and clothes in skins appeared to her while she
was washing and asked if she would give herself to him, to which
she assented," reports John M. Riddle in *Eve's Herbs: A History of
Contraception and Abortion in the West*. She alleged she was trans-
ported to the Sabbath, basically a Black Mass, a ceremony often
performed by Satanists for ritual or just a damned good time.

The Black Mass is a perversion, a blasphemous version of the
Catholic Mass. In the modern era, most Black Masses, such as
the failed attempt to host one with a student group affiliated with
the Harvard Extension School in 2014 by the Satanic Temple,
are, at best, political theater and, at worst, simple trolling. In this
case, the group backed out at the last minute due to pressure from
influential Boston Catholics connected to the school, and Harvard
University, which no longer postpones events due to eclipses, had
former president Drew Faust release a statement that included
the line: "The decision by a student club to sponsor an enact-
ment of this ritual is abhorrent." The cloaked ritual featuring a
fake sacrificial virgin (the woman inhabiting this role was not
a virgin) took place in a Chinese restaurant near the university instead. But if we are to believe Anne-Marie de Georgel's
confession, it sounds like her Black Masses were far more mental
than political theater.

She may have been referring to honest-to-Lucifer rituals, such as dancing naked in the woods, with nature unrestrained, and away from the literally bloody patriarchy and their damned inquisitors. Anne-Marie had the balls to share that she'd boiled poisonous herbs and animal and human body parts, sometimes robbed from cemeteries, to create potions we now sometimes call "flying ointment."

Step aside, evil witches, and let a nice, trusted physician tell us more about this potion and all the wonder it could provide. According to Jeremone Cardan, a doctor, in 1554: "It was smear[ed] all over themselves. It consists, if it is to be believed, of that fat of infants torn from graves and the juices of parsley and nightshade, as well as cinquefoil and soot. Incredibly they [the witches] may persuade themselves that they have seen large areas, theaters, green gardens, fishing, garments, adornments, dancing, handsome young men, and lovemaking of whatever kind they desire." Nearly all accounts of such witches' ointments at the time contain unbaptized babes, in addition to contraceptives and abortive herbs. Whether the actual fat used was taken from an animal or a dead baby, it's believed it could have acted as a carrier for other ingredients.

While it's tempting to write such potions off as legend and lore, some women did concoct devilish and deadly brews. Meet La Voisin, poisoner of the 1 percent.

Catherine Monvoisin (ca. 1640–1680), known as "La Voisin," was a French midwife and proud witch. She performed abortions and openly provided more obvious occult services, such as creating potions and poisons, telling fortunes, and even holding the real kind of Black Masses; she was far too legit for political theater. In a relationship that would one day be echoed by Nancy Reagan, who would consult an astrologer to help aid her husband in political decisions while simultaneously facilitating Satanic Panic propaganda nationwide in the 1980s, one of La Voisin's clients was Madame de Montespan, King Louis XIV's mistress. In fact, this client would be her downfall. (Be careful when creating poisons to kill the people in charge.)

La Voisin, the wife of a jeweler and silk merchant, lived well in Villeneuve-sur-Gravois, a cultural hot spot in Parisian society. But her comfortable life was at stake because her husband was, by all accounts, a terrible jeweler and silk merchant and drove the family into debt. So La Voisin, likely still called Catherine at the time, began supporting the family through her work as a midwife, which naturally included abortions. She also figured out that she could make money by reading fortunes. Through her work as both a fortune teller and an abortion provider, she noticed a theme in her clients' desires: men. So she tapped into her herbalist skills and began branding herself as a potion maker. With no moral hang-ups about hexing or healing, and fully understanding that she who knows how to heal knows how to destroy, La Voisin created both love potions and, well, the heavier stuff.

La Voisin also opened a home for unwed mothers; if the rumors are to be believed and she did kill infants or at least use fetuses in Black Mass ceremonies, she had access to the materials. In a Black Mass, a naked woman is typically used as the altar, and La Voisin often volunteered to take this role herself.

Many of these ceremonies took place underneath churches, facilitated by priests—many of whom were her lovers. Who needs a love potion when you have the simple power of pussy? Her body count (history records at least six of her lovers) contains executioners, magicians, and members of the aristocracy, in addition to priests.

Through her booming business in potions, midwifery, and the type of witchcraft that would make the Moral Majority's Satanic

Panic of the 1980s seem well deserved (86 the rose quartz, extra dead baby, please), La Voisin gained power and had no fear of using it. Forget political theater; she preferred a much more direct approach to change-making. La Voisin was one of the heads of the *affaire des poisons*, a cult that poisoned many members of the French aristocracy. The bold witch even planned to poison the king himself, as ordered by her client Madame de Montespan, the king's mistress, who wanted him dead because he wouldn't become monogamous with her. And Madame de Montespan was only one of her high-connected clients.

While La Voisin always collected her bills, she used the money she made cooking up potions for the rich to offer midwife services to peasants for free—making her hard to hate, other than the potential actual baby-killing she carried out in church basements. And if you're feeling a bit of déjà vu, yes, that reads like a synopsis of the QAnon Pizzagate conspiracy of 2016, which alleged that high-ranking Democratic officials like Hillary Clinton were running an underground Satanic pedophile ring headquartered in the Washington, DC, pizzeria Comet Ping Pong.

La Voisin wasn't the only name in town. Her competition in the dark arts was a woman named Marie Bosse. Unfortunately for both women, King Louis XIV, a.k.a. the Sun King, was (rightfully) very paranoid about being poisoned. The rumors are true: he had servants taste his food before he ate it to make sure it wouldn't kill him. Marie Bosse was caught in a round of arrests related to his fear, and she pointed the finger at La Voisin, who was then arrested, kept drunk on wine, and ultimately convicted of witchcraft and burned to death in a public execution in 1680.

In case you have a morbid curiosity, being burned alive hurts the most at the beginning, before the nerves turn to crisp, and the lucky ones die quickly from suffocation.

Before she was caught, it's believed that La Voisin helped poison more than a thousand people, and some historians speculate she killed twenty-five hundred children for her Black Masses. It's hard to say if this number is inflated due to fear. At the time, people were scared of witches, but they were *really* scared of their organized meetings, whether it was a poison cult or your run-of-the-mill baby-killing Black Mass. Such groups were considered more dangerous than a solitary witch.

Some folks who used potions and herbal remedies at the time might have just been . . . high. Often, the potion described as a witch's "flying ointment" contained atropine, which can cause hallucinations and occurs naturally in the nightshade family. Some women may not have been lying in their testimonies by blaming their "crimes" on the devil, and they may not have been actually worshipping him; they might have just been tripping their faces off and hallucinating.

Today, modern-day witches sell safer versions of this "flying ointment," containing cannabis rather than anything poisonous. "My flying ointment recipe is very similar to the old-school kind and includes many of the classic ingredients," Natalie Reyes, owner of the online boutique the Skeleton Key Shop, tells me. "However, after much research and testing, I found that it was not necessary to include the few plants that are considered toxic or lethal when ingested, and the result was very much the same as all of the solanaceae [nightshade] and entheogenic plants are imbued with the same kind of liminal energies needed to alter consciousness and enter a trance state." While her original recipe contained hemp, she switched it up due to the unfortunately murky laws surrounding hemp and CBD sales. The witches of yore may have been brewing up psychedelic potions for the same reason a self-proclaimed weed witch today turns to cannabis while sick or after a medical procedure, including miscarriage or abortion: pure pain relief.

The church often told the poor that disease and discomfort were necessary suffering. They believed that pain, especially women's pain, was Eve's curse and meant to be experienced. The related Bible passage Genesis 3:16 in the Revised Standard Version reads: "I will greatly multiply your pain in childbearing; in pain you shall bring forth children, yet your desire shall be for your husband, and he shall rule over you."

If this line of thought is applied even to giving birth—because, of course, some painkillers could harm a fetus—then it would have been ludicrous for people to expect any pain relief when deliberately ending a pregnancy. Childbirth without the aid of a midwife would continue to be an unmedicated exercise in stamina and self-control for hundreds of years. Allegedly, Queen Victoria was the first person to give birth with the aid of chloroform sedation— much later on, in 1853.

So, when witches and midwives offered painkillers such as ergot, it only added to their reputation of evil. Even in modern times, women continue to struggle to have their pain taken seriously. Taking the abortion pill often results in what's described as a "heavy period," but it can be as excruciating as a spontaneous miscarriage. (And, of course, as many people are aware, a heavy period can itself be excruciating for some.) Regardless, patients are typically directed to manage the pain with nothing but over-the-counter options.

In 1583, Johann Weyer (1515–1588), a Dutch physician, occultist, and demonologist known for scientifically challenging claims of witches practicing anything supernatural, asserted that many of the accused should not be held responsible for their Inquisition testimonies, as they were likely the result of having hallucinations. (We love a man who can do it all.) Weyer also openly criticized the *Malleus Maleficarum*, which was called "possibly the most misogynous text ever written" by the aforementioned activist and historian Silvia Federici. Weyer was an early ally, using his ratio-nal knowledge to challenge claims of witchcraft. He was also one of the first people to talk about the role of mental health conditions in witch hunts—not as a jab at the inquisitors, whose moral panic is its own long story, but in reference to possible medical condi-tions experienced by those who were persecuted. Like eugenics programs to come, witch hunts were an excellent excuse to get rid of any perceived stain on society, including those who struggled with mental health in an era of devils, rapist priests, and wrongful imprisonment. (And, yes, I'm aware that I could be talking about any point in history when I list those factors.)

The Middle Ages indeed earned their dark reputation. It's no won-der that by the time the Renaissance came about, the likes of La Voisin were all about poisoning the 1 percent and reveling in the Dionysus-approved theatrics of the Black Mass. These unholy cel-ebrations were an answer to the death and disease of the plague, a backlash to the pathetic attempts by the people in charge to blame marginalized groups for the unprecedented horrors of the illness.

And, as humans were unable to stop the decay, women (espe-cially the likes of Béatrice de Planisoles, who enjoyed sex with mul-tiple lovers, was born into the wrong religion, and took health and protection into her own hands, as demonstrated in the contents of her infamous purse) bore the brunt. The misogynistic tabloids of the time, such as the *Fournier Register* and *Malleus Maleficarum*, changed many attitudes for the worse, transforming birth control into an enemy of life. And through changing terminology, these shifts linked reproductive rights, lay healers (especially women), and witches, categorizing all as evil and fit for death or prison.

And it was only the beginning. For the people native to North America and the Black folks brought there through enslavement,

both forced to bloodily assimilate and drop their inherent religions, as well as the women rooted out by the Puritans during the
fascinating (if overhyped) Salem Witch Trials, the erasure of and
ascription of evil onto spiritual practice was already beginning to
simmer across the pond, too.

CHAPTER 3

WITCH HUNTS IN COLONIAL AMERICA (THE REAL AND THE HYSTERICAL)

1

The air is frigid and smells like the pine trees that poke through it, revealing spots of sunlight. You're warm in your leather leggings and fur robe. It's the winter of 1692 in your ancestral land of Naumkeag, which was renamed Salem, Massachusetts, some sixty years ago when it was settled by English colonists. Your clothing may mainly serve to keep you warm, but you're partial to a bit of decoration. While such attire is acceptable for both the men and the women in your tribe, the Naumkeag band of the Massachusett, you identify as neither.

In the present day, folks would call you a two-spirit person, an umbrella term coined in 1990 for Indigenous people who identify with male and female genders but don't fit neatly into either. Instead, you occupy an alternative gender status and enjoy duties typically distributed to more than one gender role. You likely know how to find and identify useful plants, a task usually assigned to women, whether they are foods, such as wild rice or hardy tubers, or medicines, like slippery elm bark to prevent a pregnancy (and perhaps treat a bullet wound). You've also obtained a warrior reputation status for your hunting and fighting skills. Rather than being treated as an outcast, you are revered and considered the divine result of supernatural intervention sanctioned by your people.

While you like to both defend your community and sew, because you're a two-spirit member of your band, there's a decent chance you also hold a spiritual role as a healer.

More than three hundred years later, trans and nonbinary folks not so unlike yourself will face unique battles in their fight for reproductive justice (and this is especially true for Indigenous people). However, you may have already realized how much you freak the shit out of European immigrants, who were often shocked by the gender-defying role of the two-spirit. The recently established Wabanaki Confederacy, encompassing tribes such as the Mi'kmaq, Maliseet, Passamaquoddy, Penobscot, Abenaki, and smaller bands like the Massachusett, was one of the earliest Indigenous groups in North America to encounter English and French colonists. By your era, the Wabanaki peoples have engaged in nearly two hundred years of trade and frequent conflicts with both the English and the French. And still, the settlers are unsettled by your gender expression. While being two-spirit is not synonymous with being gay, you do form romantic and sexual relationships with people of the same sex as you. As you peer through the pines at the Puritans, who are still just a few decades new to the area, your intuition pings with discontent. But you're bored by the machinations of their daily life and ready to go home to the colorful comfort of your tribe and partner.

You can see these Puritans, but they can't see you, and you can hear them, but they can't hear you—until you're ready for them to. When they stomp around in their buckled leather boots, the snow crunches loudly. You've watched many of these immigrants bust their asses trying to walk on it. You may go on to lose the war, but you'll win a few battles against these guys—in particular, during King William's War (1689–1697), the first of four French and Indian Wars. However, even if you kick their asses a few times, their arrival and resulting hysterics will be turned into a beloved story of persecution by self-proclaimed witches to come—even if the tale is also part of the story of your demise. But right now, you take a moment to judge the people who will bring hell, in the literal Christian sense, through their beliefs and, in the metaphorical sense, through what your people will experience in the era of colonization.

You are a vibrant contrast to the Puritans. They are dressed conservatively in drab colors. Clear gender roles are established through their attire; you find no trace of anything like a two-spirit. The women and girls mend clothing, milk cows, and make candles, wearing depressing dresses, perhaps some kind of gray, if you can call it a color, with high-necked smocks and wide collars, and, of course, aprons. The women with husbands cover their hair with a linen cap. The men and boys who herd cattle (and even attempt to hunt now and then) wear hats that look like steeples. They pair this with too-big shirts with funny sleeves that look like clouds. They have knee-length breeches, perhaps also made out of leather such as yours, vests, and jackets (this makes sense; gotta stay warm), but they are unadorned. These are not people concerned with beauty. And in a contrast with your rich storytelling and oral tradition, the Puritans read obsessively from a single book known as the Bible.

As you observe these off-worlders from your post, you notice that they rarely show affection, especially not to their kids. They work their children *hard*, nearly as hard as they work their livestock, little fingers spinning, and stitching, and plowing. Work is valued, and tears are met with whippings. However, traumatizing children has a price. It will be these asshole kids who will eventually perform a childish strike in the form of tossing and turning and biting one another, all the while blaming their poor behavior on witches. And their parents won't only buy their story; they'll imprison one another and even kill to prove it true (not to mention claim to fuck ghosts and see jellyfish floating in their fireplaces). Over temper tantrums, nineteen people will be executed.

Conversely, you'll get smallpox, and 90 percent of your people will die from it.

The way you rear your children is different. Your kids frolic around campfires and play fetch with dogs. Your kids know how to have a good time, but they can also kill a deer and then transform its fur and meat into a coat and meal. You notice that the Puritans hoard their children the way they guard their land, crops, and cattle. While you love your little ones, nurturing relationships are rarely limited to blood, and they learn much from the village elders. The Puritans—who call *you* "heathens," by the way (and that's one of the nicer terms)—fear this kind of collectivism.

Right now, despite the fear spreading (not to mention new diseases your immune systems are unprepared for) through tribes, for the most part, you still enjoy your community- and nature-based way of life. Roughly two hundred years later, not only will there be more Europeans in town, but they will be running the whole damn continent. Legislation, notably the 1887 Dawes Allotment Act, will seek to treat Indigenous people as individuals rather than members of a tribe. Settlers enact this by taking, then splitting, tribal land. Yet they ironically use this weapon to enforce their own idea of a tribe on you: the nuclear family. If you or any other Indigenous families want a chunk of this land, you are required to register a male head of household. Each head of a family gets one-quarter of a section, while every single person over eighteen gets one-eighth of a section and those single folks under eighteen years receive only one-sixteenth of a section. The legislation fails to mention your fellow two-spirit people.

While the fear of the wilderness and its primal sounds will fuel the frigid courtrooms and pews of Salem, in their infamous, yet overplayed, witch trials, your magic is the personification of nature. Your healers are medicine men and women (or persons), who, like the many two-spirits who occupied the role, are considered sacred and thus further blur the line between science and magic, not unlike the Egyptians' Heka. Folk magic, which is just another word for magic of the people, is both a source of ethnic identity and a rite of initiation. "To be an effective conduit of supernatural power, a folk healer must maintain a balance between magic and medicine," as the misuse of magic can affect one's healing abilities, writes anthropologist and second-generation Cherokee scholar Alan Kilpatrick.

The two-spirit and their hunting comrades walk away from the Puritans, frighteningly unaware, or perhaps all too certain, of the violence that is to come.

While it is tricky to know precisely how many Indigenous peoples lived in North America before Columbus got there, the estimates range from 3.8 million to 7 million people. Experts give the high end of the range at 18 million. The European settlers' forced removal of them from their ancestral lands, especially burial locations (which people will continue to swear are haunted for centuries), and prohibited use of their language and oral history resulted in an irreparable loss of history. While it's broadly true that Indigenous cultural beliefs were nature based, capable of seeing shades of gray, and containing both magic and medicine, it is impossible to describe them in broad strokes or as a monolith. As Jonnette Paddy, former Miss Native UNLV, told Catherine Daleo for a *Millennials in Motion Magazine* article on the spiritual ritual of smudging: "We're all so incredibly different, so we don't all practice the same things. The spirituality differs tribe by tribe; there really isn't one 'Native American spirituality'—a lot of people tend to think that of our religion. Our religion and culture intertwine, so they're as different as the languages we speak."

While one can't make too many sweeping statements, there are some folk magic practices that many tribes shared, not only with one another but with the rest of the world. Many tribes, including the Cherokee, Pueblo, Seminole, and Lena (not to mention the Puritans), used "witch dolls," which are similar to voodoo dolls, or effigies created to perform magic on a living person. Dolls in general are a common gift to give to infants—and in our gendered world, dolls are especially accepted as gifts for girls, often with the intention of encouraging them to play house and embrace gender roles, while boys get Transformers and GI Joes. With dolls already so ingrained into the human experience throughout history, it tracks that the rebellious, magical version also took hold globally in so many societies. In 2002, the American Girl doll company released Kaya'aton'my, or Kaya, of the Nimíipuu tribe, marketed as the earliest American Girl with a story set in 1764, acknowledging that Indigenous American culture *was* American culture before the influence of any European immigrants. More than a decade after Kaya's release, the company became an unlikely ally for reproductive rights and an enemy of American conservatives by raising money for Girls, Inc., an organization that supports abortion rights. Today, you can find great memes of American Girl dolls performing séances with captions like, "Wanna come over and hex Brett Kavanaugh?"

While we don't know if they used them to prevent pregnancy, some people indigenous to North America also commonly used magical amulets in ceremonies, like what Pierre Clergue may have adorned our friend Béatrice with before getting busy across the pond, or like the ancient Egyptian uterine amulets adorned with the crocodile god Sobek. Traditional medicine people in certain tribes typically carried a small pouch around their neck filled with tokens that, like the Pythagorean theory that influenced Hippocrates, represented the four elements: earth, air, fire, and water.

As is true for their magic, any generalizations about people indigenous to North America's family planning is doomed to leave a lot out. However, what white settlers did to the Indigenous people is critical to the story of reproductive justice and witch hunts in America. Not only did Indigenous people practice many forms of magic, from divination to love charms, but their cultures continue to be looted by modern-day pagans and "spiritual" white people. Whether it's the overharvesting of white sage (a plant with a use you may not be familiar with—stay tuned) for Instagrammable space cleansing or models posing in feathered headdresses at Coachella, a festival whose parent company donates tens of thousands to anti-choice groups, Native practices are among the most appropriated. Indigenous people were already using herbs for abortion and birth control for centuries before the Puritans showed up (in addition to the withdrawal or pull-out method), and while Salem steals the spotlight, America's Native peoples are the victims of perhaps the greatest actual political witch hunt in history. In *Defenders of the Unborn: The Pro-life Movement Before Roe v. Wade*, author Daniel K. Williams writes, of folks seeing images of abortion, "What made abortion liberalization efforts so frightening was that, for the first time, a majority of Americans wanted to legitimize the killing of particular classes of people solely because they inconvenienced those who had the power to determine their fate." Clearly, they forgot about the people indigenous to North America.

This book cannot encompass the entire history of these peoples' participation in the reproductive justice movement or religious practices. Therefore, the focus will be on the perspective of witchcraft and witch hunts, beginning with the events of the early nineteenth century.

∽ͼ

Thomas Jefferson, who was the third president of the United States from 1801 to 1809 and is more prominently featured later in this chapter, was the first US president to suggest the implementation of a reservation system. Despite definitely wanting to get Indigenous people off any valuable land, he was fascinated by their cultures, even decorating Monticello, his home in Charlottesville, Virginia, with their art. Another Jefferson cultural fact: he also loved the violin, a tidbit that loses its charm for classical music lovers once you learn he kept up his practice only because he whined about the music being played in North America at the time as being in a "state of deplorable barbarism," according to the National Constitution Center.

Andrew Jackson, the seventh president of the United States (1829–1837), was also a music lover. He was an early champion of having music as part of a political campaign, although he preferred British ballads (everyone knows Jefferson was a voracious Francophile). Andrew Jackson ardently supported "Indian Removal," enacting the 1830 Indian Removal Act. This law was all about money, really. It let the government trade lands where the cotton grew like crazy east of the Mississippi for spots out west in the "Indian colonization zone"—land the United States picked up in the Louisiana Purchase. (Cotton will play a major and multidimensional role in this chapter itself.) The Indian Removal Act is the legislation that sanctioned the Trail of Tears, a term coined by a Choctaw leader who referred to it as a "trail of tears and death" in an interview with an Alabama newspaper reporter.

At first, in the southeastern United States, many Choctaw, Chickasaw, Seminole, Creek, and Cherokee people initially agreed to assimilate, believing it better than relocation, which they rightly assumed meant death, and they thus became known as the "Five

Civilized Tribes." (America's first president, from 1789 to 1797, George Washington, was a big proponent of assimilation, an idea that continued even when removal efforts ramped up.) Back in the early 1830s, around 125,000 people indigenous to North America lived on lands their families had been on for ages—millions of acres across Georgia, Tennessee, Alabama, North Carolina, and Florida. But by the time 1840 rolled around, after a mass genocide, you'd find hardly any of them there anymore.

During the brutal winter of 1831, faced with pressure from the US Army, the Choctaw people, a tribe that absolutely kicked ass at agriculture, not to mention sports, such as stickball, were first forced on the relocation journey on foot, some bound in chains, without any food, supplies, or help (but under orders) from the government. Thousands died along the way. They were not allowed to enter towns or cities for fear of disease spreading, and they often were lucky to have shoes while marching on the bitter ice and snow.

In another harsh winter, that of 1838–1839, more than 15,000 Cherokee were uprooted from the Smoky Mountains in Tennessee and made to head out to new territories in eastern Oklahoma, a devastating march known as the Trail of Tears. Meanwhile, about 1,400 managed to avoid the relocation and stayed behind in North Carolina, Alabama, Tennessee, and the Georgia mountains. But even they weren't left in peace—their lands and means of making a living were taken from them. The Cherokee who endured the journey finally arrived in Oklahoma when spring came around in 1839, where they began the unfathomably arduous process of restarting their lives while trying to hold on to their culture.

Considering the high death count and the reliance on oral history, records regarding the Cherokee rituals are scarce today, but not extinct. Cherokee wrote down their magical texts in the native script of the Sequoyah syllabary in pocket-size notebooks. As Cherokee scholar Kilpatrick found while researching the magic of his ancestors, the Western Cherokee (and other tribes) used love magic, divination, and the accumulated wisdom of the medicine person, or *dida:hnvwi:sgi*, a gender-neutral term for "curer of them." Keep in mind that Cherokee magical texts in such books are considered "ritually dead," meaning they no longer contain their tribal power. "That is, their powers to heal or harm anyone [has] expired over time and [has] now been strictly nullified," Kilpatrick writes. If only modern doctors could consider the much-abused Hippocratic oath ritually dead and write a new one that encompasses reproductive rights or had Christians stopped taking the Bible passage Exodus 22:18, from the King James Version, "Thou shalt not suffer a witch to live," so seriously sometime before the Inquisition.

But different cultures have different moral codes. The Trail of Tears is often seen as one of the most violent examples of the varying viewpoints regarding landownership between the people indigenous to North America and colonists. But the violence went beyond the land—the Indigenous people forced into relocation were stripped of their culture, too. For example, the Indian Removal Act meant changes in gender roles for many tribes, including the Cherokee, who historically practiced a matrilineal kinship system before being made to assimilate into the European idea of the nuclear family.

Part of the reason tribes were forced from their homes was the expansion of production and land needed for agriculture, expansion that occurred due to the inhumane enslavement of Black people from Africa, which soared after the invention of the cotton gin. These threads of liberation and reproductive rights are impossible to untangle: Cotton root bark played a prominent role as an abortifacient for enslaved women, who notably used the herb as a form of reproductive resistance. Of the herbal abortive remedies available in North America at the time, research shows that cotton root bark, which Indigenous people were also aware of, exhibits some of the lowest toxicity.

And there were many such remedies. More dangerous than cotton root bark was pennyroyal oil, from the periwinkle pennyroyal plant, which smells of spearmint and can induce abortions by causing uterine contractions. Indigenous people used the plant for this purpose—although the dose needed to abort could kill the pregnant person or cause lifelong kidney and liver damage, so it was risky and had to be closely titrated.

According to folklore, slippery elm bark, the red, orange, and brown branch with a distinct butterscotch scent and a chewy texture, can also induce a miscarriage. The plant grows everywhere from South Dakota to Tennessee (across the Trail of Tears). The Cherokee used it for abortions and also to treat bullet injuries. Before colonization, Indigenous tribes engaged in tribal warfare, but the introduction of guns greatly heightened violence. But without them, tribes were at a major disadvantage, so they often traded fur or joined European conflicts (such as the French and Indian War) to obtain firearms.

The Shoshone and Navajo people used stoneseed as an herbal birth control. It was most often taken orally, and, like so many herbal remedies, one should drink only a little bit to avoid complications such as dizziness and nausea (although, let's be real, those symptoms and so many more are also side effects of the modern hormonal birth control prescribed today). Stoneseed is a species of flowering plant native to the western United States. The perennial herb grows from a taproot (like a carrot), and its woody stem is covered in little upright hairs. Its flower has five lobes (like a pentagram) and is light yellow with hints of green (just like that crocodile dung we talked about in earlier chapters). As with other ancient herbs, studies on mice have shown that the plant reduced their fertility, though their efficacy in humans has never been proven.

In *13 in 1: The Authentic Native American Herbalist's Bible*, Hakidonmuya Kimama mentions that juniper, a woody masculine scent lovely in perfumes, can induce uterine contractions in pregnant people, which you may remember from our discussion of ancient Greece in the time of "filthy sorceress" Theoris of Lemnos.

On social media, you can find instructions for saging your genital area after a bad breakup, and on celebrity wellness sites, you can find sage shaving cream that costs more than what plenty of Americans make in a day. Sage is a holy plant known by Indigenous peoples for its cleansing properties, which very well may have included clearing out an unwanted pregnancy. Bees, butterflies, and hummingbirds adore the plant for its lavender flowers, accented by its gray-green leaves and revered for its calming properties when one lights and fans the smoke from dried bundles tied with rope. In modern-day times, some forms of the plant will be overharvested in real life and overplayed on Instagram. White sage, native only to California, is currently at risk for extinction due to the unfortunate combination of a limited bioregion and unlimited poachers due to its trendiness. Although various cultures have embraced the practice of smudging herbs like sage, there was a time when Indigenous peoples in the Americas were prohibited from this tradition. In the 1800s, both Canada and the United States outlawed smudging. It wasn't until the 1950s that Canada revoked this ban, and in the United States, the American Indian Religious Freedom Act of 1978 finally reinstated the right for people indigenous to North America to use sage for their rituals. Considering this, despite its widespread use, many find burning sage as a non-Native person to be cultural appropriation. Lavender and rosemary are some lovely aromatherapeutic alternatives.

As white Americans enacted horrors like the Trail of Tears, they were simultaneously creating the concept of Indigenous folks not as humans but as spirits to be appropriated. This was demonstrated with the rise of Spiritualism, a nineteenth-century religious movement based on communication with the dead and riddled with scam artists—although that last fact didn't stop both the Protestants and the Catholics from taking it seriously enough to issue dire warnings about the practice, which they considered witchcraft. These were smoke-and-mirror rituals to "channel" the dead to ask them questions, much like the modern use of a Ouija board. And at the time (and even today), folks often sought to summon knowledge from Native spirits specifically.

Brad Steiger, the author of some 170 books on the occult, whom this author frankly finds to be a charlatan and a quack, writes in his book *American Indian Magic: Sacred Pow Wows & Hopi Prophecies*, "In essence, since the advent of modern Spiritualism in 1848, we have had a native Anglo-American religion based upon metaphysical insights of the Indian." He's not wrong, but that doesn't make it ethical.

Over the very same years Indigenous people were dying of exposure on the Trail of Tears, their ghosts were already being hijacked for party tricks. Spiritualists said Native Americans, with their deep connections to nature, were better than others at crossing spiritual planes ... to show up at a party of Victorian ladies who wanted to know if their husbands were cheating? They probably were, but leave the Indigenous spirits out of it. The first woman to run for president, Victoria Woodhull (1838–1927) was dubbed "Mrs. Satan" for believing in Spiritualism, suffrage (for white women), and reproductive rights (for white women—Mrs. Satan also believed in eugenics).

Eugenics takes away reproductive rights by attempting to stop someone, or a group of people, from reproducing—or by blazing ahead surgically through sterilization without their consent. Even Spiritualism probably has more evidence backing it than the debunked "science" of eugenics. Perhaps the only good thing eugenics ever did was help spark the impetus for the reproductive justice movement (which the progenitors of eugenics would *hate*, you'll be happy to hear). The utter cruelty of eugenicist practices demonstrated the importance of protecting the right to have children safely just as much as the right *not* to have children.

Indigenous people were on top of this.

As Abaki Beck and Rosalyn Lapier, the grandchildren of Annie Mad Plume Wall, a respected healer among the Blackfeet Nation of Montana, write in the essay "For Indigenous Peoples, Abortion Is a Religious Right":

> Our grandmother taught us that Blackfeet women used both medicinal plants and ritual practices for reproductive health. The Blackfeet used over a dozen plants to regulate menstruation, for abortion, for the birth process, and to address symptoms of menopause. Blackfeet women also held a religious ceremony during which a sanctified belt decorated with religious symbols was worn to regulate fertility and prevent pregnancy. Whether using medicinal plants or religious rituals, Blackfeet people viewed reproductive health and bodily autonomy as part of our relationship with the sacred realm.

Assumptions and generalizations are dangerous. Keep this in mind when reading conservative hot takes on any group of people's beliefs. It's not unusual to see conservative news outlets hijack historical violence to try to paint a culture as anti-abortion.

In one Indigenous religious ritual, water was called upon to bring on a pregnancy (just like with the Nile half a world and quite a few centuries away). According to a Hilibi (of the Creek Tribe) legend recounted by tribal member Woksi Miko, as reported by Bill Grantham in *Creation Myths and Legends of the Creek Indians*, a woman who wasn't married but was ready to be a single mom went to get water from the spring and became pregnant. Because she went to the spring instead of chasing down some sperm, some of her brothers assumed the father was a leopard, known within the tribe as a water tiger (*wi katca*). Like the uncle of Rhea Silvia, mother of Romulus and Remus who was impregnated by Mars, they were not happy about this potential half-water-tiger niece or nephew and wanted to put an end to it. However, the woman escaped and went to live happily ever after with the leopard, which can be understood as her surviving by integrating with nature.

In addition to recipes for birth control, Indigenous records also contain recipes for health and well-being while expecting, like a delightful-sounding goldenrod oil to massage swollen joints in the knees and arms as well as the belly during pregnancy.

Today an interested mother can expect to pay anywhere from $125 to $425 to have someone encapsulate her placenta so she can consume it, which many choose to do to continue to nourish the baby with nutrients like vitamin B6, vitamin B12, and iron from the womb through breast milk. Be warned that eating your placenta comes with risks, as it isn't sterile and could contain bacteria and viruses. The Navajo tradition is quite the opposite—they place importance on burying the placenta after childbirth so it can merge with nature. Magic and medicine. Cherokee folklore discusses using the placenta as a tool for divination. It's believed that by studying the placenta, you can tell if the parents will be "blessed again in the future," Kilpatrick writes. Among Eastern Cherokee, it was believed that a pregnant or menstruating woman could make a man sick by standing too close, making eye contact, or cooking his food. The use of menstrual blood, from Béatrice de Planisoles's purse contents to the New Orleans Voodoo trick of dosing a love interest's coffee with the stuff, is another one of those witchy similarities found across cultures. In a far more morbid tale of pregnancy and magic, in ancient Mexico, Aztec sorcerers would use the severed left forearms of women who passed away during childbirth to paralyze or disarm their enemies.

If only Persephone had the severed forearm of an enemy who died in childbirth to protect herself when Hades dragged her off to hell and got her pregnant (while also crowning her queen of the underworld). Persephone's mother, Demeter, a goddess of fertility and agriculture, could have helped her out if better prepared, as, remember, she's associated with the chaste tree, which the ancient Greeks (and Indigenous people) used as a contraceptive—and an aphrodisiac. Get yourself an herb that can do both. According to *13 in 1: The Authentic Native American Herbalist's Bible*, it is "one of the best herbs for nourishing women's and men's reproductive organs and restoring female energy and tone." It tastes like black pepper and can be used as a tea, tincture, or ground into actual black pepper and used in cooking.

For members of the Creek Tribe, who originally lived on the flatlands of present-day Georgia and Alabama, love spells involved tobacco. Long before sage became coveted, Europeans went apeshit for tobacco, which has a very powerful magic outside of love spells: it's addictive. While tobacco is likely the most famous herb of the "New World," its connection to reproductive justice pretty much ends in modern scientific studies of its adverse effects on a pregnancy, namely, tissue damage in the lungs and brain of the fetus. While using enough theoretically could cause a miscarriage, it should not be used as an abortifacient. As long as mifepristone and misoprostol are available, no one should opt for an herbal abortion of any kind.

As Kilpatrick recounts, in ancient Western Cherokee lore, seven menstruating women killed the monster Stoneclad, a human-witch with stone for skin. They did so under the direction of a medicine person called a conjurer, one advanced in occult powers. In an act of penitence, Stoneclad gave up his plethora of secret information by singing aloud sacred chants until he died.

In some Indigenous traditions, any gender could be a witch, but they were not immune from the fear of the crone. Traditionally, elderly folks with extensive knowledge of plants and animals were the go-to candidates for healers, who would use everything nature provided to treat ailments. However, even Cherokee were guilty of assuming the weirdo single woman over the age of thirty-five was a witch. "She lived alone in the woods, never married, and was considered an 'outsider' by the family," writes Kilpatrick describing "Lucy," the half sister of his grandmother. "Formerly . . . the Indians have been known to knock old women regarded as witches on the head and throw them into the water. Now there is a law against it, but even last year an old woman was killed by a witch," reads text from 1928 referencing an anti-witch-killing law passed among Western Cherokee in 1824. Like what happened in the witch hunts of Europe after the Black Death, in the era of smallpox, if a medicine person failed to heal someone, they put themselves at risk for accusations of witchcraft.

While Indigenous people had plenty of legends before Columbus arrived, colonization made the fear of the witch soar. And it was a two-way street: they also inflicted the fear of the witch in the Puritans. The witch archetype often arises to describe very real horrors.

While the Trail of Tears is associated with the most psychic trauma inflicted on the Indigenous peoples by the colonizers, the wound began forming long before that. Natives were forced to shun their languages and use English, and children were forced into mandatory American assimilation schools inspired by the military, which forbade Native practices (and abused and sometimes even murdered the kids) in a continued effort to smother their culture and, as one would describe it today, "Westernize" the children (an ironic description considering the hemispheres from which these groups originate)—and of course, in a tale as old as time (or, better yet, Ramses the Great), to create new soldiers. As assimilation continued, fear of witches spread.

A Cherokee woman disclosed, in 1812, to the missionaries at Brainerd Mission that all of her relatives had been charged with witchcraft and executed. The only reason she survived was because she was pregnant. From 1816 to 1838, Brainerd Mission operated as a government-sponsored Christian mission and school, established with the aim of educating Cherokee children, while also introducing them to Christian teachings and cultural practices. It was constructed along Chickamauga Creek, in the area that's currently known as Chattanooga. It was the largest mission school of its kind and closed only because its students were forced to relocate along the Trail of Tears. All that remains today is the school's cemetery.

As stated in an account by missionary Cephas Washburn in 1822, about an eleven-year-old Native girl named Jane Hicks in another assimilation program:

> The first convert was a little girl. . . . She had suffered much
> from superstitious fears, she was especially afraid of witches.
> As this was very common . . . one day, at the opening of school,
> I read a portion of Scripture, in which was some mention of
> witches. . . . She looked at me with a countenance of terror,
> as though she expected that one of these mysterious beings

> *would seize upon me. . . . She laid aside her book and could*
> *not attend to her lesson, so deeply was this superstitious*
> *belief inwrought in the very depths of her soul.*

While it's tempting to blame the fear of witches entirely on Europeans, some Indigenous people believed in witches all on their own, and we cannot chalk up Native beliefs purely to white influence. "Witches and sorcerers remain, in some form, a vital ontological reality to my mother's [Cherokee] people," Kilpatrick wrote on the subject as recently as 1997.

While Kilpatrick's writings suggest most Cherokee believe that witches are a creepy product of nature, they also believe that they can be created by ritual. To do so, potential witch recruits are taken away from their moms shortly after birth for seven to twenty-four days and fed only a diet of "liquid or fermented hominy" or a "specially decocted herbal tea," according to Kilpatrick. It's in this brew that ergot appears again, which the Dutch physician, occultist, and demonologist Johann Weyer believed accounted for the strange behavior of accused witches back in the Inquisition. The four ingredients in the witch-making brew are algae from rocks on a mountain stream, two kinds of insect, plants containing the hallucinatory ergot, and "phosphorescent wood extracted from a petrified stump," Kilpatrick writes.

If one were to concoct a potion to create a witch, based on cross-cultural usages, this seems like as valid a recipe as any. Kilpatrick's field notes share that the rise of giving birth in hospitals has therefore reduced the number of witches, as they can't be safely taken from their mothers and given to the tribe to turn into a witch. The rise in hospital births may have lowered the number of tribally sanctioned witches, per legend, but they still give the Indigenous people who created such folklore plenty to worry about. Hospitals are seen as ritually unclean places, perhaps because of discrimination and death. Here folklore's basis in reality is revealed: A 2020 study revealed that Indigenous women experience higher rates of severe maternal morbidity and mortality compared to white women, with the highest rates observed among Indigenous individuals living in rural areas. Also keep in mind that Black women have the highest maternal mortality rate in the United States, at 69.9 per 100,000 live births, according to data from 2021, which is nearly three times the rate for white women, according to the Centers for Disease Control and Prevention.

Additionally, Indigenous and Alaska Native people face more than double the risk of death from pregnancy-related conditions or complications than white people. This disparity is evident not only in rural settings, where limited access to treatment might be a factor, but also in cities. In 2019, Stephanie Snook of Seattle, a member of the Tsimshian and Tlingit tribes of Alaska, was pregnant with twins and agreed to be interviewed for NBC about the disparity of care white and Indigenous women receive. Due to a heart condition, the mother of two changed care from her community health clinic to a high-risk maternal-fetal specialist at Seattle's Swedish Health Services hospital system. Despite being told she was in the best hands, Snook—an activist for murdered and missing Indigenous women (search for #MMIW, #MMIWG, and #MMIWG2S for more info)—went into cardiac arrest and died on August 2, 2019, along with her twins. The three became part of the same heartbreaking statistics that Snook spoke out about.

Today, sometimes conservatives will tell you that Indigenous people or their ancestors are anti-abortion as a result of the reproductive violence inflicted on them. Some Indigenous people *are* against abortion and do find it to be a form of continued repression. There are also those who are pro-choice (just like in any group of people). And as Charon Asetoyer, director of the Native American Women's Health Resource Center, stated, "Native women have abortions . . . and anyone who tells you differently is out of touch with their communities." There are currently 574 federally recognized Native nations. About 300 or so of these have reservation homelands, and some of those have bans on abortion, like Pine Ridge Reservation in South Dakota. However, this could say more about the United States of America than the people who came before it.

As of June 24, 2022, abortion has been fully prohibited in South Dakota, with only limited exceptions to preserve the life or health of the pregnant individual. Counties with Native American reservations, such as in South Dakota, in addition to those housing prisons, continue to be among the poorest places in America. The Indian Health Service is funded at a federal level, and thus subject to the Hyde Amendment, which bans federal money for Medicaid for almost all abortions. There are only three circumstances in which an Indigenous woman can access abortion through IHS: rape, incest, or endangerment of the mother's life. As if the point hadn't been driven home enough, in February 2008, the Vitter Amendment, attached by the Senate to the Indian Health Care Improvement Act, passed, applying Hyde's restrictions permanently to IHS beneficiaries. "It's a very racist amendment," said Asetoyer, "[because] it puts another layer of restrictions on the only race of people whose health care is governed primarily by the federal government. All women are subject to the Hyde Amendment, so why would they put another set of conditions on us?"

But it's not just BIPOC *women* who are subject to such hurdles. April Matson, a former grocery store worker who identifies as two-spirit and uses "they/them" pronouns, drove a friend more than nine hours to a Colorado clinic to get an abortion just months after the South Dakota ban went into effect. Matson, a parent of two who lives in Sioux Falls and is Sicangu Lakota, had an abortion themself at the same clinic in 2016. Matson, who lived in Rapid City at the time of their abortion, told AP News that their IHS staff didn't even discuss abortion as an option. So, instead, at thirteen weeks pregnant, they made the trip, like so many after them will do, across state lines. After the procedure, unable to afford a hotel, while still bleeding and experiencing pain, they slept in a tent by a horse pasture. "That's a lot of barriers," said Matson. "We're already an oppressed community, and then we have this oppression on top of that oppression."

2

According to the Smithsonian Center for Folklife & Cultural Heritage and just about everyone else, the Salem Witch Trials, which occurred during the winter of 1692 and spring of 1693, were the deadliest witch hunts in North American history. Witch hunts tend to occur across cultures more often during cold periods, possibly because people look for scapegoats to blame for all the crops failing and how much pain everyone is in. A century and a half before the Cherokee faced the deadly winter of 1838–1839 on the Trail of Tears, the Puritans created their own sad, snowy saga. For supposed charges of witchcraft, they put to death fourteen women, five men plus one who died during torture, as well as two dogs. Of course, that's not good—no number of deaths on these trumped-up charges would be acceptable. But given that about twelve million Indigenous people died in what is today the United States between 1492 and 1900, and our slave trade killed millions of Black enslaved people—plenty of whom were called witches, heathens, devils, or something of the sort, too—it seems that modern-day witches may have picked the wrong injustice to obsess over.

When they landed in Salem, the Puritans did have to deal with battles with the French-supported Indigenous Wabanaki people. While the data shows which group of people suffered the most in the end, at the time, the Wabanaki outnumbered Puritans by six to one, and the settlers did not come out of these conflicts in good shape. About half of the "bewitched" children who began thrashing about in church, screaming about dark-skinned devils in the run-up to the witch trials, were orphans from the war. Several of the women exhibiting "bewitched" symptoms—such as convulsions, screams, or a desire to get on a broom and fly far, far away—were widowed by it. The Puritans described the Indigenous peoples as "horrid sorcerers and hellish conjurers," as Pulitzer Prize–winning nonfiction author Stacy Schiff reports in *The Witches: Salem, 1692.*

Basically, the victims of the Salem Witch Trials caused a completely unnecessary stir out of boredom from their lives of tireless work, gossip, violence, and most important, fear. Modern-day witches and feminists continue to refer to what happened in Salem as the pinnacle of wickedness, but the truth is, compared to the other persecutory evils going on at the time, it was just a bunch of paranoid, God-fearing settlers who were all too ready to throw their own people into a nasty and freezing cold prison and perhaps even kill them (and your little dog, too). Familiars, animal sidekicks for witches, played a major role in the trials. Offering insight into the perversion harbored in the accusers' repressed minds, witches were often accused not only of having familiars but of suckling them. Familiars came in the form of dogs (RIP), toads (one hilarious servant woman placed a frog in a fearful family's milk jug), and mostly cats. Many also believed that Native Americans could change into animals, such as tigers or lions (that is, big frightening cats).

Life in Salem in 1692 left much to be desired. The drab clothing, the endless labor, and the omnipresent fear of hell from constant Bible study were as hard-core as they appeared to the Wabanaki peering at them through the woods. But from executing dogs for witchcraft to having sex with ghosts, they still managed to get some fun in.

The Puritans back across the pond not only found the Church of England too similar to Catholicism, but found both far too liberal as well, at least as far as prioritizing the Bible goes. After a spiritual revival movement called Puritanism emerged within the Church of England toward the end of the sixteenth century, they finally fled to the "New World" to live freely under their own rigorous conviction during the 1620s and 1630s.

Not all of them came to America. Some Puritans, such as Sir Matthew Hale, stayed in England. The famous Royalist would conduct his own witch trial across the pond, sentencing at least two women to death for witchcraft in 1662. (Many years after his death, his convictions—which included staunchly believing in witches and even more staunchly not believing that marital rape exists—would forever change the country whose existence he once saw as an ache in his mother nation's womb: centuries later, a man named Samuel Alito cited his work in *Dobbs v. Jackson Women's Health Organization*.)

All Puritans frowned upon pomp and religious ritual and believed that they had a direct line to God. Screw the priests and religious 1 percenters with connections to the queen. Their strict moral order can still be seen today in Christian extremism's influence on our government. The Puritans viewed themselves as the chosen ones, God's favorite children, and, with the confidence of a nepo baby, they kind of believed everything would just work out for them. And for a long time, they weren't wrong.

They arrived a few generations after the Bay Colonies' founding. The Bay Colonies are the seventeenth-century settlements in North America around Massachusetts Bay and Chesapeake Bay. The Massachusetts Bay Colony, established in 1628 with Boston as its capital, was a center for Puritanism and notable for its early democratic experiments. The Chesapeake Bay area, the Virginia and Maryland colonies, was more known for its agricultural economy, particularly tobacco cultivation. Before the Puritans began swearing that they'd signed the devil's little red book as a way to get out of chores, the earlier North American colonists had already seen their spooky share of happenings, such as the Lost Colony of Roanoke. Meant to be the first permanent English settlement in North America, it was founded in 1585, but when a ship arrived in 1590 with supplies, all 112 to 121 colonists had disappeared without explanation. Due to the one word, "CROATOAN," ominously carved into the settlement's surrounding stake wall, some believe that the colonists relocated to Croatoan Island or either were massacred by or assimilated with the nearby Indigenous people. To this day, no one knows exactly what happened. (And, FYI, the *first* Europeans to land in North America—at least the first for whom there is solid evidence—were Norse, voyaging from Greenland, where Erik the Red created a settlement around the year 985.)

While 1692 is the highlight of the era of New England colonial witch hunts, it was not the only instance. Of the 200 women accused of witchcraft in this time and culture, 22 were midwives or healers, including the famous Anne Hutchinson. A well-known Boston woman, midwife, and iconic preacher, Anne was tried and banished from Massachusetts in 1637 after attracting a religious following of her own (good New England ladies weren't supposed to do that). Hutchinson was never directly accused of being a witch, but because she delivered a stillborn and "deformed" child (their ableist language, not mine) to a client, she was assumed to be in cahoots with the devil. Drawings of the poor child were used as image-based propaganda to prove that witchcraft exists—a trick that the anti-choice crowd would also invoke centuries later by parading around with photoshopped pictures of aborted fetuses in an attempt to scare and shame people out of supporting reproductive rights.

The climactic Salem Witch Trial spectacle took off when the Reverend Samuel Parris, the minister of Salem Village, called a doctor to examine his nine-year-old daughter, Betty, and eleven-year-old niece, Abigail Williams. They were both "having fits," which is probably accurate because it just sounds like a tantrum—the symptoms were writhing around, screaming, and pretending to be a dog, barking and all, relatable to the parents of any small children—but the girls were diagnosed as victims of witchcraft. Ironically, these girls had a penchant for occult practices themselves. During breaks from their chores, they loved playing fortune teller to learn whom they'd marry. Tale as old as time.

Mary Sibley, an older Puritan lady apparently familiar with the occult—in her case, sympathetic magic, or the ritual using something associated with a person or thing to achieve influence (such as using the waning moon for removal spells and the waxing moon for attraction work)—lived near the Parris home. She suggested that Tituba and John Indian, a married couple enslaved by Reverend Parris, solve the problem by baking a "witch cake." The infamous Salem witch-cake recipe produces something that resembles a donut mated with a sea urchin. Made with rye flour, it looked like a stale bagel with many points jutting out from it. Sibley explained that if Tituba added some of the bewitched girls' pee to the recipe, and then fed it to a dog, she could transfer the devil-spirit from the girls into the pup—a species, as we know, that is not above suspicion themselves. So while the reverend and his wife were away, they did just that.

Tituba was implicated. One of the three women first accused of witchcraft in Salem (along with the unhoused beggar Sarah Good and the elderly Sarah Osborn), despite being enslaved, Tituba is the only member of this unfortunate trio to survive the year. Her husband, John Indian, was an Indigenous man likely originally from Tibitó, Colombia.

The Reverend Samuel Parris, who honest-to-God believed in witches, had purchased the couple while he was living in Barbados.

Samuel Parris, born to Thomas Parris, a cloth merchant in London, in 1653, inherited land in Barbados after his father's passing. In Barbados, he managed the family's sugar plantation and worked as a credit agent for fellow sugar growers, at a time when sugar was as lucrative and influential as tobacco. A hurricane in 1680 wrecked his holdings, prompting him to relocate with his family to Salem Village, where he took up the role of a minister.

Unfortunately, it's tricky to know the exact details of Tituba's life. There are shockingly few surviving records from the trials themselves. Despite typically detailed epic recordkeeping by the industrious Puritans, there are few from 1692—people seemingly stopped diligently writing in their journals (or burned them later out of rightful shame after surveying the wreckage). In the court documents that do exist, Tituba's identity is starkly listed as "Indian Woman, servant." In colonial accounts following 1692, she is often called the "Black Witch of Salem." While this indicates that she is associated with black magic (but you should know by now that most magic is gray), it could also have a more straightforward explanation: her skin color.

Nine-year-old Betty, a child in Salem in 1692, described the devil as a "great black man," which, whether for racist reasons, the settlers' fear of nature and the dark, or a combo, is how just about every description from the Salem Witch Trials describes the, well, Dark Lord. Sometimes he wore a "great high-crowned" hat. Every now and then it's a Black woman. But in Salem, the devil's skin color is almost always dark. And the willing—those who *wouldst* like to live deliciously—signed their name into his red book, the infamous Devil's Book, and took part in Satanic rituals, such as flying on brooms, sneaking into beds of people other than their spouses at night (many bewitched Salem men argued that the women in their beds were succubae), and even enjoying coven meetings naked at night in the woods. Many Salem women who claim they were approached by the devil said that, in exchange for singing their name, he offered some time off work, pretty clothes, and often protection from neighboring Indigenous tribes.

Tituba confessed to signing the Devil's Book, but she also said that Parris beat the confession out of her. According to her forced confession, Satan said he was God and that if she served him for six years, he would give her "many fine things." To be fair, it sounds like a better bargain than being enslaved by colonialists. Tituba was imprisoned for more than a year but never actually convicted. No one knows what happened to her after a grand jury dismissed her case in May 1693.

The witchcraft trials were chaotic, unreliable, and disorganized. The colony had set up a special court just for these trials, long before the principle of "innocent until proven guilty" was recognized. This cornerstone of justice wasn't adopted in the United States until the 1895 Supreme Court case *Coffin v. United States*, which laid down the presumption of innocence in criminal cases. In Salem's courts, an accusation of witchcraft was practically a one-way ticket to jail. Judgments were made based on coerced confessions, the testimonies of two witnesses who claimed to have observed witchcraft, and spectral evidence, such as the fits suffered by young girls. One Salem resident claimed to see twelve pulsating glow-in-the-dark jellyfish in his fireplace. For some helpful context: No one really wore glasses. If what they saw wasn't actual witchcraft, the visions were probably stress reactions coupled with poor eyesight. Or everyone was tripping balls on ergot. As Schiff writes, "It was as if Tituba had handed out hallucinogens."

Anything considered sketchy in your past could lead to guilt. Fifty-eight-year-old Dorcas Hoar, who had been telling fortunes for years (she also had a fondness for robbery), was found guilty but given a temporary pardon. The trials ended before the courts could execute her. Another one of the accused, Martha Corey, was doomed before the witchcraft allegations began, in part because she was a white woman with a biracial teenage son, which made you more of a suspect at the time than telling fortunes or stealing. At her trial, Martha made quite the reasonable statement: "We must not believe all that these distracted children say." Between having a half-Black kid and suggesting something rational, she was a goner for sure. She and her husband, Giles Corey, were among the few actually put to death. Giles was likely found guilty simply for marrying a woman with a mixed-race son from a previous sexual encounter. While Martha was hanged to death, Giles was "pressed" to death, in a form of torture known as Peine *forte et dure*, meaning that they put heavy stones upon his chest, and when he did not confess, the increasing pressure of such stones eventually unintentionally killed him.

Another form of spectral evidence that could land you in prison was the "witch's mark," which could be anything from a blemish to a mole. God help you if you had a third nipple. According to a sixteenth-century physician who consulted for King Henry IV of France (1553–1610), known for amping up France's economy, in part because he established French colonies in the Americas, any doctor who could not tell the difference between a witch's mark and a natural blemish was a poor physician. Remember, this was an era when the contents of a first-aid kit hadn't changed much since antiquity. A 1676 autopsy identified someone's heart as their stomach. And, at the time, dissection was often limited to the bodies of criminals, which meant that they mostly happened on men, and knowledge of the female body was limited as a result.

Many who confessed in Salem did so because it was safer than continuing to assert their innocence or because the person who enslaved them beat it out of them. The more one denied being a witch, the more likely they were to anger folks and end up freezing to death in a shit-stained prison. On the stand, accused witches might fess up to abortions, for which they were not being charged, but that didn't help their cause. Describing women on the stand in Salem, Schiff writes, "While women tended to lament their vile natures, earlier misdeeds tumbled out too: an attempted suicide, a theft, a bout of drinking, an abortion, an adulterous liaison."

If it hadn't been for the witch trials, such women likely could have gone their entire lives enjoying the right to privacy. While the Right likes to cast America as a land that's always been against abortion, even its most conservative settlers took a more liberal stance than today's conservative extremists. While the Puritans were indeed pious people, this was still the time of the quickening, where pregnancy began when a mother (the Puritans recognized only two genders) first felt her child move (or told people that she did). Not only did single women get abortions from local midwives, but, like today, so did mothers who already had children and couldn't keep up with or afford any more.

Most abortions of the time went unmentioned, at least in public forums, because they occurred early in the pregnancy using herbs— ones they may have learned about from the folks who knew much more about North American land than they did. According to the author of the 1991 article "Taking the Trade: Abortion and Gender Relations in an Eighteenth Century New England Village" Cornelia H. Dayton, a UConn history professor: "Indigenous women were quite good at spacing children more widely apart than settler women. We've often wondered to what extent Indigenous women passed on knowledge to settler women." A famous colonial abortion people like to trot out is one with a sad ending: Sarah Grosvenor, who died from a late-term surgical abortion in Connecticut in 1742, which she sought out after herbal abortions earlier in her pregnancy failed. Medical or late-term abortions were rare because they were quite dangerous in a time before antibiotics, but herbal options weren't as effective as the abortion pill we have today.

One Salem midwife, Mary Toothaker, pulled into the paranoia, was absolutely positive that she herself was a witch. As a midwife, she'd know about such herbal remedies better than anyone. Mary pointed the finger at eleven others, including her sister and daughter. She was also utterly terrified of and obsessed with tribal attacks and said she made a pact with the devil because he promised "to deliver her from the Indians." One of her most prized possessions was her book on astrology, and perhaps the stars told her something to make her so paranoid. Upon her release from prison, where she had been held on charges of witchcraft, she returned to find her home reduced to ashes. She managed to rebuild her life, but it was cut short on August 5, 1695, when she and fourteen others perished in a raid by neighboring Indigenous tribes. In the same attack, her twelve-year-old daughter, Margaret, was taken and never seen again.

The fear of the locals was so great that Cotton Mather, the minister of Boston's Old North Church, a guy who claimed to be instrumental in the court proceedings of the Salem Witch Trials but may have just been smart enough to write books about it, later worked Indigenous people into the courtroom testimonies. Like Parris, Mather very much believed in witches. Before shit hit the fan in Salem, after watching "bewitched" children writing and screaming firsthand, he concluded that the devil was to blame. He wrote about his beliefs in one of the best known of his 388 books, the 1689 *Memorable Providences*, in which he vowed, "Never use but one grain of patience with any man that shall go to impose upon me a Denial of Devils, or of Witches." One of his reflections on his Massachusetts home: "The New-Englanders are a People of God settled in those, which were once the Devil's Territories."

Cotton was the son of Increase Mather, president of Harvard College (the same university whose associated club backed out of hosting a Black Mass in 2014) from 1685 to 1701. If such men believing in witches sounds strange, know that Harvard's 1683 commencement was rescheduled due to an eclipse. Harvard, the first college in the American colonies, was founded on September 8, 1636; it's a Virgo. And the stars actually did warn about the year 1692. According to that year's almanac, a March alignment of stars indicated chaos: "In short, mankind in general are about this time inclined to violence."

In one tale of such violence, Ann Foster, accused of witchcraft in 1692, died while waiting in prison. Accused at seventy-five years old, she was the perfect problematic crone to rot to death in service to setting an example for other women. She was still recovering from a family tragedy, one that, due to its moral implications, likely made her guilty in the eyes of the court rather than garnering sympathy: Three years before the Salem Witch Trials began, her son-in-law and daughter, Hannah, had fought over a land sale. The son-in-law, a horrid drunk, slashed Hannah's throat. She was massively pregnant with their eighth child, who died along with her.

In Salem, witch-hunting exacerbated existing anxiety, mostly about attacks from Indigenous peoples, which led to paranoia, which led to more hysteria and further accusations of others practicing witchcraft. While the words "Salem Witch Trials" are nearly synonymous with witchcraft in colonial America, compared to other horrors at the time, few people died. Not only did the Puritans own slaves (and accuse them of witchcraft), but by this time the full-scale arrival of enslaved folks from Africa and the Caribbean had begun in earnest, creating injustices in the realm of family planning and witchcraft that even the Puritan most bored of chopping wood and spinning wool couldn't dream up.

As stated in 2021 by Richard M. Mills Jr., deputy representative of the United States to the UN General Assembly, at the Commemorative Meeting for the International Day of Remembrance of the Victims of Slavery and Transatlantic Slave Trade:

> *The raw statistics are horrifying. An estimated 12.5 million Africans were put on slave ships during the transatlantic slave trade. More than one in twelve would die during the Middle Passage. And after they arrived on our shores, they were auctioned off like chattel, forced into hard labor, beaten, raped, killed, and deprived of all forms of freedom. And on those scarred backs, they helped build America—my country. Even the White House was constructed by enslaved peoples.*

3

Africans abducted to America through the wretched Middle Passage didn't separate the sacred from the profane. Through ritual, one could harness these energies and manifest them into action on the material world. What is considered magic in the colonial world, including use and knowledge of herbs, was perfectly normal in African societies. The Middle Passage was the route of horrors between Europe, Africa, and the Americas that carried recently captured people, including children, from the West Coast of Africa to the American colonies. While the lack of accurate recordkeeping makes it tricky to report exact figures, the New-York Historical Society Museum & Library reports that the slave trade stole more than 2 million people and took them across the Atlantic between 1500 and 1700. Only 1.7 million survived the initial trip.

While on the monstrosity that was the Middle Passage, an enslaved person was bound in what any rational person understands to be a torture device. Cramped conditions are an understatement. If one was lucky, there was rotting rice or corn served with filthy water once a day. Widespread dysentery. Smallpox. Sexual abuse of enslaved folks by their capturers was rampant. If anyone got pregnant, they couldn't expect an upgrade in accommodations, but they could expect their pregnancy to be seen as a monetary gain for those who enslaved them. Most who went into labor on the ship died. If a mother and her children were lucky enough to live, they were likely going to be separated at auction after arrival.

While history books tend to focus on nineteenth-century cotton plantations, the transatlantic slave trade began in the fifteenth century. America was actively practicing slavery while the Puritans bickered over the glow-in-the-dark jellyfish someone saw in the dark without glasses while possibly tripping on ergot.

The bondspeople, another term for the enslaved, who first arrived in what is now the continental United States did so in Virginia in 1619 after being taken from present-day Angola, a land of beautiful waterfalls and the only place in the world where you can see giant sable antelope, which were once believed to be extinct. At the time, Angola was a Portuguese colony. First, about 350 bondspeople were taken onto a Portuguese slave ship called the *São João Bautista* headed to the Spanish colony of Veracruz, in Mexico. It didn't get there. Two other ships with malevolent motives, English privateer boats called the *White Lion*, which also had carried enslaved people, in an event described as the start of slavery, and the *Treasurer*, intercepted the *São João Bautista* and stole the already-stolen Angolans on board. This was executed under the control of an English nobleman known as the Earl of Warwick Robert Rich. Rich (fitting surname) loathed both the Spanish and Catholicism, so he loved getting in their way, especially if he could find a way to make money off it. The *White Lion* landed in Virginia first in late August 1619 and the *Treasurer* four days after.

There's not a lot of information around about what happened to the bondspeople on board. The most quoted record of the oceanic enslaver-on-enslaver battle comes from the letter to the Virginia Company of London, a joint-stock company chartered by King James I, charged with the Jamestown settlement since its establishment in 1607. The letter was penned by John Rolfe, one of the early English settlers there, who was famously a tobacco farmer and, more infamously, Pocahontas's husband (not to be confused with John Smith, the guy from the *first* Pocahontas Disney movie).

Born around 1596, Pocahontas was actually named Amonute. Pocahontas was her nickname, which means either "playful one" or "ill-behaved child." (This name would go on to become Trump's nickname for Democratic senator Elizabeth Warren, who had previously claimed Cherokee ancestry. According to a DNA test, she allegedly does have some from six to ten generations ago, but this is still sus on her part, making this one of the rare Trump jokes to strike home with liberals.)

Pocahontas was the daughter of Wahunsenaca, a.k.a. Chief Powhatan, the *mamanatowick* (paramount chief) of the Powhatan Chiefdom. Her infamous meeting with John Smith happened in the winter of 1607, long before she met John Rolfe, and when she would have been around eleven years old. By Smith's account, he was captured by the Powhatan. Two large stones were placed on the ground. They held Smith's head on the formidable rocks, and a warrior lifted a club ready to bludgeon his brains out. But Pocahontas ran in and placed *her* head there instead to save him. Much of this is speculative. According to other accounts, Smith met Pocahontas some months later, when she was visiting his settlement to play with friends (because, remember, she was eleven years old). Smith returned to Europe. They never married, but there is evidence that they at least became friends.

In 1613, it was Pocahontas who was captured and held for ransom by the English during one of their ongoing wars. During her captivity, they converted her to Christianity, as would happen to so many Native children, and baptized her with the Western name Rebecca. Pocahontas was seventeen or eighteen when she married Rolfe that same year. They had a son, Thomas Rolfe. Three years later, in 1616, the family traveled to London. Pocahontas became an It Girl; she was shown off as proof Indigenous people could be Westernized, attending 1-percenter balls and exclusive shows. However, the Marie Antoinette lifestyle did not last. Pocahontas died in Kent, England, around the age of twenty or twenty-one of illness, likely pneumonia, smallpox, or dysentery.

Back across the pond, the transatlantic slave trade was growing daily. If a family made it off the ships intact, they were fortunate (though that feels like the wrong word here) if they were able to stay together at auction and end up at the same place. And it's not as if the threat of separation went away after that moment. Fear of your child, mother, friend, or husband being sold to another plantation or household was just part of everyday life. Marriages of enslaved people were not recognized by law, but as always, love found a way, and people continued to find joy in unions despite it all. One wedding ritual involved the practice called "jumping the broom." While Salem witches (in children's dreams and coerced confessions) flew across the sky on brooms to attend a devil's meeting, bondspeople jumped over the symbol of the house in an act of love and defiance.

Likewise, couples continued to have children because they wanted to. On "nicer" plantations, enslavers would even encourage this, as allowing families to live together meant they were less likely to run away.

According to data from 1850, the infant mortality rate among enslaved people was twice that of whites, due to their poor treatment—and the fact that there was often little downtime allowed after giving birth. They were put back to work so quickly that sometimes women would breast-feed while working in the fields. They tied their child to their back in a homemade wrap with sweat dripping down both of their bodies under the scorching sun as Dorothy E. Roberts reports in *Killing the Black Body: Race, Reproduction, and the Meaning of Liberty*. When the child needed to feed, the mothers would bring the child to their breast, often while they continued to work (although "torture" is a better word than "work" for the unpaid labor inflicted upon bondspeople). Other times mothers worked while elderly enslaved folks (the women who met the definition of a crone) watched over the children. While none of this was voluntary, whole communities did come together, under unspeakably terrible circumstances, to help one another.

However, mothers were, at least at first, still physically bound to their kids through the need to breast-feed, which is why the average runaway was a single Black male between the ages of eighteen and thirty, reports Michael P. Johnson, a member of the Department of History at the University of California, Irvine, in "Runaway Slaves and the Slave Communities in South Carolina, 1799 to 1830." Some Black men would opt not to marry or have kids because of the fate they knew would befall their families. As Black author Henry Bibb stated after escaping slavery himself, the daughter he didn't take with him "was the first and shall be the last slave that ever I will father for chains and slavery on this earth." According to his autobiography, the famed abolitionist Frederick Douglass, and as reported in Yvonne Patricia Chireau's *Black Magic: Religion and the African American Conjuring Tradition*, who escaped at age twenty, was once helped by a conjurer, Sandy Jenkins. "Conjure," also called "rootwork" or "hoodoo," described a variety of folk magical practices used by Black Americans. According to novelist and fellow abolitionist William Wells Brown, "Nearly every large plantation had at least one, who laid claim to be a fortune teller, and who was granted more than common respect by his fellow slaves." Jenkins gave Douglass an enchanted root before he had to meet with a man with a nasty reputation for disciplining bondspeople. It wasn't unusual to seek the help of a conjurer in efforts to avoid physical beatings and other cruelties, including being separated from one's family.

For some enslaved men, opting out of marriage was impossible. Sometimes enslaved folks were forced to marry one another, or at least sleep in the same bed and have children. Both genders had to decide between nonconsensual sex and intentionally producing a child with the knowledge that they would never be free, or the thrashings they'd receive for refusing. More bondspeople meant more money. Depending on the man in charge, pregnancy was sometimes rewarded, such as with breaks from field work, extra food, and clothing, and even the rarity of a gift that made a mother feel feminine, such as a bow for her hair, shares Roberts, thus encouraging procreation by offering crumbs of humanity.

The children legally belonged to the property owner who enslaved the parents from the day of their birth. All of this was legal. It wasn't just legal; one of America's very first laws was about this issue. A 1662 statute, *partus sequitur ventrem*, passed in colonial Virginia, mandated that the children of enslaved mothers would also be bondspeople and, thus, property. The legal principle of *partus sequitur ventrem* (that which is born follows the womb) derives from Roman civil law precedents for slavery. It also meant that white mothers, like the witchcraft-accused Puritan Martha Corey, assumed ownership over any biracial children. Courts held the belief that a slaveholder's moral dominion over the family was sanctioned by divine will. Enslaved women who didn't or couldn't conceive were often punished or sold.

Partus sequitur ventrem also further legally sanctioned rape. Owners of bondspeople could literally profit from impregnating any women and girls they owned and selling their children at auction. This sort of treatment didn't even end in 1808, when legally bringing enslaved people into America ended, thanks to the Act Prohibiting the Importation of Slaves. If anything, the lack of ships completing the torturous journey through the Middle Passage meant that enslaved women's childbearing became even more of a business interest. In 1820, beloved founding father Thomas Jefferson told his plantation manager: "I consider a woman who brings a child every two years as more profitable than the best man of the farm." Slave births were recorded in the business ledger, which is how Jefferson likely kept track of some of his own children (not to mention their mother).

Sally Hemings was only fourteen when Thomas Jefferson, forty-four, began raping her in 1787, in Paris, where she worked as a domestic servant from 1787 to 1789. In Paris, bondspeople were allowed to petition for their freedom. Hemings survived and convinced Jefferson that she would go back to Monticello only if he promised "extraordinary privileges" for herself and freedom for her children; she would go on to have at least six of Jefferson's kids. According to Monticello's website, four survived into adulthood: Beverly, a son, became a carpenter and fiddler; Harriet, the only daughter to survive, was a spinner in Jefferson's textile factory; Madison, a son, became a carpenter; and their last child, a son named Eston, became a carpenter and musician. Beverly and Harriet Hemings left Monticello without being legally emancipated and reportedly passed in white society; their heritage was never discovered during their lifetimes. When Jefferson died in 1826, Sally wasn't officially freed, but she was *unofficially* freed by his daughter Martha Jefferson. Thomas Jefferson's will freed Hemings's younger children, Madison and Eston. In the 1830 Census, Sally Hemings and her sons Madison and Eston were recorded as free white individuals. Then, in a unique Census conducted three years later after the 1831

Nat Turner Rebellion, Hemings identified herself as free.

And, by the way, carrying on the 1-percenter tradition of keeping it in the family, Sally Hemings is believed to be the daughter of Thomas Jefferson's wife's father, John Wayles, and Elizabeth Hemings, an enslaved woman—making First Lady Martha Jefferson and Sally Hemings half sisters. (This situation wasn't unusual, and court documents surviving from nineteenth-century divorce records show that many white women married to men who enslaved people changed their minds and decided they were against slavery real quick once they realized their husbands were having sex with them.)

Unfortunately, most enslaved pregnant people had it much worse than Sally Hemings's already horrific life, and it's a mistake to think that births were valuable to those who enslaved people only from an economic perspective. Pregnancy was also weaponized to further dehumanize. In the discussion of reproductive justice, people talk about "maternal-fetal" conflict. This is a term to describe laws, policies, and other practices pitting mother and child against one another. It's a feminist term that typically refers to medical decisions that must be made when a mother's life and child's life cannot both exist. But for enslaved people in America, this conflict was present in a different way. Perhaps the most horrible thing you will read in this book, reported on in the highly recommended text *Killing the Black Body* by Roberts, is this: when slaveholders wanted to whip an enslaved pregnant person, they would make them lie facedown in a ditch—protecting the fetus while torturing the mother.

Considering all of this, obviously, many bondspeople undertook methods to prevent or stop pregnancy. The article "'She Had Smothered Her Baby on Purpose': Enslaved Women and Maternal

Resistance," by Signe Peterson Fourmy, recounts interviews conducted by Fisk University and the Works Progress Administration during the 1920s and 1930s with formerly enslaved women. One was with Mary Gaffney, who shared that when her enslaver forced her to "marry" a man she loathed and sleep with him, she "kept cotton roots and chewed them all the time" to not get pregnant. Cotton root bark, stripped from the very plant people were enslaved to grow for use in clothing and textiles, contains oxytocin, which triggers uterine contractions. Bondspeople would also drink tea made of cotton root bark, at night, by candlelight, perhaps with the help of a midwife. The thin, flexible, brownish yellow root is almost odorless, making it a wise choice if you need to hide it, and has an astringent taste.

Such herbal remedies sometimes showed up in southern medical journals at the time, Roberts writes. For instance, Dr. E. M. Pendleton of Hemlock, Georgia, wrote in 1849 regarding enslaved patients: "The blacks are possessed of a secret by which they destroy the fetus at an early stage of gestation." Another doctor, John T. Morgan, reported the same in 1860, stating that Black women used medicine "to effect an abortion or derange menstruation." His report does give us some insight into what herbs were used, such as "the infusion or decoction of tansy, rue, roots and seed, of the cotton plant, penny royal, cedar gum, and camphor, either in gum or spirits." While some of those plants also exist in Africa, and such knowledge may have originated there, there's also evidence that Black and Indigenous peoples shared information about herbal remedies as part of an exchange of both magical and reproductive knowledge.

Some Black conjurers of the time cited a spiritual connection between themselves and Indigenous peoples and learned from their traditions, weaving such knowledge into conjure. In *Black Magic: Religion and the African American Conjuring Tradition*,

Yvonne Patricia Chireau defines conjure as "The categories of healing and harming were morally neutral attributes of the same powers of predisposition and control. The Western idea of delineating
good from evil as 'obverse and reverse' concepts has no parallel in
the African tradition. A more accurate dichotomy for character-
izing the amoral principle underscoring such practices might be
'powerful' versus 'powerless.'" For instance, the many uses of conjure included both preventing a pregnancy from happening and
increasing fertility for those who wanted children. And sometimes,
when one is powerless, a powerful action seems the best course of
action. The most extreme form of preventing the continuation of
slavery was infanticide, Roberts writes in *Killing the Black Body*.

Terminating a pregnancy and, in rare and extreme instances,
killing a child were about not only bodily autonomy but also sub-
verting slavery. Infanticide was a radical means of maternal resistance, and, as so many enslaved newborns died because of lack of
access to prenatal care, there were likely cases that were not actually infanticide but were treated as such. For some mothers, death
was indeed a better option for their children than slavery, especially
when herbal remedies such as cotton root bark had failed to stop
the child's birth before it happened. But as Roberts writes, we "do
not know, for example, whether slave mothers practiced abortion
and infanticide selectively, terminating pregnancies or the lives of
children that resulted from rape or forced mating. Moreover, while
infanticide spared children from the horrors of slavery, it was not a
desirable strategy for overthrowing the institution." But while they
did not come without consequence, revolutions were.

The New York Slave Revolt of 1712 (shout-out to the supernatural
Eunus, who kicked off the Servile Wars of ancient Rome) saw at
least twenty-three enslaved Black people (some sources say that

this number is higher and that free Black and Indigenous peoples joined in) riot against city whites to retaliate against inhumane treatment. There were no plantations in the city, of course; bondspeople here worked in households. On the night in question, enslaved people first set fire to a building on Maiden Lane, near modern-day Wall Street. When people started running out of their homes to avoid being burned, the group came at them with axes, knives, and guns. Nine white people died and six were injured before the rebellion was halted by local militia.

Six bondspeople died by suicide rather than go to trial. Of those brought to trial, eighteen were acquitted, and several more were pardoned. The rest were executed; many were burned alive; one was crushed by a wheel. Another was put in chains until he died by starvation. The rest were hanged, and a pregnant bondswoman was kept alive until she gave birth, at which point she too was executed. The rebellion has been painted as a fight against Christianity. A letter from the chaplain of the English garrison in New York City claimed that there was a sworn blood oath between members of the community and an African "sorcerer," which involved a blood-sharing ritual among everyone involved, in conjunction with the use of an enchanted protection powder.

The fear that enslaved folks from Africa would rise up against Christianity is as telling as the anxiety in Salem regarding Indigenous peoples. The religious revival known as the Great Awakening soared across America during the 1700s, asking enslaved people (and just about everyone else, frankly) to drop the ancestor worship and reverence of nature and get monogamous with Jesus. At first, enslavers wanted to keep Christianity as far away from the people they worked as possible, as they worried that the message of spiritual equality could lead to revolts. However, most historical accounts say that the majority of enslavers thought it was their "Christian duty" to let the enslaved hear the good news about the Lord.

This is bullshit. Like the Christian boarding schools imposed on Indigenous kids, the Great Awakening was another method of social control. This doesn't mean that bondspeople were pawns. They quickly formed their own congregations, listened to Black preachers, and of course, like the Egyptians and so many before them, incorporated this new god slyly into their preexisting African beliefs.

Chireau writes, "Among enslaved Blacks, older cosmologies gradually merged with concepts that were extracted from newly formed Afro-Christian ideas such as a radical monotheism, dualistic notions of good and evil, and concepts of spiritual intervention. Elements of the older African worldview also intersected with a network of Anglo-American supernatural traditions. The simultaneous emergence of Africa-based supernaturalism (later identified as Conjure and Hoodoo) and black Americans' embrace of Christianity resulted in the reinforcement of magic and religion and convergent phenomena," defining magic as "the beliefs and actions by which human beings interact with an invisible reality," and adding, "Although magic is generally characterized as the antithesis of religion, it seems just as often to reflect the latter, to be its mirror image."

Conjure, a form of "resistance, revenge, and self-defense," had a fluid relationship with Christianity, constantly shifting and learning from one another. Magic, herbal knowledge, and religion could coexist. For example, John Henry Kemp, a bondsperson in Mississippi, was part of the True Primitive Baptist Church, which preached "one faith, one Lord and one religion," yet he was also known for his divination abilities, palm reading, and healing through "charms, roots, herbs and magical incantations and formulae" for "those who believe[d] in him," Chireau writes. And even before New Orleans Voodoo existed, Black Americans of African descent practiced magic with effigies. For instance, Clara Walker, a former bondswoman from Arkansas, talked about a Black witch doctor who would punish slaveholders by creating a "little man out of mud" and shoving thorns into the doll.

Voodoo arrived in New Orleans in the 1700s with the enslaved folks brought from Haiti. During the Haitian Revolution (1791–1804), many white Americans who'd been living in Haiti fled and brought their bondspeople with them. Vodou, which means "spirit" or "god" in the Fon and Ewe languages of West Africa, is a blend of African religious traditions and Catholicism. The term has also come into common use as the name for the spiritual practices of Haiti, but it is now part of the American religious landscape as well. "Voodoo" is an Americanized spelling of "Vodou," but if you're in Haiti, always use "Vodou" and make sure to capitalize it. You also may have heard of "Hoodoo," which refers to folk magic and is sometimes also called "conjure."

Largely due to the Catholic influence, abortion is not always embraced in Voodoo, but like with any religion and any people, it happens, especially when its practitioners are often enslaved, or the descendants of enslaved people, and more likely to be subject to sexual violence. Marie Laveau of New Orleans is perhaps the most famous witch of all time and became known for alleged practices of cannibalism, ritual child sacrifice, and abortions.

Laveau, a woman of color, was born free in 1801, but was still treated like she was inferior due to her race and gender (although her New Orleans residence is now among America's top tourist attractions). However, her unique position allowed her to move throughout various classes of society. Laveau provided beauty and hair services, relationship advice, and information on herbal medicine to everyone from enslaved people to rich white ladies. There is no information confirming she ever actually dealt with abortions.

However, we do know that Prince Dawson, a male Voodoo doctor in Cincinnati, was accused of performing one in 1888. While slavery officially ended in 1865, implementing abolition didn't happen overnight, and many would argue the process is ongoing even still. By the end of the 1800s, all states in the Union except Laveau's Louisiana had therapeutic exceptions in their legislative bans on abortions. But when a woman and an aborted fetus were connected to Dawson, they charged him with a crime. He was acquitted after he testified that he couldn't have done so because he had no surgical tools, save a knife to remove corns, and he wasn't even in town on the day in question. According to the *Cincinnati Post*, on May 8, 1888, "To hear his story one would think him the most innocent man on earth—only an herb doctor who went about doing good and paring corns."

Dawson himself said he was the father of forty children. While most accounts indicate he was Black, Dawson would also claim Cherokee descent. Living up to the eccentric reputation of witches and wizards, Dawson often added twenty to forty years to his age, asserting to be eighty-six or even one hundred years old when he was actually in his sixties. He was well over six feet tall and wore his hair in a mohawk. He's also remembered for his epic overcoat made of several animal pelts and adorned with medals. Although most conjurers were men, all of them were known for fucking with gender, not unlike practices that earned two-spirit people spiritual status. One male conjurer in Virginia, Revered Dr. H., wore "his hair braided like a woman and [had] rings in his ears." From Prince Dawson to rock star Prince of the modern era, gender fluidity is associated with creativity and counterculture.

In 1906 Dawson was arrested for stealing chickens (likely for a ritual). They shaved his gorgeous mohawk off. After being released on the chicken-theft charges, he died on his way home from jail when he was hit by a train. Perhaps most important, Dawson worked as a doctor in a poor neighborhood where "regular" doctors wouldn't set foot. By now, midwives and other healers were called "irregular" doctors, compared to the trained "regulars" of the medical establishment (white men). Caribbean midwives were taken aback by the scarcity of their trade in America. Immigrants brought their knowledge and used it, especially for lower-class citizens who could not afford a Western doctor.

Facets of the modern medical movement—still often unavailable to the disenfranchised—were birthed from experiments on folks whom such doctors wouldn't deign to treat save for use as guinea pigs. Notably, we owe advances in Western gynecology to experimentation on bondspeople. J. Marion Sims, commonly known as "the father of modern gynecology," developed the surgical cure for the vesica-vaginal fistula through experimentation on enslaved women between 1845 and 1849. Three of those women were named Lucy, Anarcha, and Betsey; we don't know the names of any other of Sims's patients. The surgeries were done without anesthesia, as its use wasn't common practice yet. At times he used opium, too weak to truly stop their pain but strong enough to leave them with an addiction. It's as if Sims got off on the power—or simply loved money. By his admission, "If there was anything I hated, it was investigating the organs of the female pelvis." But gynecological advances were lucrative at the time, and Sims was persistent.

For most of history, even if there was money to be made, many men in the medical profession didn't want to go anywhere near "women's problems" simply because the idea grossed them out (or scared them). The vesica-vaginal fistula is a nasty complication of prolonged labor, forming a hole between the vagina and the bladder. Women who develop the condition, like the enslaved women Sims experimented on, often become social outcasts because of the incontinence, infection, smell, and pain—all symptoms that persist until the fissure is repaired. For too long, the argument was that because this procedure saves lives, people should just be thankful that it exists at all and shut up about how it was developed.

Unfortunately, Sims was not alone in using bondspeople who could not—either by law or within the dynamics of forced servitude—consent in medical experiments at the time. Even in the past decade, many doctors have stood up for his actions due to the importance of his medical contributions, despite the cultural backlash against him and the extreme human suffering as the result of his surgeries, as our society rethinks what we decide to showcase and monument. His statue was finally taken down from Central Park in New York City in 2018, and in an article from that year in the *Atlantic*, Sarah Zhang described the inherent tensions in assessing his significance: "To implicate him, his defenders implied, is to implicate medicine in mid-19th century America."

In honor of Anarcha, Lucy, and Betsey who underwent Sims's cruel experimentation and the nameless others who endured forced medical torture to advance modern surgical procedures, artist Michelle Browder created a sculpture called *Mothers of Gynecology*. Likenesses of three women, as imagined by Browder, were erected in Montgomery, Alabama, in 2021, near the location of J. Marion Sims's infamous surgical theater. "They were experimented on without anesthesia, without consent—of course, they were enslaved, so of course there wouldn't be any consent—but it's just the mere fact that their dignity was stripped from them. So I wanted to create a piece of art that gives them dignity, respect, and identity," Browder said in an interview with the American Independent Foundation.

Unfortunately, we know how the story ends. After the Civil War (April 12, 1861–April 9, 1865) ended, it wasn't smooth sailing for Indigenous people . . . or Black Americans. By reframing the reproductive rights movement to one of reproductive justice, society can begin to offer a more reparative system. The Salem Witch trials are attention worthy, by and large, for much of the same reason that reality TV is: they were absolutely bonkers. But those who identify as witches or who are just fascinated by the occult may wish to reconsider how they look at them now. The executions that did occur were likely the result of misplaced fear, and memorializing those events as the "deadliest witch hunts in North America" might continue the tradition of unknowingly misplacing our terror. Why does this attack loom larger in some witches' cultural memory than the assaults on enslaved and Indigenous peoples over that same time period?

The era of colonization in North America is in need of new narratives, whether that means realizing that Pocahontas should have been just eleven when the Disney film took place or unveiling the gruesome history behind some of the most important gynecological medical advancements in our history. And prepare yourself: the same holds true for some of the most revered icons of the left-handed-path tradition.

CHAPTER 4

EUGENICS, ORGIES, GLAMOROUS ABORTIONISTS, AND THE CARNIVAL WORKER WHO STARTED IT ALL

1

You're in a quaint coffee shop built out of New York City's signature dusty red bricks. It's in Lower Manhattan—Greenwich Village, to be exact. Called "America's Bohemia" by the poets who reside there and the aging Victorians who fear it, whispering about the sex and the drugs and lack of a nuclear family structure, the way America's political Right will one day gossip about Bushwick, Brooklyn. You do have a slight hangover, but the espresso fills your nose as you sip, and after the reefer you enjoyed before walking over from your tenant-style apartment, you feel just fine. The year is 1915. You're flipping through a newspaper when you see an ad penned by a painter asking for "Dwarfs, Hunchbacks, Tattooed Women, Harrison Fisher Girls [after a New York City illustrator of beautiful women], Freaks Of All Sorts, Coloured Women, only if exceptionally ugly or deformed, to pose for artist."

It's been placed around this time by Aleister Crowley, the "most wicked man in the world," who will go on to become one of the most famous occultists in history. When he arrived in New York (the man would spend his life living all over the world), as Richard

Kaczynski reports in *Perdurabo: The Life of Aleister Crowley*, he was met at the dock by Henry Hall, a reporter from the *New York World* Sunday magazine, who described him as "the strangest man I ever met. He is a man about whom men quarrel. Intensely magnetic, he attracts people or repels them with equal violence." Today, Crowley continues to be as divisive as he was more than a hundred years ago, as this author discovered when writing this section. He is best known for founding the religion of Thelema, calling himself the prophet responsible for leading the world into the "Æon of Horus."

While the ad claimed to be seeking art models, Crowley was also probably looking to use such people in magical rituals. Tangentially, Crowley is often credited as the one who started spelling occult "magick" with a *K*, to make it more official than the everyday word "magical." Let it be known that while the man is intentionally cryptic, when he described things as "magical" without a *K*, Crowley usually actually meant "sexual."

All you really need to know about Aleister Crowley is that he didn't just think his penis was holy; he devoted his entire life to proving it. He even *looked* like a penis. While a Google image search reveals that he's no Ryan Gosling, apparently, there was something glamorous about Crowley—perhaps that stare—that made the bald-headed, problematic, charismatic, hashish-smoking British man *very* fuckable.

Aleister Crowley (October 12, 1875—December 1, 1947) was born in England to a wealthy family of the Plymouth Brethren, hard-core Christian fundamentalists whose sect started in the 1820s and, like the Puritans, thought the Bible was the ultimate and only authority. Crowley's father, a preacher, died of cancer of the tongue—an ironic way to go out for someone who spit sin-fearing sermons for a living—and left Crowley a fortune, although he'd go on to spend it all and eventually file for bankruptcy. One could argue Aleister's own sin is what killed him: he died at the age of seventy-two of myocardial degeneration and chronic bronchitis, also heavily addicted to heroin and likely experiencing syphilis. "It was sex that rotted him. It was sex, sex, sex, sex, sex, all the way with Crowley. He was a sex maniac," Vittoria Cremers, one of his followers, once said.

Crowley, like so many of us, rebelled against his family. "I simply went over to Satan's side; and to this hour I cannot tell why," Crowley once said, reports Gary Lachman, countercultural historian and founding member of Blondie, in *Aleister Crowley: Magick, Rock and Roll, and the Wickedest Man in the World*. From an early age, Crowley followed the "left-handed path," an umbrella term for a life based on enjoying earthly pleasures (such as sex and heroin) rather than shunning them and opting for individuality over collectivism. This is, of course, also associated with Satanism.

While this author is about to talk a lot of shit about Crowley, it should be understood that today, many lovely, warmhearted people walk the left-handed path and see it as a path to a more inclusive world, rather than the manufactured one Crowley tried to create. Crowley pushed everything to the extreme. "I want none of your faint approval or faint dispraise. I want blasphemy, murder, rape, revolution, anything good or bad, but strong," Crowley once wrote.

Crowley has been called a "spiritual nihilist." Whether he believed his own shit is up for debate. The man was also called "the Beast," after the Beast in the Book of Revelation, a nickname first given by his mom, which he held onto for life. Not unlike a specific brand of art-school fuckboi many readers may know, at times he would state that "nothing matters." In his more uplifted moments, he was able to find the hilarity in existence in a poetic way that one interested in life's strange synchronicities might find appealing. In a 1920 diary entry regarding an internal debate with Buddha, Tobias Churton reports in *Aleister Crowley: The Biography*:

Spiritual Revolutionary, Romantic Explorer, Occult Master and Spy (some biographers claim that he worked as a British spy) that Crowley wrote: "The Mystery of Sorrow was consoled long ago when it went out for a drink with the Universal Joke." Yet by his own admission, Crowley was at one point "intellectually insane," per Lachman. He loved drugs and said hashish helped him greatly in all his workings, but later in life, heroin did him in. He got debilitating migraines and had asthma. At the time, heroin was prescribed frequently by doctors as a cough suppressant, among other common uses. The heroin prescription a doctor gave Crowley would screw with him for the rest of his life but not get in the way of building massive influence. Crowley's followers claimed the guy could make himself invisible and that he practiced astral projection and jumped across the Atlantic to chat with his bougie Los Angeles followers while his body was dying in England. "Would it not be surprising if he was somewhat mad?" writes Churton. "He was like a stoned Atlas, with a world on his head."

That Stoned Atlas would become an epic influence (if an overly glamorized one) on the modern occult. Ozzy Osbourne sang about him, and today you'll find his works on the bookshelves of even the most leftist witches despite the fact that he was vehemently anti-abortion (among other things). He didn't always treat fully formed adults with humanity, either.

Victor Neuburg was a close friend and follower of Crowley, though others said he looked more like Crowley's familiar, given his obedience and habit of literally following him around. Neuburg worshipped Pan, an ancient Greek god of sex, drugs, and rock and roll, a deity also close to Crowley's heart. His relationship with Crowley likely had elements of dominance and submission as well. The issue of Crowley treating lovers such as Neuburg as less than human isn't based on consensual S&M but allegations of him both beating Neuburg (and others) and berating him with anti-Semitic slurs. Neuburg shaved his head save for two tufts framing either side, which he dyed red and styled to resemble horns, and trotted about after Crowley, who led him around tied on a chain at times. Neuburg was present for a moment pivotal to Crowley's decision to devote his life to sex magic. Once, prior to Crowley's move to New York City, where he would place his infamous newspaper ad, the pair walked out into the African desert and erected an altar on which, as the introduction to this book teased, Crowley "sacrificed" himself—code for receiving anal penetration. This moment cemented Crowley's never-ending love of sex magic, which he is most known for.

Sex magic is the practice of using sexual energy to cast a spell. The easiest way to perform sex magic is to throw your orgasm toward a goal. This doesn't have to be about finding love or anything related to sex; you can use sex magic for money, power, or glory. While some folks, Crowley included, are into partners or orgies for sex magic, you can also do it through masturbation. Ethical modern-day witches say that this is the best way to perform sex magic, as it's just you; you don't have to mess with anyone else's aura. Orgasms are called *la petite mort*, French for "the little death," for a reason; again, as Crowley will tell you, it's powerful stuff. Full moons, the moon phase representing manifestation, are ideal for sex magic. And if you're doing one for money, it doesn't mean you have to jerk off to cash, exactly. It's best to think about what you want that purchasing power for beforehand and build up an excellent visualization of it. Then, think of sexy things until you're about to come, and switch your mind to your goal. It doesn't hurt to try!

Crowley's followers in Thelema included Jack Parsons, the sexy scientist who invented the rocket engine, and L. Ron Hubbard, the villainous founder of Scientology. Unlike Neuburg, a true believer, it's possible that Hubbard was there more to learn the art of the scam, as he stole moves from Crowley when it came time to start his own religion. Or did he want to believe? Jack Parsons once told Crowley that Hubbard was "the most Thelemic person I have ever met." From lessons on attracting followers to views on abortion, Crowley and Hubbard are undeniably intertwined. As Hubbard wrote in *Dianetics*: "The child on whom the abortion is attempted is condemned to live with *murderers*, whom he reactively knows to be murderers, through all his weak and helpless youth!" Despite such seemingly anti-abortion writings, the Church of Scientology has been sued by a former member for coercing her to get an abortion when she was a teenager. They denied such allegations and settled the lawsuit out of court. But back to Crowley, "the Beast."

In late summer 1898, Crowley met chemist Julian L. Baker in Switzerland. This crowd loved scientists with a spooky streak. Through this acquaintance, Crowley was introduced to George Cecil Jones and the Hermetic Order of the Golden Dawn, founded in 1888, considered the founders of modern occultism. This clandestine group had a significant impact on the ritual magic still observed in pagan traditions like Wicca, and they embraced activities favored by contemporary witches, including astrology and tarot. Despite their progressive stance on gender equality, uncommon in elite societies of their time, it's important to note that they also apparently engaged in spiritual eugenics—a concept also adopted and reformulated within his own religious framework by Crowley.

One had to advance up the ranks to be taken seriously within Golden Dawn, which ultimately proved challenging for the controversial Crowley. One of their temples is called the Amen-Ra, named after Ra, the Egyptian sun god (though it is located in Edinburgh).

Crowley was initiated on November 18, 1898, in London. He learned much about ceremonial magic through Golden Dawn. Perhaps his desire to form his own order was galvanized by the rejection he experienced once he was in. His bisexuality, drug use, and party lifestyle made him unpopular among the group, who, despite their mysterious and salacious reputation, in many ways maintained Victorian-era ideas about morality. There was a whole lot of messy wizard drama, complete with Crowley later being sued for publishing Golden Dawn secrets. However, Crowley won the lawsuit, and the drama helped build his bad-boy reputation.

Like many occult groups, Golden Dawn was reportedly into eugenics—the "science" of beliefs that personality traits and intelligence are genetically determined, inherited, and differ from race to race. Texts describe how Golden Dawn members wanted to both become ultimate beings and then create more of them by manifesting an ideal human race. As writer Jules Evans wrote, "The Golden Dawn believed they were midwifing this evolution." It was unabashedly an elitist organization—in many ways, just a witchy version of any number of exclusive London gentlemen's clubs. You know how in *Dune*, Lady Jessica's occult group, the Bene Gesserit, are trying to produce a biologically perfect baby god-human? It was kind of the same deal going on in these circles at the time. Whether it was secret societies or just Crowley on a regular Saturday night, occultists were very into spiritual eugenics during the nineteenth and twentieth centuries (and bits of this persist even today).

Crowley was vehemently anti-abortion. "Abortion was anathema to Crowley," per Churton, describing Crowley's reaction when learning that Jack Parsons apparently gave someone he got pregnant money for one. "Not only were abortions frequently due to money-worries but Thelema insisted on the 'true wills' of parents *and* children." However, looking at Crowley's actions, it appears that he didn't always care too much about being a parent to his own children himself, no matter how much he desired heirs. He reportedly had at least five, although some would die at quite a young age, and when this happened, he tended to blame the mother, as he did when one miscarried.

In *The Equinox of the Gods*, a book first published in 1936 that was intended to tell Thelema's origin story, Crowley writes that one should "consider abortion the most shameful form of murder, and loathe the social codes which encourage it." If we are to continue to take his writing at his word, he didn't consider women—let alone "Tattooed" and "Coloured Women"—to be people, either, once writing, "Morally and mentally, women were for me beneath contempt. They had no moral ideals. They were bound up with their necessary preoccupation with the function of reproduction.... [I]ntellectually, of course, they did not exist." Hypocritically, of course, his description of women's supposed moral failings sounds suspiciously like one of Crowley himself. And it was one of his many so-called Scarlet Women who helped him write *The Book of the Law*, the chief canonical work of Thelema. (Crowley preferred to view her assistance as some sort of spiritual download of his own knowledge.) The Scarlet Woman is a form of female perfection in his Thelema religion, a take on the Whore of Babylon, a left-handed-path dream girl, who appears in the Bible together with "the Beast" or the antichrist Crowley saw himself as. Crowley thought that the Scarlet Woman should be "loud and adulterous," and "shameless before men," and that "eyes shall burn with desire as she stands bare and rejoicing."

"Thelema" derives from the Greek for "to will, wish, want or purpose." Thelema's mission statement is "Do what thou wilt shall be the whole of the law," which means to follow one's own path, recognizing the human as an animal, but trusting one's own will—rather than the Christian God—to get what you want. Within Thelema, Crowley saw himself as the prophet assigned with the mission of leading humanity into the Æon of Horus, or the age of Horus, in the early twentieth century. Some of Crowley's works were just repackaged perverse beliefs from ancient Egyptians and Kabbalah, the brand of Jewish mysticism in which Lilith, ballsy first wife of Adam, makes her grand entrance to the world.

Another deity Crowley identified with was Isis, the Egyptian goddess of magic. Perhaps Crowley was unaware—though you, dear reader, are not—that Isis also appears in a prayer from the Roman poet Ovid calling upon the deity to heal his lover, Corinna, after she had an abortion. Crowley, too, fancied himself a poet, although his works were much more on the lewd side.

Crowley's life took him all over the world. His true love was mountain climbing; despite all the rituals and notoriety, he was likely happiest when literally on top of the world. But Egypt is where he rebranded himself as a prophet.

He honeymooned in Cairo with his first wife, Rose Edith Kelly, whom he married in 1904. While they eventually fell in love, that's not why they initially married. They got hitched because they were both the type of people who make irresponsible spontaneous decisions. Back in Edinburgh, Rose—who once lied about needing an abortion and used the money to buy clothes, bringing a bad name to the Scarlet Women of the world—accepted two marriage proposals. Truthfully, she wanted neither man. But her family was like, *Rose, you have to get away from us and settle down, so you'd better decide on one husband, and stat*. Crowley, a mere acquaintance of her brother, offered to marry Rose instead to get her out of the bind. She accepted. Impossibly, like a rom-com starring the wickedest man in the world, they actually fell in love, and she became one of his many ill-fated Scarlet Women.

During a brief respite from all the sex the newlyweds were having in Cairo, Crowley managed to convince a guard to let them stay a night in the King's Chamber of the Great Pyramid, the largest of the Egyptian pyramids, where god-men, as Crowley saw himself, enjoy the afterlife surrounded by the bodies of their wives . . . and perhaps a mummified alligator or two. While in Cairo, Crowley called himself the Persian prince Chioa Khan, which is Hebrew for "Great Beast." Rose, during their magical marathon that likely included mind-altering substances, had some bad news for her husband: Crowley had offended Horus. But she also informed him that his guardian angel, Aiwass, wanted to relay a massively important message. Maybe he didn't think women were equals, but he trusted Aiwass, who, apparently through Rose, had some information that he could use to redeem himself.

Rose then "channeled" Horus, telling Crowley that "the Equinox of the Gods" had come, and, of course, Crowley was the chosen one. It was amid these meetings with Egyptian gods and guardian angels and newlywed women that Crowley penned *The Book of the Law*, which Lachman describes as the crux of his philosophy. According to his followers—so we can assume this report first came from Crowley—he lit up the chamber with so much astral light that candles were no longer needed. And it was around this time that Rose became pregnant.

Rose gave birth to a girl, appropriately named Nuit Ma Ahathoor Hecate Sappho Jezebel Lilith. Crowley wrote a collection of X-rated stories, *Snowdrops from a Curate's Garden*, in 1904, which was apparently used to amuse Rose as she recovered. The work contains romantic titles such as "The Cocksucker's Crime."

Unfortunately, baby Nuit Ma Ahathoor Hecate Sappho Jezebel Lilith died at age two of typhus, a feverish and deadly disease spread from the bacteria of mites, fleas, or lice. Crowley blamed Rose, and she sank deep into alcoholism. Crowley "had no interest in the practical, day-to-day work of raising children and wanted the freedom to do as he wilt," writes Lachman. And he wasn't very consistent in his expectations of women. On the one hand, he believed that if "pity and compassion and tenderness" visit the heart of the Scarlet Woman, then Aiwass's "vengeance shall be known," and he will "slay me her child." On the other hand, he expected them all to be such perfect mothers that they could even cure typhus. Rose gave birth to another daughter, Lola Zaza, who grew up and rejected

Crowley. Rose and Crowley divorced, and he carried on his carnival of Scarlet Women. Lola died in 1990.

Crowley was always mixed up in an early kind of poly drama. Once, in the early 1920s, while living at his Abbey of Thelema, which was a harem, temple, and commune in a fishing port near Palermo, Sicily—home of Eunus and, later, where the "death ships" that brought the Black Plague docked—Leah, one of Crowley's partners, became pregnant, miscarried, and blamed fellow compound member Ninette for causing it with black magic. Ninette, Leah, and Crowley were in a throuple of sorts. Crowley read Ninette's diary and said he concurred. Ninette was kicked out of the compound but quickly allowed to reenter the community to give birth to Crowley's child as she, too, was pregnant. Ninette would give birth to his daughter, Astarte Lulu Panthea Crowley, who died in 2014, according to internet records.

Crowley really wanted a male heir, and he carried out many "magical operas" with the goal of having one. He ultimately did have a son in 1937, Randall Gair Doherty, who died in 2002. Magical mission accomplished.

Crowley was obsessed with the idea of the merging of masculine and feminine energies. He stated once that mixed bodily fluids from the two sexes is "the most powerful and radiant thing that existeth in the universe." Crowley also adored anal sex, likely because it was a fuck-you to traditional sexual expectations (especially during his time) and, honestly, probably because he just thought it felt good. Can't blame him for that. Crowley said that sex between two men was holy because he considered it "magician on magician." He loved to bottom. And yes, we're allowed to gossip about his sex life; the man basically took credit for inventing sex magic. Sorry. *Sex magick*. Crowley was bisexual and thought sex itself was very rebellious. By his own words, he loved to "satanize," which basically meant to freak people out in a glamorous and very horny fashion.

He wrote of how "wine, women, and song" could be used in magical ritual. Lachman explains that sex, drugs, and rock and roll were welcome and necessary to Crowley's brand of religion. Crowley's Gnostic Mass, one of his many Thelemic rituals and a perversion of the Roman Catholic Mass, includes digesting a Communion wafer soaked in period blood. For music, he leaned toward the tom-tom drum, as it was supposed to raise women's libidos. S&M, such as sex magic through bondage, showed up whenever possible.

Remember, Crowley was a poet. His rituals and religions show a ritual and pompous yet erratic energy not unlike free verse. This is a guy who loved sex and violence. When Crowley was fourteen, he tested whether a cat had nine lives by inflicting deadly torture nine different ways: "arsenic, chloroform, hanging, gassing, stabbing, slashing, smashing, burning, and drowning," Lachman writes. Crowley eventually threw the poor cat out the window. Crowley also tends to contradict himself even in the same sentence. In *The Equinox of the Gods*, Crowley writes that he "can attack an unsuspecting stranger, and torture him cruelly for years, without feeling the slightest animosity toward him. Fond of animals and children, who return my love, almost always." I guess the tortured kitty cat didn't make the cut.

Additionally, "A male of perfect innocence and high intelligence is the most satisfactory and suitable victim" is a commonly repeated Crowley quote, suggesting he'd go so far as to include murder in his left-handed rituals. Except this: That male heir? He was actually talking about his sperm. His writings have more hidden meanings than a Taylor Swift song. Once again, what Crowley believed in was mostly just fucking or jerking off... but surrounded by sigils and robes.

Apparently possessed by an evil spirit—not on his own accord, of course—he was eventually presented with the idea of human sacrifice. Crowley says he was informed that "the supreme sexual-magical act was the ritual rape, murder, and dismember-ment of a virgin," although there is no evidence that he ever actu-ally killed anyone. As an adult, Crowley reportedly did complete a ritual that involved crucifying a frog before cooking and eating its legs. Unsurprising, knowing the cat story. And while there's no indication he ever murdered anyone (although people blamed him for the deaths of porters who perished accompanying him on mountain-climbing expeditions as well as that time a man died after drinking dirty spring water at the Abbey of Thelema), he definitely left a trail of socially destroyed Scarlet Women and neglected offspring.

People argue over his last words. The most famous account is that he said, "I am perplexed." Others insist these were the last words muttered on his deathbed: "Sometimes I hate myself." Either way, Crowley remains an emblematic figure who reminds us that even the occult icons whose works are read by most well-meaning folks interested in magic have complicated and sometimes hateful stories, which, as much as the left-handed path loves a rebrand as the path of the liberated individual, frankly, shouldn't be so surprising.

2

It's hardly shocking that secret societies from the Gilded Age through World War II were invested in spiritual eugenics, consid-ering how downright mainstream the actual practice was. More than sixty thousand people were sterilized in the United States during the twentieth century, thanks to normalized "science" founded in the racist, ableist beliefs of eugenics.

Eugenicists twisted and applied burgeoning theories of biol-ogy and genetics to human reproduction. The eugenics movement began in late-nineteenth-century England, gained scientific sup-port in the United States, and then quietly whimpered into the darker corners of bigotry after Hitler's reign ended. After World War II, like a canceled acquaintance, most people simply pretended that eugenics didn't exist.

Eugenics' origin story stars Francis Galton (1822–1911), an English scientist. Make that *Sir* Francis Galton—he received a knighthood from King Edward—and he was influenced by Charles Darwin, who happened to be a half cousin. (Though Darwin's work fueled the false beliefs of eugenicists, he was not responsible for the evils carried out by those who embraced them.)

Galton was operating after slavery was officially over, so his theories opened up a new avenue for racists once his ideas landed in the United States. Galton was a different breed of sex-obsessed, problematic, eccentric British gentlemen: he had an axe to grind with the church for reducing great men to celibacy—thus rendering them unable to make more babies—during the Middle Ages. (Sure, it was an *old* axe, but Galton was going to grind it anyway.)

In *Control: The Dark History and Troubling Present of Eugenics*, Adam Rutherford calls Galton eugenics' midwife, and considering the level of pseudoscience involved in the movement and the unshakable fervor of its adherents, he could almost be considered another cult leader who found success in America's deeply bigoted past. Like Crowley, Galton viewed most humans like animals. He wholeheartedly approved of contests like "Better Babies," which debuted at the 1908 Louisiana State Fair among the carnival games and the lion tamers and involved human babies being judged like pups at the Westminster Dog Show, a new kind of human-animal exhibit influenced by his work. Some eugenics archivists are quick to point out that these competitions took hold at fairs because they *were* influenced by animals, agriculture, and the judging of stock and reduced humans to the same level.

Also like Crowley, he loved travel and had a complicated relationship with women. The guy didn't write poetry, but he did pen a best-selling travel book and invent the modern weather map, the dog whistle, and a three-point scale to rate the hotness of women: "attractive, indifferent, and repellent."

The word "eugenics" was coined by Galton in 1883. It comes from the Greek root *eu* for good and *genos* for offspring, meaning "well born" or "good in birth." While we attribute the official origins of eugenics to Galton, he surely wasn't the first to consider the notion. After all, other people had to feel similarly, or he never would have gained such a following.

Plato said that charms and incantations worked for the soul, while drugs healed the body. But he also wrote a quite thorough plan to control reproduction in the utopian state depicted in his book *Republic*, penned circa 375 BCE. In his story, men and women were set up by the state based on their desirable qualities. Children deemed inferior were shuffled into the working class and discouraged from having kids.

This was basically still the goal of the twentieth-century version of the concept. The eugenics movement was funded by the nation's richest families, such as Carnegie, Harriman, and Kellogg. They felt certain that America would be better if more Anglo-Saxons and Nordics had children because these groups, according to eugenics' dicey "science" and a biased definition of intelligence, were assumed to have the highest IQs. Anyone who did not fit into this category—which was most everyone, but especially Black and Indigenous people, immigrants, poor white people, and those with disabilities—was to be sterilized against their will. This often happened without their knowledge, as it was frequently done during childbirth or other medical procedures.

Before you judge this thinking as a thing of the past, remember what Trump said about "shithole" countries. And think about how, in 2020, he told a crowd at a rally in Minnesota, a state that's 80 percent white: "You have good genes. A lot of it is about the genes, isn't it, don't you believe? The racehorse theory. You think we're so different? You have good genes in Minnesota."

Eugenics worshipped the IQ test, believing that it could accurately quantify how smart someone was, thus indicating their value to society. While eugenicists considered themselves men of science, and surely not occultists, we once again see the attempt to rationalize bigotry and glaze over perversions with the high-class air of a gentlemen's club. While the IQ test may be useful in some settings, it's not a surefire way to categorize the vast ability of human intellect or abilities. And, at the time, intelligence tests were often used to categorize people: who to sterilize, but also which immigrants to send back home. As penned in *Scientific American* in 1915 by public health official Howard Knox: "The purpose of our mental measuring scale at Ellis Island is the sorting out of those immigrants who may, because of their mental makeup, become a burden to the State or who may produce offspring that will require care in prisons, asylums, or other institutions." Terms such as "moron" (IQ between 51 and 70), "imbecile" (IQ between 26 and 50), and "idiot" (IQ below 26) were scientific labels used in eugenics. (When it comes to Trump's own intelligence, he is a self-described "very stable genius." Surely, all very stable geniuses agree.) Despite their less than stellar track record on reproductive rights, the Catholic Church stood as the sole national organization to consistently oppose eugenics.

"Positive" eugenics encourages "better" people to reproduce, as Crowley's sex magic did, whereas "negative" eugenics tries to stop "inferior" people from doing so through forced sterilization or other such nasty methods. In the United States, negative eugenics was all the rage, and the government either looked away or outright systematized the damn thing. The practice of forced sterilization was considered humane, like spaying or neutering a feral cat. In North Carolina alone, during the 1930s and 1940s, almost eight thousand "mentally deficient people" were sterilized. Sixty-five percent were Black, despite making up only one-third of the state's population. And all over America, state institutions were given the power to sterilize people without their consent. The doctor Harry C. Sharp proposed sterilizing criminals to help with "race degeneration" in 1899, writes sociologist, law professor, and advocate Dorothy E. Roberts in *Killing the Black Body*. Sharp went on to perform vasectomies on more than four hundred inmates—and this wasn't a practice that ended with the twentieth century.

Anyone deemed unfit for reproduction could be sterilized or committed for "feeblemindedness," a reality that persisted through the 1960s. According to Roberts, "Labeling a young woman feeble-minded was often an excuse to punish her sexual immorality. Many women were sent to institutions to be sterilized solely because they were promiscuous or had become pregnant out of wedlock."

The concept of feebleness was connected to eugenics icon Charles Davenport, a Harvard-educated zoology professor at the University of Chicago. He believed that everything from "feeble-mindedness" to alcoholism to hemophilia to, oddly, as Ruther-ford points out, "seafaringness" (yes, that means people who enjoy spending time on boats) was the result of genetics and could be corrected by eugenics. And as Roberts writes, one of the indicators of feeblemindedness was the inability to demonstrate "the normal aversions of a white girl to a colored man who was perhaps nice to her." There were no such tests for men, of course, and we all know Thomas Jefferson was excused for raping a fourteen-year-old enslaved Black child.

As BIPOC women were forced into sterilization, middle-class white women fought for their right to have the procedure vol-untarily. At the time, doctors followed the recommended "120" formula created by the American College of Obstetricians and Gynecologists: "If a woman's age multiplied by the number of children she had totaled 120, she was a candidate for steriliza-tion." They additionally needed the approval of two doctors and a psychiatrist. Author and activist Angela Davis writes about how "what was demanded as a 'right' for the privileged came to be interpreted as a 'duty' for the poor."

Margaret Sanger (1879–1966) is a household name that most people think of as a reproductive rights icon. Hailed by some as the reason we have birth control and one of the greatest feminists of all time, she's also become a controversial figure. Sanger popularized the term "birth control" and founded the American Birth Control League in 1921. Sanger also opened the first Planned Parenthood in 1916 in Brownsville, Brooklyn. Despite the anti-choice movement's insistence on associating Planned Parenthood with abortion, only about 3 percent of what the organization does today is abortions. Mostly, Planned Parenthood provides exams, birth control pills and intrauterine devices (IUDs), and information to patients.

Sanger wasn't in favor of abortion herself, and she saw birth control as a way to avoid the whole thing. Born Margaret Louise Higgins, Sanger was the sixth of eleven children; her mother, Anne Purcell Higgins, had seven miscarriages, adding up to eighteen pregnancies within twenty-two years. Anne was often ill and died of tuberculosis at age fifty. Margaret was only nineteen. Appar-ently, Margaret confronted her dad at her mother's funeral and blamed him, stating, "You caused this. Mother is dead from having too many children."

From the mid-nineteenth to mid-twentieth centuries, America underwent a makeover to medicine, which was most often a career reserved for men. Women could become nurses or midwives or take care of home duties, while their husbands became doctors and lived their dreams. Despite her ambition, Sanger couldn't afford medical school, so she enrolled in a nursing program in 1900. Although her reputation is stained with conservatism in the modern age, Sanger was quite liberal back in the day: she hung out in Greenwich Village and wrote sex-education columns for the *New York Call*—a socialist newspaper. Her column was censored thanks to those infamously restrictive Comstock laws, which weren't just sex negative but fully choked free speech. After her column was canceled, she started her own newspaper, the *Woman Rebel*, an eight-page monthly newsletter supporting contraceptives. She picked the bold slogan "No gods, no masters" and wielded her newsletter to give Comstock's bonkers laws the middle finger, which deemed her educational information on STIs and other sexual health obscene and illegal. She was indicted in August 1914, but she escaped to Europe to evade arrest. She came back to face trial, but the obscenity charges against her were dropped.

Sanger, at first, was a feminist crusader for female pleasure. She was indeed sick of the Victorian ideas of morality, which said that good women became good mothers without complaint. But Sanger operated like a politician, and therein lay her success. People—especially people wealthy enough to fund her projects—didn't get on board with Sanger when she was evangelizing for worry-free, pleasurable sex. But she saw a chance, and she took it: just as her birth control movement was beginning to garner attention, eugenics was taking a stronghold in American society.

Sanger could sell birth control as a way to keep what were considered undesirable populations down *and* as a feminist tool for responsible family planning. She left behind the bohemian Greenwich Village scene (just as Aleister Crowley—a very different kind of bohemian . . . even if they kind of did agree on abortion— was moving in) and got to work advocating for her chosen causes. Sanger began to weave eugenics into her birth control pitch, solidly entrenching it as an instrument in the eugenics movement. She even asserted that "eugenics without birth control seemed to me a house built upon the sands." Sanger was undeniably a positive influence on the reproductive rights movement, and her involvement in eugenics, unfortunately, made more sense when viewed through the scope of her time. As Roberts writes, "It appears that Sanger was motivated by a genuine concern to improve the health of the poor mothers she served rather than a desire to eliminate their stock." However, eugenics is also evil, and it's okay if one wants to hate her for it. Understanding the complexity of her as a character in the narrative is crucial to understanding that, in the history of birth control, while there may be obvious villains (hi, Comstock), even the heroes don't exist purely on a binary of good and evil. Binaries are most often bullshit.

Eugenicists operated pretty much unchecked in America until the Nazis called everyone on their bluff by revealing the movement's true nature on the world stage. The Nazi regime forcibly sterilized an estimated four hundred thousand people, and then, of course, there was the Final Solution. By the 1940s, eugenics was no longer in vogue and discredited as the poor science and fuel for racism that it was. Eugenicists in America, like someone today deleting now problematic old tweets, pretended like they'd had nothing to do with it.

At the Nuremberg trials, meant to hold high-ranking Nazis accountable for crimes against humanity, three were acquitted, twelve hanged, and four got away with under twenty years in prison. The infamous Josef Mengele, known as the "Angel of Death," had performed twisted and deadly experiments on prisoners at Auschwitz; he escaped and (allegedly) died by drowning in Brazil in 1979, having served no time for his many crimes against humanity. Documents suggest that following World War II and until his death, Mengele was a well-known abortionist in Buenos Aires, Argentina.

But it's time to talk about a different abortionist, one who didn't inspire *The Human Centipede*.

3

When Madame Restell, "hell's representative on earth," unknowingly met Anthony Comstock for the first time, she was dressed in black silk mourning attire. Her outfit would have included a full skirt enhanced by a petticoat, her waist snatched by a whalebone corset. (Incidentally, whalebones were what she performed her surgical abortions with.) During the Victorian era, it was customary for a woman to wear black for two years following the death of a spouse. Her husband, Charles Lohman, had died the year prior. They had enjoyed a long, passionate power-couple relationship, which broke norms at the time—as did Restell's solo success and modern point of view. She was a mother, but she often spoke about how marriage could be awesome even without kids—a radical notion for the time. Restell was not the sort of person who worried about getting canceled; she played politics and treaded into controversy just like Sanger had. But unlike Sanger, Restell was a proud abortionist. She was good at her job, and it made her a millionaire.

The *Police Gazette* printed a caricature of Restell in 1847: a witch, complete with a devilish bat, hungrily holding a baby. Restell fitted the bill for a witch, the Scarlet Woman, a Lilith who dared to make money through business—like a *man*.

Madame Restell had piercing brown eyes and brown hair streaked with gray like lightning. At sixty-six, she was just as beautiful as—and even more fabulous than—she had been in her youth. Refusing to let age fuck with her glamour, she was far from the stereotype of postmenopausal women as sad crones. She was hot and proud of it.

On this cold January night, a stout man with a doughy face, impressive side whiskers, and a bow tie looked back at her when she opened her door. The man, who behaved and appeared as if a stick was permanently shoved up his ass, was Anthony Comstock, the leader of the New York Society for the Suppression of Vice—the very Comstock responsible for the Comstock Act of 1873, which made it criminal to distribute information on contraceptives and classified birth control as obscene. Comstock was there to entrap Restell so that he could arrest her.

"May I speak to Madame Restell?" Comstock inquired, standing on the doorstep of her glamorous brownstone on Fifth Avenue and Fifty-Second Street, once described as a house "built upon a mound of baby skulls," as brilliantly detailed by *Madame Restell: The Life, Death, and Resurrection of Old New York's Most Fabulous, Fearless, and Infamous Abortionist* by historian Jennifer Wright. Like Crowley after her, she was described as a "beast" by journalists, but unlike Crowley, those were not her own words. Restell built that mansion on land that she won in a bidding war with the archbishop of New York's Roman Catholic Church after he publicly denounced her. Restell enjoyed engaging in beefs with her rivals.

It was likely Restell's passion for her work that made her assume the man was there to help get a woman out of trouble. In addition to surgical abortions, she offered herbal abortive pills for those early in pregnancy. She also let women stay with her and give birth and helped them put their children up for adoption if they chose. So more often than not, when a rich man showed up at her door, it was because his mistress was pregnant and it was a problem that needed solving.

Restell sent Comstock away with the nineteenth-century medical abortion: some of her pills, with directions inside the bottle rather than on the outward labels most medicines have, as it was illegal to show them on the outside due to Comstock's own laws. "It is not infallible," she warned. "No medicine is. In nine cases out of ten, however, it is very effective." If his friend needed further help, a surgical abortion cost $200, or the equivalent of $5,000 today. While she did take in folks who couldn't afford the procedure, Restell charged high-end fees for high-end abortions for wealthy clientele. (A surgical abortion today, depending on your insurance, where you go, and how far along you are, costs anywhere from $0 to upward of $1,000.)

Two weeks later the man returned—but not with a pregnant mistress. Nope, his companions were a cluster of cops with a warrant for her arrest. "You've brought quite the party with you," Wright describes Madame Restell commenting without breaking a sweat. When she was arrested, she walked like the boss that she was, insisting on having a lunch of oysters before she came to the station, and they allowed her to do so. People listened to Restell even if they despised her. Thanks to the magic of confidence, her words had power.

She insisted on traveling to court in her infamous over-the-top carriage pulled by two gray horses. The coachman wore purple, associated with royalty in color magic. A self-made millionaire and an immigrant, Restell had earned the right to be arrested in style.

Restell was born Ann Trow in a small English town called Painswick in 1811. Her upbringing was, in fact, rather witchy and may have played a role in her rebellious streak. Painswick was known for its pagan customs and even had a yearly festival dedicated to Pan that may have included "nocturnal orgies," according to historian Timothy Mowl, as detailed by Wright. Sounds deviant enough to make Crowley proud.

As a girl, Restell worked as a butcher. Experience with animals was often the most hands-on training any medical practitioner saw before going to work in those days. In America at the time, most medical schools didn't even make their students study at hospitals to learn; only half asked them to dissect a human cadaver. Medical students were expected to learn, essentially, by experimenting on patients. This is also what Madame Restell did.

There was a boom of medical schools in the nineteenth century, but that doesn't mean that they were good. Surgery was gory at the time. About 50 percent of patients died bound to the surgical table with leather straps, which is why patients were required to pay up front. Because surgery was so dangerous, it was usually a last resort, which also may explain the extraordinary death rate.

Surgical abortion would remain dangerous until the invention of penicillin in the 1940s. Charles Meigs, an American obstetrician who worked as chair of obstetrics and diseases of women at Jefferson Medical College from 1841 to 1861, Wright writes, wrote in 1854 that doctors shouldn't bother washing their hands, as "a gentleman's hands are clean."

Restell saw herself as a gentleman. While she eventually rose through the ranks of New York society and became the woman she sold herself as, Madame Restell, the persona, was an advertising tool—the Ziggy Stardust to her David Bowie. Madame Restell, the immigrant from France, was invented as a way to advertise and market Ann Trow. France was considered chic, sex positive, fashionable, and ahead in medicine. Restell was so good at exuding glamour that no one questioned her English accent. Why would they when her conversation included so much progressive commentary? She was known for asking, "Why should women have no say over if and when they become mothers?"

Trow immigrated to America in 1831 with the hopes of pursuing the American dream. She succeeded. Prior to becoming a famous abortionist to the wealthy, she was Ann, the seamstress, living in downtown Manhattan. While Lower Manhattan is associated with high-end boutiques and martinis now, at the time it was a poor area for immigrants with an epically high mortality rate. Trow's first husband, Henry, a tailor and horrid alcoholic, died of typhoid in 1833, leaving her alone with their toddler daughter.

At the time, one-third of the deaths in New York City were kids under five years old. There were an estimated thirty thousand unhoused kids on the streets of New York. Thanks to *Hamilton*-famous Eliza Schuyler, the socialite wife of Alexander Hamilton, the city's first orphanage was founded in 1806, but the New York Orphan Asylum wouldn't help *all* children. Foundlings, or abandoned children, as described by New York's first chief of police, were considered "embryo courtesans and felons." Foundlings were not allowed in the New York Orphan Asylum, which accepted only orphans of the wealthy or infants given up for adoption by wealthier women. So-called foundlings, as Wright writes about, wouldn't get a home of their own until the Infant's Home was founded in 1865.

It was a hard time to be a poor kid with immigrant parents, and it was a hard time to be an immigrant mother like Restell was. Due to round-the-clock working hours not yet regulated by labor unions or federal laws, very little pay, and the social and economic limitations of being a woman in the early-nineteenth-century United States, many moms couldn't afford or find child care. So it was common to just drag your kids in the hopes that they'd sleep while you were away. Wright describes a 1859 cartoon from *Harper's Weekly* depicting opium as "The Poor Child's Nurse." Heroin was commonly prescribed for a child's cough, and other common cough syrups of the era contained a potent mix of substances that a modern American would serve decades in prison for possessing. There was also a lot less social stigma around unaccompanied children at that time. But Restell wanted a better life for herself and her child. She achieved that . . . even if she did disown her daughter later in life for marrying a cop.

As Sanger learned decades later, if a woman wanted to work in the medical profession in America in this era, she could either be a nurse or go into business with her doctor husband and take over midwifing duties. Restell ignored all the rules. She first learned about pill compounding from her neighbor Dr. William Evans. She started making her own, and they sold so well that she could quit her day job and give up tailoring. Her first pills were marketed to treat lung problems due to consumption, in addition to treating the liver and stomach (it's pretty safe to say they were not actually effective). Before too long, women were coming to her for abortive pills on the DL, which she made through the 1830s, that contained ergot of rye (we meet again) and cantharides. Later, Wright writes that Restell used oil of tansy and spirits of turpentine.

There were many menstrual-stimulation pills on the market at the time. One popular brand was Dr. Champlin's Red Woman's Relief—note the similarity to Crowley's carnal Scarlet Woman. But the big players in the medication abortion market were men, and Restell wanted a piece of the pie.

At first, everyone assumed her second husband, Charles, was the chemist behind the capsules. It was unheard of for the wife to be a breadwinner, let alone a shrewd, money-loving, glamorous millionaire. Charles was a friend and colleague of George Matsell, a bookstore owner who also sold occult and spiritualist texts and would go on to be the first New York City police commissioner. Charles published the book *The Married Woman's Private Medical Companion* in 1847 under the name A. M. Mauriceau. It openly supported abortion and shared that "until men and women are absolved from the fear of becoming parents, except when they themselves desire it, they ever will form mercenary and demoralizing connections, and seek in dissipation the happiness they might have found in domestic life," Wright shares. In contrast to Trota of Salerno, the twelfth-century gynecologist whose work wasn't properly credited to a woman until 1985, in this case many people assumed that Restell wrote the book rather than Charles. The *Louisville Daily Courier* expressed concern that the text was crafted to "express benefit . . . in furtherance of [Restell's] hellish schemes." *The Married Woman's Private Medical Companion* contained advice on healing postmedical abortion by either applying ice or using a rag soaked in snow on the genitals (it's okay if this makes you squeamish; there are more germ-proof options such as store-bought ice packs available today), among an abundance of other novel and thoughtful reproductive medical advice. In this author's opinion, they likely penned the book together. It was the bit about icing one's genitals with snow that got Charles arrested for selling "obscene publications," but his wife would spend far more time in prison than he ever did.

In 1840, a patient of Madame Restell's named Ann Maria Purdy became deathly ill from tuberculosis. While it was unrelated, all Purdy knew was that she had an abortion and then became very sick. Shockingly, given the lack of sterilization at the time, few of Restell's patients died. Purdy could have gotten sick for many reasons; tuberculosis is spread easily through coughing, and it was common at the time. But when Purdy confessed to her husband about the abortion, he reported Restell to the police and charges were brought. The press made her out as a monster, charging her with acts against God. (Ballsy, given that slavery was still legal.) During the appeal, the charges were overturned. Purdy died later of the tuberculosis she likely got anywhere *but* Restell's office.

Then there was Mary Applegate. She came to Restell in 1845, not for an abortion, but to give birth and recover under Restell's care. The father, Augustus Edwards, wanted nothing to do with a child and arranged for Restell to give the baby to a nurse. "Baby farms" were cheap, dirty, crime-riddled places where wet nurses fed babies while moms recovered. They were common, too, and disreputable, but it was better than pumping your baby full of opium and crossing your fingers.

When Applegate was on the mend, she asked Edwards for her child. He lied and claimed that Restell gave the child away without his consent, asserting he had never said anything about sending the child to a nurse. When Applegate came back to ask Restell about her child's whereabouts, Restell said she had no idea how to find the nurse and it was out of her hands. When Edwards eventually also came to Restell to try to locate the baby, Restell claimed that she had no idea even whom Applegate was. To this day, no one knows what actually happened, but Applegate never found the child, and Restell never told.

In a case that became public in 1847, Maria Bodine, a housekeeper, went to Restell for a surgical abortion. Initially, Restell turned her away, stating she was too far along. Bodine was six months pregnant, but she insisted until Restell performed the abortion. But Bodine became sick. A doctor, Samuel L. Smith, wrote to the mayor of New York that Bodine's illness was the result of Restell's care. Though Bodine hadn't been the one to bring the charges, she *was* very ill and appeared so during the trial: she was dealing with health issues including syphilis, though she didn't know it. Smith, her doctor, hadn't told her—standard practice at the time, as doctors assumed a woman patient's husband or male friend would be the one to foot the bill for her care, and they didn't want to out the men for cheating and passing along an STI.

The case went to court. Restell's defense claimed Bodine's illness had nothing to do with her, but Restell was found guilty and spent a year in prison on Blackwell's Island, now known as Roosevelt Island—the infamous madhouse that journalist Nellie Bly would expose in a series of articles decades later. Restell's stay was much better than Bly's, considering she used her money to bribe everyone possible, ensuring that she had fresh peaches and a storeroom transformed into her own cell, complete with a closet full of dresses. Other inmates lived communally in tiny cells, cramped in with other inmates, all sleeping on a strip of canvas, sharing a single chamber pot and a tank to wash in. When Restell's sentence was over, she went right back to work.

During Madame Restell's trials, no one spoke of her intelligence and abilities, as one would today. Describing Madame Restell, Wright writes, "Intellect in a woman such as her wasn't necessarily laudable—it could easily be perceived as canniness. Rather than use her mind for good, as a man might, she might use it to manipulate the feebleminded members of her sex, in the manner of a witch." Restell was smart, and she knew it. The anonymous account of someone identified as a "Physician of New York" described her in 1847: "She positively thinks that she is one of the nicest, best, bravest little women in the world; and she would be very indignant, if anyone should offer to dispute it." Infantilizing language, but okay. Maybe she *was* one of the bravest little women in the world. During the Purdy trial, one letter written in defense of Madame Restell, allegedly penned by an actress, ended with this line: "God bless you dear madam, you have taken off the primal curse denounced upon Mother Eve in Eden. I am bound to pray for you every night of my life." Like a rock star, the witchy abortionist once portrayed with a baby-eating bat demon had fans to reinforce her high self-esteem.

As her fame soared, it was only a matter of time before she caught the attention of Comstock and got herself arrested. Restell had become a member of New York City's elite, a fashionable, glamorous, rich, beautiful woman who was also an abortionist with the influence to take over a prison. Comstock knew very well about Madame Restell and thought she was a Satanic murderess— unfortunately, her rise to fame happened at the same time he was soaring to power, demonstrating the polarized views on sexuality at the time.

He may have successfully arrested Restell, but she never made it to trial, and what happened instead actually helped the public turn further against him. Restell's trial was set for Saturday, March 29. That Monday morning, on April Fools' Day, the body of the "wickedest woman in New York" was found. Madame Restell had killed herself by slashing her throat in a bathtub the day before the trial.

Some people insisted that she faked her own death. Among them was Egyptian astrologer Charles Malogole, who was asked in 1879 if he ever did business with Restell. He replied: "I did business for Mm. Restell, but not the late Mme. Restell because that woman is not dead.... She is now pursuing her vocation in Paris. She had good reasons for leaving the city, and it was part of the programme that she was reported dead." There's no evidence that Madame Restell faked her death. There's no evidence that she had any interest in eugenics, either, or was actually guilty of any malpractice. By all accounts, she genuinely loved her work . . . almost as much as she loved making money. Performing abortions undoubtedly made her evil in the eyes of men like Comstock, but enjoying her profession, and, without shame, wanting to get properly compensated for it, might have been what tipped her over into the image of a *witch*.

4

Let's talk about symbolism. The history of reproductive rights— and the longer history of hunting witches both real and imagined— is one with a heavily illustrated timeline.

The Star of David is composed of two overlaid equilateral triangles. Together, they form a six-pointed star. The symbol dates back to antiquity. It's also known as Magen, or the alternative spelling Mogen. *Magen David* means "God as a protector," which caught traction with Jewish mystics. When used properly, the Star of David is a protection sigil and a religious symbol of pride. But the Nazis turned a sacred symbol and protection spell into a death marker.

On September 1, 1941, Reinhard Heydrich, a high-ranking German SS official who was pivotal in implementing the Final Solution, ordered that all Jews in the Reich six years of age or older wear a badge with a yellow star on a black field adhered to the chest, inscribed with the word "Jew." Remember how during the Inquisition our girl Béatrice had to wear a yellow cross as a mark of religious shame? The Nazis took persecution to levels so evil and abhorrent that they shamed people into dropping eugenics—at least in polite company.

Now might be a good time to pause and observe that the Jews have historically been pretty chill regarding reproductive rights. As Rabbi Danya Ruttenberg—an author, scholar in residence for the National Council of Jewish Women, and creator of Rabbis for Repro, a national network of Jewish clergy working to support reproductive rights in their communities and on a national level— explained in an interview with Marin Cogan for *Vox*:

> *Abortion is permitted in Judaism, and when the life of
> the pregnant person is at stake, it is required. Judaism's
> approach to abortion finds its basis in the book of Exodus.
> There's a case where two people are fighting, and one
> person knocks over a pregnant person and causes a mis-
> carriage. It says very clearly, if it's only a miscarriage,
> then the person who caused the harm is obligated to pay
> monetary fines as damages, and if a pregnant person dies,
> then it is treated as manslaughter. So we see right away
> that in the book of Exodus it's very clear that the fetus and
> pregnant person have different statuses, and causing a
> miscarriage is not treated as manslaughter.*
> *The fetus does not have the same status as a born human.
> It's treated as potential life, rather than actual life.*

The Universal Hexagram, as used by Aleister Crowley's Thelema, squeezes the middle of the six-pointed star—remember, this guy *loved* Jewish mysticism, even if he was on a very different page regarding abortion—turning it into the Unicursal Hexagram. In the Thelemic version, there's often a five-petal flower in the middle as a nod to the pentagram, a universal symbol of the occult. The hexagram represents the divine macrocosmic, as in the holiness we cannot see or control, the union of opposites. The petals represent the five magical elements (fire, water, air, earth, and spirit) of the flower represent the microcosmic forces of five elements of the magical formula *YHShVH*, an allegorical form of the Hebrew word for Jesus. Together, the inner flower and outer star symbolize the interweaving of planetary and elemental magick—the outer world meets the inner. Stars, representing the sun from Ra to Wicca, show how the magic permeates the mainstream and vice versa.

If one is to look at the cover of *The Satanic Bible*, penned by Anton Szandor LaVey, another bald man of the left-handed path, one will notice that the pentagram adorning the cover is upside down. LaVey often added a lightning bolt through the middle of his beloved upside-down pentagram that, rather unfortunately, does look as much like a rock-band logo as he probably hoped it would. In most pagan practices, the pentagram represents the self with its five points—one for the head, two for arms, and two for legs. When the pentagram is inverted, the corresponding body is reversed, too: genitals face the sky. This is why the upside-down version is employed by those walking the left-handed path, in contrast to pagan religions such as Wicca, which view man overriding animal instincts using the brain and spiritual wisdom.

Wicca, a neo-pagan nature-based religion whose followers identify as witches, originated in England but spread like wildfire through America during the 1960s and '70s. It was part of the countercultural revolution that also included the free-love movement. During this time, openly discussing sex, and considering the enjoyment of sex a valid reason for using contraception and valuing reproductive rights, reached mainstream America. The term "pro-choice" and its counter, "pro-life," entered the chat. Simultaneously, anti-abortion activists organized and radicalized, especially after the Supreme Court decided *Roe v. Wade* in 1973 and as reproductive rights became associated with free love and (gasp!) even the gay rights movement.

Pentagrams have continued to be important symbols in the modern era and even made an appearance at the end of *Roe*, too. Here's how it went:

Norma McCorvey was not the ideal candidate to change the face of abortion in America. For starters, McCorvey was a lesbian. She liked her drink and she liked her drugs. She'd been in trouble with the law since she robbed a cash register at the age of ten. She survived many abusive relationships, from her alcoholic mother to her first husband, and while we're sympathetic to that now, for a very long time, women were blamed when they got beat up.

This was her third pregnancy. Her first child had been put up for adoption, and her mother took her second. The third time, she discovered she was pregnant while working at the carnival show. She tried to abort herself, unsuccessfully, by drinking castor oil, which some research suggests can induce labor later in a pregnancy. But Lady Luck rarely smiled on Norma McCorvey. She turned to an illegal abortion clinic. However, it had already been shut down by the police, and no one was there to help her. Of the clinic, according to James Risen and Judy L. Thomas in *Wrath of Angels: The American Abortion War*, McCorvey said, "Nobody was there. It was an old dentist's office. Then I saw dried blood everywhere and smelled this awful smell."

Around the same time, Sarah Ragle, the daughter of a Methodist minister, went to get an abortion in Mexico for $400 during her third year of law school, after getting pregnant with the child of her eventual husband, Ron Weddington. She loved to ride horses and played the drums like nobody's business. Abortion was illegal in Texas, and needing to travel out of the country for a medical procedure really pissed Ragle off. At the urging of friends, she started doing legal research for an abortion referral project. The service boldly asked her to file a lawsuit to challenge Texas law, which was the same since 1854. Because she needed help, in 1969, she teamed up with Linda Coffee, whom she knew from her law school class. They needed a plaintiff, so they were introduced to McCorvey by Henry McCluskey, a Dallas abortion attorney.

The three women met at a pizza parlor (before the days when the Far Right associated such restaurants with ritual sacrifice and child trafficking). Even though Texas has no exception for rape, McCorvey lied to Ragle and Coffee and said she had gotten pregnant as the result of rape. Perhaps this was due to the social stigma around abortion; perhaps she knew that she'd be a poor lead plaintiff otherwise. McCorvey was given the pseudonym "Jane Roe."

Coffee filed a class-action suit against the district attorney of Dallas County, Henry Wade, on March 3, 1970, and the ball was in motion. Wade was already known for another high-profile case: he had been supposed to prosecute Lee Harvey Oswald for President John F. Kennedy's murder, but Jack Ruby had shot and killed Oswald before he could go to trial; Wade's assistant conducted the proceedings against Ruby.

On June 17, the federal court ruled that Texas's abortion bans were unconstitutional. The court refused to grant the women the injunction they wished for but said the criminal abortion statutes were void. Both sides cross-appealed. By then, it didn't even matter for McCorvey, who was ready to pop and gave her third child up for adoption after birth. "It was really for all the women who came along after me," she said, feeling upset and used.

The case was appealed and went to the highest court in the nation. In January 1973, the Supreme Court issued a 7–2 decision in McCorvey's favor, holding that the Due Process Clause of the Fourteenth Amendment to the US Constitution provides a fundamental right to privacy—which protects a pregnant person's right to an abortion. At one point, Jay Floyd, the assistant attorney general of Texas, said: "It's an old joke, but when a man argues against two beautiful ladies like this, they're going to have a last word."

When *Roe* passed, Norma McCorvey was at home with her lover, Connie Gonzales, looking perturbed. Gonzales asked Norma what was wrong. She had no idea that the landmark case had involved her own partner. Risen and Thomas relay the conversation:

"They've legalized abortion," McCorvey said.

"That's good," Gonzales replied.

McCorvey looked at her directly and asked: "How would you like to meet Jane Roe?"

While most of liberal America slept comfortably under this ruling for forty-nine years, the Right radicalized. They joined forces and put together a detailed plan. Even McCorvey—Roe herself—had switched sides and become an anti-abortion activist, although she later claimed that she did this because conservative anti-abortion groups gave her money. But by the time the plan was in place and already rolling, most progressives were too busy applauding themselves for voting for Obama to notice.

Following *Politico*'s May 2022 report of Justice Alito's leaked draft opinion in the US Supreme Court case of *Dobbs v. Jackson Women's Health Organization*, which would overturn *Roe v. Wade*, people finally woke the hex up. Alito's opinion included language regarding "quickening," by then a long-forgotten term, and Matthew Hale—the seventeenth-century English jurist responsible for the belief that husbands can't rape their wives who was passionate about sentencing women to death for witchcraft.

The day after Alito's draft leaked, Catholic churches, including St. Joseph's Priory in Michigan, woke up to find pentagrams—in 2022, a symbol of witchy, feminist resistance—spray-painted on their doors. Perhaps not the most effective or considerate form of protest, but at least someone was awake to what was still happening even in a world where you can put "witch" in your Instagram bio and not get torn limb from limb. Perhaps some women had become too comfortable, because the anti-abortion crowd had had *their* spray paint ready to go decades earlier, as soon as *Roe* passed in the first place. In the next chapter, you'll meet their "activists" who blew up abortion clinics. But most anti-abortion activists used their brains and community organizing rather than explosives. They created an intelligent and detailed plan, published books about the mission to overturn *Roe*, vowed to overturn *Roe* in every election, appointed judges bent on overturning *Roe*—all public, intentional, and methodical. And they succeeded.

Roe herself campaigned for the anti-abortion cause (though money was involved). Margaret Sanger, whose name is now nearly synonymous with Planned Parenthood (an organization the Right has deemed synonymous with abortion), wasn't even into the idea, preferring to frame birth control as a preferable alternative. And, truly, until Wright penned her must-read book, Madame Restell, a glamorous woman, unafraid of her identity as a self-made millionaire and abortionist, was largely lost to history.

Plenty of folks would like the practice of eugenics, finally discarded after the unspeakable evils of World War II, to stay in the past where it belongs. But its foundational ideas unfortunately live on through the words and actions of some of the most powerful politicians in this country. And these same hypocrisies and inconsistencies are further highlighted by the fact that Aleister Crowley, the "most wicked man in the world," was anti-abortion but seemingly pro-eugenics himself (much as modern-day witches and those who embrace the left-handed path would like to ignore this or simply don't know about it).

The lesson in all this? In the war for reproductive rights, nothing is as it seems. In our narrative, the Far Right will soon be murdering doctors and the Republicans' most-beloved icon will depend on astrology to decide when to fly Air Force One. They will also hijack occult imagery and repackage it to stoke baseless fears of child sacrifice. Buckle up: we are now entering 1980s America.

CHAPTER 5

SATANIC PANIC, REAGAN ASTROLOGY, AND BOMBS OVER CHRISTMAS

1

It's Christmas morning, 1984. You're in Pensacola, a city on the coast of the Florida panhandle. Incumbent Republican, jellybean-eating, former Hollywood star President Ronald Reagan has just last month beaten the Democratic former vice president Walter Mondale in a massive victory.

Pagans have been celebrating the Winter Solstice, the shortest day of the year, as a time of rebirth and renewal—complete with a party involving presents decorated with evergreen plants and greenery meant to remind practitioners and partygoers alike that life exists even in the harsh winter—at least since the ancient Norse thousands of years ago. Saturnalia, an ancient Roman pagan festival celebrating Saturn, agricultural god (like the winter version of the Sabine woman's Neptunalia), was held in mid-December and is said to have influenced modern-day Christmas. They even used wreaths as decorations.

Your Winter Solstice tradition isn't that different. There's a wreath on your door—even if it is store-bought—and your living room is littered with wrapping paper adorned with reindeer as your young children bound about wildly. The weather is perfect: high sixties with an ocean breeze. You always did have a thing for snowmen made from sand, and with your lovely nuclear family, you can enjoy the Christian holiday with a cup of rum eggnog to take the edge off your kids arguing over who got the better Cabbage Patch Kid from Santa. Your cozy living room smells like gingerbread accented by the salt air that flows through your open window. "It's the Most Wonderful Time of the Year" plays on the radio.

And then you hear something like fireworks, but the reality is far more sinister: it's bombs set by extremists at the nearby Ladies Center and the offices of two other doctors who provide abortions. Kaye Wiggins, one of those charged in the bombings, would call this "a gift for Jesus on his birthday." You weren't ready to have the "birds and the bees" talk with your kids yet, much less a conversation about abortion, and you're definitely not prepared to get into why people justify heinous acts by proclaiming themselves Christian. But here you are.

Dr. David Gunn would be killed in Pensacola eight years later, on March 10, 1993, at the age of forty-seven. Gunn and several other physicians who performed abortions were murdered in the '90s in a wave of violence during the Reagan administration, although the seeds had been planted long before.

Gunn was a guy with a great smile and a fabulous mustache who walked with a limp from childhood polio. He graduated from the medical school of the University of Kentucky and became an obstetrician who provided abortions. Outside of Pensacola clinics, he traveled to perform abortions in Georgia and Alabama; even during *Roe*, thanks to reactionary Christian extremism, his was a dangerous profession, and few wanted to take up the work.

Despite knowing that anti-abortion terrorism was on the rise, Gunn refused to wear a bulletproof vest to work. He was murdered by a man named Michael Griffin in front of the Pensacola Women's Medical Services Clinic. Griffin (1961–) was a follower of John Burt, a former Ku Klux Klan member with beady eyes and a drooping face who had created a home for girls called Our

Father's House, meant to "save" them from a life of drugs and sex work.

Griffin claimed it was divine intervention that led him to Gunn. Griffin watched the doctor for five hours on March 5, 1993, before following him to his car. Griffin said, "David Gunn, are you going to kill children next week?" and Gunn apparently replied, "Yeah, probably," as reported by Risen and Thomas, according to an interview Griffin gave in prison. (You can decide whether to take him at his word.) Griffin then recited a Bible verse, Genesis 9:6, the verse that would become the motto of the deadly anti-abortion activists: "Whoever sheds man's blood, by man his blood shall be shed," per the King James Bible. Five days later, Griffin returned and shot three .38 caliber bullets—into the back—as Gunn exited his car.

Before he succeeded in becoming a famous murderer, Griffin was in the US Navy on submarine duty, working as a nuclear power-plant supervisor. His personal life raised red flags. Griffin's wife, Patricia, citing abuse, requested a restraining order in their divorce proceedings, which Michael initiated. Patricia wrote that her husband "suffers from great fits of violence." He denied it. The divorce was ultimately dropped when the couple got back together.

Griffin and his wife were both followers of John Burt, although quick to turn against their leader. During his trial, Griffin's attorney, Robert Kerrigan, argued that Burt had brainwashed Griffin and driven him to commit murder. Burt had shown the couple (and their two little girls) graphic anti-abortion propaganda films and aborted fetuses kept in saline solution that, like some Christian Jeffrey Dahmer, he kept in his office.

It was during *Roe* that the anti-choice crowd started using this kind of graphic imagery of abortion to make their point. The truth is, many common medical experiences are ugly. Most people undergoing a medical procedure are spared from seeing gory photos of it. The use of graphic imagery moved abortion out of the realm of medical privacy, which, after all, was what *Roe* was all about, and into a public spectacle designed to further villainize generations of women. Sometimes the images anti-abortion crusaders use are distorted or edited, and some pro-choice folks find it comforting to believe that none of the images are to be trusted. But the truth is, others are not edited. Looking at photos or videos of abortions *can* be graphic—but so is video footage of a colon resection, if you're bad with blood. The point is, the way it looks has no bearing on the fact that it's a medical procedure and it's often necessary or simply desired and that is perfectly fine.

Anti-abortion activists have used this type of graphic imagery to harass people going into clinics for decades, but they've also used it to recruit folks to the anti-choice cause, as was the case with the Griffins. In 1984, *The Silent Scream* was released, a controversial (and medically disputed) half-hour documentary created with footage of an ultrasound exam during an abortion that would wind up in high schools and colleges across the country. It is regarded as one of the most successful propaganda films of all time.

After watching the movies, the Griffins completed a five-hour weapons training program facilitated by the Pensacola Police Department. Three days before Griffin shot Gunn, he stood up at Burt's fundamentalist church, Whitfield Assembly of God, and asked, "Would you agree with me in prayer that David Gunn should get saved and stop killing babies?" as reported by Risen and Thomas. The congregation did agree; after all, their leader, Burt, was already protesting outside his clinic with a life-size effigy, like some witch at Burning Man, of David Gunn wearing scrubs and bloody gloves, inscribed with, you guessed it, the Bible verse Genesis 9:6.

Gunn's murder inspired "Get Your Gunn," the first official single Marilyn Manson ever released, back when the only ones trying to cancel the disgraced shock rocker were Christians.

Griffin was sentenced to life in prison with no chance of parole for twenty-five years. In 2017, the State of Florida Commission on Offender Review denied Griffin's parole, setting his next hearing date for March 9, 2043. He remains incarcerated at the time of this writing. Burt wasn't convicted in Gunn's murder, although he did get hit with a wrongful-death suit. And, by the way, if Our Father's House sounded creepy to you, your instincts are spot-on. In 2003, Burt was arrested for molesting a fifteen-year-old girl living at the home. He was convicted and sentenced to eighteen years. He died in prison in 2013.

While Griffin was in jail, he got fan mail from people like Rachelle Ranae (Shelley) Shannon, a thirty-seven-year-old house-wife who wrote to Griffin that what he did wasn't murder, but "anti-murder," and called him "the awesomest, greatest hero of our time." Shannon was a member of the Christian extremist orga-nization called the Army of God, also involved in incidents such as the 1982 kidnapping of an abortion doctor and sending death threats to Supreme Court justice Harry A. Blackmun, who, despite being appointed by Republican president Nixon, left a lib-eral legacy, including authoring the Court's majority opinion on *Roe v. Wade*.

On a frigid February night in 1985, a bullet shattered the window of Justice Blackmun and wife Dorothy's suburban home in Arlington, Virginia. Reasonable folks assume this was connected to *Roe*. The day of the shooting, Blackmun received a typewritten postcard from Buffalo, New York, that read: "Sir, I do not like the way you are doing your job. One day I am going to see you and shoot your brains out. I am going to shoot you dead and I will be coming to your funeral," Risen and Thomas report. However, the FBI decided—at least pub-licly—that the incident with the window was a random accident and not connected to the threatening postcard, likely to avoid the polit-ical heat associated with abortion. Co-opting the Holocaust, much to the dismay of reasonable Jews, Christian extremists would dub Blackmun "the Butcher of Dachau." By his retirement, Blackmun had received over sixty thousand pieces of hate mail.

While Blackmun's *Roe* decision was a massive win for reproductive rights, he was likely more interested in protecting the medical profession than a woman's right to choose. His ruling read that it "vindicates the right of the physician to administer medical treatment according to his professional judgment up until the points where important state interest provides compelling justifications for intervention. Up until those points the abortion decision is inherently and primarily, a medical decision, and basic responsibility for it must rest with the physician." He equated viability with the twenty-four to twenty-eight weeks after conception, continuing the ongoing debate about when life begins, a debate that has included the quickening, ensoulment, and a fetus being the property of the person carrying them until they exist outside of their body over the course of our journey so far. In the first trimester, *Roe* (RIP) allowed nearly no regulation. In the second, it allowed regulations to protect the health of the mother, and in the third, states can ban abortions as long as there are exceptions made to protect the life and health of the pregnant person.

The Army of God and other extremist groups were able to rise in the 1980s in part thanks to the passage of *Roe*. Christians were still reeling from the sexual revolution of the 1960s and '70s and saw legal abortion as the continuing downfall of America. Shelley Shannon, the fangirl who wrote to Griffin in prison, was a firebug who just wanted to blow shit up and burn things down like a villain out of a *Mad Max* film. She'd dress in men's clothes (it's odd which instances of drag conservatives find tolerable) and attack clinics by throwing jugs filled with gasoline onto the roofs. On August 18, 1992, she concocted homemade napalm to firebomb an office building that was home to the Feminist Women's Health Center of Sacramento (she actually hit the offices of the California Board of Chiropractic Examiners), and then she allegedly firebombed another women's health center in Oregon a month later. There are apparently a *lot* of instances like this. A judge (and others) described her as a terrorist. Like a twisted country song, Shannon seemed happiest driving around America's highways, our nation's veins, with a trunk full of butyric acid, singing along to the radio while praising Jesus.

But she soon needed something stronger than napalm. She arrived in Wichita, Kansas, in 1993, once again in costume, and shot Dr. George Tiller in both of his arms, but he survived. (Tiller was killed on May 31, 2009, when anti-abortion extremist Scott Roeder shot him in the side of the head while he was in *church*.) Shannon stands by her actions, telling Thomas, "Even if I spend the rest of my life in prison, I did the right thing."

When Dr. George Tiller was twenty-nine, he tragically lost his dad, mom, sister, and brother-in-law all at the same time when his father Dean's plane crashed into a mountain east of Yellowstone, killing them all. Afterward, Tiller left the US Navy, where he had worked as a flight surgeon. While shutting down his dad's private practice in Wichita, where Dean worked as a family physician, Tiller discovered that his dad had really been running a secret abortion clinic within the clinic. Tiller had no idea about his dad's undercover practice. And he discovered that Dean Tiller had once refused to perform an abortion for a woman in the 1940s; she died after seeking help elsewhere.

Originally, George Tiller wanted to be a dermatologist. There's a great scene in *Grey's Anatomy* where the surgeons longingly hang out in the dermatology division to get away from surgery, imagining their surely far less bloody lives if they had stuck with skin. Tiller probably could have related. But after his dad died, he decided to take over his work.

Tiller hated how hospitals handled abortions at the time, forcing the women to wheel past the newborn-baby section. Hospitals at the time also charged roughly $1,000 for an abortion, while Tiller offered them for $250. Tiller, married with four kids (he also adopted his sister's infant child after she died in the plane crash and raised him as his own), struggled with drug and alcohol-use disorder his entire life; he overcame it, but the religious Right relentlessly used it against him. Before he was killed, he had to deal with anti-abortion fanatics protesting by pretending to be babies and crawling on hands and knees into his clinic. Preferable to murder, but absurd nonetheless. This guy put up with a bunch of childish antics, took many bullets, and ultimately gave his life for his profession, which, by all accounts, he was great at. Part of the reason he was targeted so often is because he was willing to perform postviability abortions when necessary.

Wichita was where 1991's "Summer of Mercy" took place, when tens of thousands, some report hundreds of thousands, many of whom got arrested, took part in a slew of abortion-clinic protests and harassment. This is when the anti-abortion organization Operation Rescue, whose slogan is "If You Believe Abortion Is Murder, Act Like It's Murder," came to fame after being founded by Randall Terry, a pot-smoking hippie turned anti-abortion activist who feels most like a charismatic street preacher. The guy did want to be a rock star, after all.

During the 1970s, Terry got high, played in a rock-and-roll band, and was beaten by his alcoholic father. He left high school and hitchhiked around for a while, living as a drifter with, in his own words, the "kind of people who take a sixteen-year-old doper into their house. People who are into Aquarian gospel, into reincarnation, into astral projection, into witchcraft. I was just hanging out with some freaky people." Terry even found his Christian zeal while stoned. "I was hanging out with wacky people, I was smoking dope, and I was reading the Bible," he once said. "But it was all this mishmash of spiritualism. I was reading the Book of Revelation. Now, if you want to read a bizarre book while you're under the influence of narcotics, it's the Book of Revelation," Risen and Thomas report.

Terry left behind weed and witchcraft, enrolled in Bible school, and got hitched to Cindy Dean from Shortville, New York, a slight woman a few years older than him. The couple, who are now divorced, strictly followed their interpretation of religious teachings that the wife must obey the husband. Terry and his wife fostered kids, eventually proudly adopting mixed-race children in addition to their biological ones. While this information does kind of make you want to like the guy, Terry was apparently one of those dudes who infuriatingly felt bad for women, as if they were all pressured by men to get abortions—an ideology perhaps most eloquently explained by anti-abortion activist Juli Loesch: "The idea that a man can use a woman, vacuum her out, and she's ready to be used again. . . . It's like a rent-a-car or something," reports Daniel K. Williams in *Defenders of the Unborn: The Pro-Life Movement Before* Roe v. Wade.

Pat Robertson helped by appealing for Operation Rescue on the Christian Broadcasting Network's *700 Club*. In a fundraising letter sent to supporters of the Christian Coalition in 1992, in an effort to drum up opposition to a proposed Iowa state Equal Rights Amendment, Robinson once wrote, "It is about a socialist, anti-family political movement that encourages women to leave their husbands, kill their children, practice witchcraft, destroy capitalism and become lesbians."

Terry would go on to run against President Obama in the 2012 election, kicking off his candidacy with a commercial during Super Bowl XLVI that featured graphic photographs of aborted fetuses. The ad begins with a brief warning label imposed over Obama's

face before Terry says solemnly, "Abortion is murder. The innocent blood of fifty million babies cries out to God from our sewers
and landfills. We must make it a crime to murder them, or heaven
will judge America." (He failed to gain traction in the race, obviously, since you've probably never heard of him.) In December
2011, performance artist, activist, and Libertarian candidate Ver-
min Supreme sprinkled glitter all over Terry's head during a debate
while claiming he was magically turning him gay.

Some people followed anti-abortion protests like they were
Deadheads following a tour. One of those people was Joan
Andrews, a.k.a. Saint Joan, who became the anti-choice movement's first (nonfetal) martyr when she was sentenced to five years
in prison for third-degree burglary, criminal mischief, and resist-
ing arrest without violence, in Pensacola, Florida, in March 1986,
just over two years after the Christmas explosions.

Andrews was a thin waif of a woman. When she was twelve, her
mom had a miscarriage and had each of her kids, including Joan,
hold the dead fetus. She was originally from Tennessee, but as an
adult, Andrews lived a home-free life not unlike Terry's. She was
even taken to the police station once on suspicion of prostitution
in Chicago's main bus terminal. She got eye cancer in 1980 and
had an eye removed. She *also* became a follower of former Ku Klux
Klan leader and convicted child molester John Burt.

Andrews didn't have to go to prison for the burglary charge.
She could have taken a deal. While the women the media dubbed
"crack moms" were terrified of giving birth in shackles due to
racist (and scientifically unsound) drug laws, Andrews reportedly craved the experience of incarceration, which she perhaps
knew would launch her into martyr status. All she had to do was
agree to stay away from the Ladies Center, the abortion clinic she
loved to harass and defile, and she could go free. She refused, and
the judge handed down what sounds like a reasonable sentence of

five years—but that was twice the maximum laid out in the state's sentencing guidelines. The Florida Department of Corrections was not happy about this. During Thanksgiving 1986, hundreds of anti-abortion activists flocked to Pensacola in a campaign to free Andrews . . . exactly as the DOC had feared.

While she was in prison, Andrews became pro-life folklore. At one point, angry that a male guard was part of a strip search, she took out her glass eye and chucked it across the room. The guards later returned her eye to her. And they weren't the only ones showing the woman deference: by 1988, even Mother Teresa was a fan. She placed her lips on and kissed a religious medal and mailed it to Andrews. It was even proposed that Andrews could be released *to* Mother Teresa, and Mother Teresa agreed, except that Joan Andrews turned the saint's offer down. She wanted to stay in the Florida prison and continue to make her point.

The Florida Correctional Facilities handled her intentionally disruptive publicity effort by transferring her to Pennsylvania over an outstanding conviction in Pittsburgh. She was free, on the condition that she'd cut it out with the protest shit. She ignored that condition entirely, returning to the Pittsburgh clinic where she previously protested. They put a warrant out for her arrest, but Andrews fled the state, and today she lives free to harass whomever she pleases; in 2020, at the age of seventy-four, she landed herself in front of a judge again for blocking entrance to abortion clinics.

All this violence, chaos, and tomfoolery did bring some change. Congress passed the Freedom of Access to Clinic Entrances Act that became effective in 1994, which, admittedly, is hard to feel super stoked about in a post-*Roe* world. But the FBI finally had to get involved, something they pretty successfully avoided under Reagan and Bush. For a long time, the FBI felt they'd had enough social drama after their involvement in the antiwar and civil rights movements of the 1960s.

After the first Bush's era came to an end, Bill Clinton entered office, and he is widely considered the first pro-choice president, even if his motto regarding abortion was "Safe, Legal, and Rare," the party line of the era.

2

Before *Roe*, Catholics were the most prominent voices fighting against abortion in America. The integration of Evangelical Protestants into the movement significantly bolstered the anti-abortion campaign. This growing force ultimately achieved their long-term and embarrassingly underestimated objective of overturning *Roe v. Wade*. According to a Gallup poll, 1976 was "the year of the Evangelical." Even Democratic president Jimmy Carter, who was in office before Reagan, had a born-again experience and identified as an Evangelical, using this morality to his advantage after the scandals of the Nixon era.

In addition to *Roe*, backlash against the sexual revolution, feminism, and gay rights—anything that was seen as a threat to the Christian nuclear family—united the conservatives, who came together under Reagan. Pre-Reagan, due to their belief in helping the poor, Catholics were largely Democrats. During Reagan's run, when many Catholics had to choose between the social welfare programs promised by Democrats and the blossoming anti-abortion stance of Republicans, they made their choice.

Reagan won largely thanks to the Moral Majority, an American political organization founded in 1979 by televangelist Jerry Falwell to advance social conservatism. He's a guy who in 1984 called the gay-friendly Metropolitan Community Church "a vile and Satanic system" that would "one day be utterly annihilated and there will be a celebration in heaven." Members of such churches, Falwell added, were "brute beasts." Falwell, who could have played ball for the St. Louis Cardinals had he not had his heart set on being a famous megachurch preacher (a lucrative decision, it would turn out), called abortion "America's national sin."

And it's tough for guys like Falwell to change—especially when their paycheck depends on Satanic sound bites. The morning of the 9/11 terrorist attacks, Falwell offered the following insight: "I really believe that the pagans, and the abortionists, and the feminists, and the gays and the lesbians who are actively trying to make that an alternative lifestyle, the ACLU, People for the American Way, all of them who have tried to secularize America. I point the finger in their face and say, 'You helped this happen.'"

Falwell is chock-full of Satanic sound bites. He once called NOW, the National Organization for Women, the "National Order of Witches." NOW is an American activist organization founded in 1966 to promote equal rights for women. It is considered the largest feminist group in the United States. Betty Friedan, a prominent American feminist author and activist, played a key role in igniting the second wave of American feminism in the twentieth century, particularly through her influential 1963 book, *The Feminine Mystique*. She was also a founding member of the National Organization for Women and served as its first president. *The Feminine Mystique* is all about women enjoying life outside the confines of homemaking and child rearing. Friedan's book seems old-fashioned and exclusionary by today's standards, but at the time, women were so desperate for someone to voice all this gendered unhappiness out loud that it started a revolution. Friedan wasn't above using the image of a witch to discredit another woman—or above minimizing the genocide of European Jews during World War II by comparing marriage to a "comfortable concentration camp."

One of NOW's biggest missions of the time was ratifying the Equal Rights Amendment to the US Constitution, basically crafted to ensure that all American citizens receive the same legal rights, irrespective of gender, predominantly concerned with equal pay, so that women would have a chance to support themselves.

During a 1973 debate with Phyllis Schlafly, a conservative activist and charismatic blonde, Schlafly provoked Friedan to display her weakness. Knowing that Friedan had been through a nasty divorce, Schlafly jabbed, "*You*, Mrs. Friedan, are the unhappiest woman I have ever met." Friedan heatedly retorted, "I'd like to burn you at the stake." And the feminists fell right into the antifeminists' hands.

Plenty of American women were, and still are, against abortion (41 percent identify as pro-life as of 2024, according to a Gallup poll). Mildred Jefferson (1926–2010) made history in 1951 as the first Black woman to earn a degree from Harvard Medical School. Regarding *Roe v. Wade*, Dr. Jefferson testified before Congress in 1981 that it "gave my profession an almost unlimited license to kill." A stylish and beautiful woman whose smile was fit for a magazine, she had no children of her own, but left a legacy. She is often credited with helping Reagan's position shift from pro- to anti-choice. (As governor of California, Reagan had supported abortion, signing the 1967 Therapeutic Abortion Act.) He wrote to Jefferson after seeing her speak on television in 1973, "You made it irrefutably clear that an abortion takes human life." As a Black Methodist woman, Jefferson brought much-needed diversity to the anti-abortion movement. (It's worth mentioning that the pro-choice side could still use help in this department as well.)

The "pro-life" crowd hates the term "pro-choice" because they want to label abortion as murder, even if they're cool with murdering a few full-grown adult doctors along the way. Likewise, the pro-choice folks hate the term "pro-life," as, from the assassinations of abortion providers to the already living people's lives that could be ruined by pregnancy, it's hard to argue that they stand for life. (A nonzero percentage of "pro-life" voters feel that having or providing an abortion is a crime worthy of the death sentence, so add "murder by the state" to the list of murders they're cool with.)

When journalists want to play it safe, neutral alternatives such as "supporters of abortion" or "opponents of abortion" or supporters or opponents of "abortion rights" are used. The term "pro-life" took hold within the context of reproductive rights in the early 1970s, and "pro-choice" came as a rebuttal by abortion rights advocates. The term "pro-life" was initially coined in 1960 by A. S. Neill in his book *Summerhill: A Radical Approach to Child Rearing*, in a very different manner, as this text promoted progressive social ideals. "No pro-life citizen would tolerate our penal code, our hangings, our punishments of homosexuals, our attitude towards bastardy," words you'd wish the lifey crowd would take to heart during their moral crusades.

In 1975, Jefferson was elected president of the National Right to Life Committee, which was previously made up almost entirely of white Catholic men. She was not one to compromise; Jefferson was against all abortions. "You can't give the individual the private right to kill, no matter what kind of justification they can come up with," she wrote for *Ebony*. "The woman who arranges her life haphazardly, relying on abortion to remove complications," she wrote, "is unworthy of being called woman."

Despite Reagan's willingness to court the Moral Majority and be swept off his feet by Mildred Jefferson, perhaps the greatest hypocrisy of the time (and an indication that the worst was yet to come) is that, despite their affiliated anti-abortion politics, Ronald and Nancy Reagan's daughter, Patti Davis, claimed that her parents' views on the topic were actually more liberal than you'd imagine—which is exactly what you would expect from a couple who went from being Hollywood elite to living in the White House.

Davis writes that her father was originally more pro-choice, as demonstrated by the 1967 bill the Therapeutic Abortion Act, signed as governor of California, which made abortion legal for victims of rape and incest and in cases where a woman's health was in danger. Ironically, this act helped make California the state most prepared to protect abortion rights when *Roe* was overturned.

"My father's views on abortion obviously shifted over the years. Throughout those years, he wrestled with his feelings," Davis writes in the *New York Times*, referring to the death of Reagan's infant child with his former wife and actress, Jane Wyman, an experience that helped him eventually solidify his anti-choice stance. "While he stated that abortions after rape or incest fell into the category of 'self-defense,' as did saving a woman's life if pregnancy or childbirth would threaten it, he couldn't accept the notion that a woman would choose to abort a fetus for other reasons," she continues. And, according to Davis, when she asked her mother whether abortion should be a choice left to the pregnant person, Nancy Reagan responded: "Yes, it should."

When Reagan was elected president, he quickly let down the Moral Majority, and they realized how easily the actor could trick and use the Christians for his own gain. As much lip service as he'd paid the anti-choice crowd, it was obvious that Reagan wasn't going to confront *Roe* head-on. And he really pissed them off when he appointed Sandra Day O'Connor, the first woman justice, to the Supreme Court in 1981; O'Connor refused to join the other conservatives and work to overturn *Roe*, even if she did personally find it "abhorrent." But Reagan had promised on the campaign trail to add a woman to the bench, and his selection of O'Connor in 1981 covertly threw liberals for a loop by advocating for gender equality. By the time of O'Connor's retirement in 2006, only one other woman, Clinton nominee Ruth Bader Ginsburg, had joined the bench. On the plus side, O'Connor was really into Halloween. Each year the O'Connors transformed their home into a haunted house for neighbors and trick-or-treaters to visit. Sandra always dressed up in a witch costume featuring an all-black gown—"a lot like her future robe would look like," her son Jay commented. Guests were served "poison" cider from a punch bowl smoking like a witch's brew thanks to dry ice. "Bottom line, our parents liked to have fun, and in a lot of different ways," her other son Brian said, per the *Arizona Republic*.

None of the justices Reagan appointed remain on the Supreme Court today. Reagan appointed Scalia in 1986, and while he would die before *Roe* was overturned, he was a crucial piece in the Republicans' long (and shrewd) endgame plan to kill *Roe*. Scalia's death raised suspicions about the inner workings of a secret society when, at age seventy-nine, he was found dead of apparent natural causes one Saturday morning at the West Texas Cibolo Creek Ranch. But there was never an autopsy. His body was found on a trip with fellow members of the International Order of St. Hubertus, a secret, archaic society for 1 percenters who are also hunters, complete with robes, grand titles, and rituals dedicated to St. Hubert, the patron saint of hunters. This led many online, especially QAnon types, to become convinced that a liberal elite deep state assassinated Scalia due to his conservative point of view. But if that had been a liberal conspiracy, it would have been an unsuccessful one: Scalia was eventually replaced by President Trump's nominee Neil Gorsuch, who voted in favor of *Dobbs*.

When it came time for Reagan to nominate an additional justice in 1987, his initial choice was Douglas Ginsburg, who withdrew before he could be nominated. The drama? His wife performed abortions during her time in medical school. And, clutch your pearls, his history includes smoking cannabis as a student and as Harvard faculty. Anthony Kennedy would get the seat instead (a seat that would one day belong to Brett Kavanaugh).

But despite all these juicy tidbits from the justices, it would be the Reagans' practice of consulting an astrologer about the timing of everything from the press briefings to Air Force One departures that would provide even better fodder for dinner-party gossip. Donald Regan, not to be confused with Ronald Reagan, was the sixty-sixth US secretary of the Treasury from 1981 to 1985 and the White House chief of staff from 1985 to 1987. Regan wrote in his book *For the Record* that Nancy Reagan had "absolute faith in a woman astrologer in San Francisco." That astrologer was a woman named Joan Quigley.

Nancy did not want this information to go public. When Quigley asked Nancy if she could discuss their astrologer-client relationship, she reportedly said, "Never, it must never come out!" Quigley wrote a book anyway as soon as the Reagans left office—seemingly partly because she was salty that Nancy had acted like a friend and then dropped her the second a White House astrologer was no longer needed and partly because the book was a guaranteed bestseller. In her book, she maintains that her reasons were simply because astrology played such a massive role in the Reagans' political history.

Giving more credence to her daughter's assertion that Nancy was actually more pro-choice than she made it out to be while courting the religious Right, Joan wrote in her 1990 book, *What Does Joan Say? My Seven Years as White House Astrologer to Nancy and Ronald Reagan*, that "Nancy was not a religious bigot."

She was, however, totally down to sell out to get her husband elected. Nancy first met Quigley in the summer of 1976 in San Francisco at a fundraiser for the Reagan campaign held on a boat. It was a luncheon, and Nancy was giving an anti-abortion speech. "If you are even considering having an abortion, just pretend there is a window in your tummy and you can see the adorable little baby inside," Nancy said. Quigley wrote, "It was saccharine and cutesy, but I guess it was the sort of speeches she was giving then."

Nancy was a woman with an instinct for glamour—some modern witches may even call it glamour magic. Whether she was tricking Republican wives into getting their husbands to donate to Ronald's campaign at luncheons or bringing everything she learned in movies to the stage on Inauguration Day, Nancy Reagan really knew how to work a crowd. She wore so much red that her preferred bold and bright shade became known as "Reagan Red." "I always liked red," she once said by way of explanation. "It's a picker-upper." Yes, it's the color of the Republican Party, but as any practicing witch will tell you, it also evokes confidence, passion, power, and lust.

The Reagans faked plenty of things, but they were genuinely in love. In their conversations, Joan and Nancy spoke in a familiar manner, referring to the former president as "Ronnie." But Nancy didn't want Joan's advice over marital woes (maybe she didn't have any); she was all politics. "Once in a great blue moon, Nancy and I would discuss her personal or family situation, but this was the exception. Mostly we stuck to matters concerned with her role as First Lady and problems that concerned the President or scheduling, according to what I saw astrologically." For instance, "I chose the time of 10:00 a.m. on November 14, 1983, for Reagan's visit to the demilitarized zone between North and South Korea." Casual, casual.

Quigley states that Nancy once said, "Joan, do you realize that you are ordering the time for the takeoff of Air Force One?" Apparently, Bill Plante of CBS said that White House correspondents speculated about the strange and erratic departure times for the presidential plane: "We wondered if there was any strategy involved and were relieved to learn that the obvious reason was astrology." Quigley maintains that she was also responsible for the timing of all presidential press conferences.

Ronald Reagan was an Aquarius, a clever but aloof air sign associated with politics and humanitarian matters; make your own judgment on that last one. Nancy was a Cancer, a nurturing water sign known for loving home and family—again, a description open to interpretation.

It's a shame astrology couldn't have helped with the administration's response to the AIDS epidemic. By the end of 1984—the year of the Pensacola Christmas bombings, and when Falwell referred to the gay-friendly Metropolitan Community Church as "a vile and Satanic system"—AIDS was raging throughout the United States. At first, doctors didn't know what was happening as hospitals filled up with people, mostly gay men, wasting away to skeletons. Scientists finally identified the cause of AIDS: HIV (human immunodeficiency virus). The US Centers for Disease Control and Prevention determined all its major transmission routes, which, at the time, were predominantly (but certainly not exclusively) anal sex and intravenous drug use—two subjects so wrought with taboo no one would speak of them candidly, especially not a conservative government. Politicians swore the situation was under control, while hospitals called in refrigerated trucks to hold dead bodies since their morgues couldn't keep up with the death count. (This may ring familiar to those of us who recall the high death tolls in the early years of COVID-19.) Reagan didn't acknowledge AIDS until September 1985, four years after it began. At that point, it was already a full-blown epidemic.

The initial awareness of AIDS surfaced in the summer of 1981, marked by the sudden and severe illnesses of previously healthy, predominantly gay men in urban areas such as New York and Los Angeles. They began experiencing rare diseases typically seen only in people with compromised immune systems. The term "gay plague" quickly caught on. In one of the most heartbreaking moments recorded, at an October 1982 White House press briefing, journalist Lester Kinsolving asked Larry Speakes, President Reagan's press secretary, about the president's plan for AIDS, which by then had killed at least six hundred people, enough that the White House certainly knew about it. When Kinsolving described that the disease was known as the "gay plague," the press pool burst into laughter. Rather than acknowledge the public health crisis, Speakes said, "I don't have it," to more laughter in the room, before turning the question around on Kinsolving, asking him multiple times if *he* had AIDS, the homophobic joke a tactic to further deflect the problem. Ironically, Kinsolving was a straight conservative and an outspoken opponent of gay rights organizations, which he called "the sodomy lobby." However, perhaps out of journalistic integrity that overrode his own bigotry, or simply because he really wanted the gruesome details for a story, Kinsolving kept asking the White House about it when no one else would. Additionally, Speakes further deflected by calling out Kinsolving's "abiding interest" in "fairies" when asked about AIDS.

Despite the unfolding horrors of the AIDS epidemic, for the majority in America, 1984 was not shaping up to be the dystopian society that George Orwell's *1984* had predicted. For much of the decade, we were still in the middle of a cold war; capitalism was *in*, and communism was the great evil. Reagan had already been solidified as a Republican icon, largely for his economic policies, known as "Reaganomics," which combined steep tax cuts, the deregulation of domestic markets, and lower government spending. Under the Reagan administration, the average GDP growth was 3.5 percent, up from the 2.9 percent average of the previous eight years. If there's anything (as much as it pains liberals to admit) that Reagan did well, it was creating economic stability . . . at least for corporations. Conversely, plenty now assert that these policies have had negative long-term effects in the decades since, as, for instance, the top tax bracket fell from 70 percent to 50 percent, drastically decreasing the tax revenue for the federal government.

Perhaps sensing that Reagan's economic policies would prove a threat, in 1980, before becoming Reagan's veep pick, then candidate George H. W. Bush referred to them as "voodoo economics," appropriating the Haitian religious tradition to basically mean "bullshit."

Voodoo economics made its way into the American lexicon so completely that journalists and politicians started taking the word "voodoo" as a preface to anything that sounded bogus. In 1985, the *Washington Post* referred to the opposition toward Title X—the sole federal grant program that puts money toward reproductive health care and family planning, which was initially enacted by President Nixon in 1970 as part of the Public Health Service Act—as voodoo biology, writing: "The reality however—the political reality—is that Title X is under strenuous attack by those who insist that a vote for the family-planning program is a vote for abortion. Remember Voodoo Economics? What we have here is Voodoo Biology."

"It's pure insanity," Faye Wattleton told the *Washington Post* on the topic. Wattleton is the youngest-ever and first Black person elected president of Planned Parenthood Federation of America. She is also the first woman since Margaret Sanger to hold the title, a position she occupied from 1978 to 1992, reigning during the infamous Satanic Panic of the 1980s, fueled by Reagan-era conservatism. While their use of the word "voodoo" likely wasn't appreciated by those who practiced the real thing, they were trying to point out the falsehood of the assumption that support for Title X, which funds birth control, was equal to support for abortion. "Half of the six million pregnancies in this country are unintentional," Wattleton said. "There is no rational explanation for this attack on Title X unless you assume that the anti-abortion people are committed to ending contraceptive practices." Considering many conservatives had given up the battle against birth control, knowing it hindered the anti-abortion movement, those against the program likely just didn't want to give more money to the government, and this was a handy excuse. In 1985, Title X served five million low-income women a year, preventing eight hundred thousand unwanted pregnancies and an estimated four hundred thousand abortions per year.

Title X is one of those programs that has yo-yoed back and forth in scale depending on which party is in office. President Donald Trump greatly scaled back money for Title X, and those restrictions were reversed under the Biden administration. Anti-choice Catholics, the primary opponents to birth control, not only had to vote for Reagan but also had to give up hopes of legislating birth control if they had any hope in eventually overturning *Roe*. By then, birth control was simply too mainstream—with a big thanks to Wattleton, who, from her wispy bangs to her big pearls to her million-dollar smile, exuded '80s glamour and pure class. Yet despite her staggering contributions to society, the press and anti-abortion critics (also influenced by racism) relied on tired witch imagery to demonize her work, labeling Wattleton the "Princess of Death."

She certainly wasn't the only bitchin' icon of the era to be called a witch. While everyone from Queen to the Beatles has been accused of hiding Satanic messages in their music, Fleetwood Mac, whose music still inspires debate over Satanic messages on online message boards today, openly wrote songs about witches (and you didn't even have to play them backward to hear them). Fleetwood Mac singer Stevie Nicks had an abortion in 1979, six years after *Roe v. Wade* became law. "If I had not had that abortion, I'm pretty sure there would have been no Fleetwood Mac. There's just no way that I could have had a child then, working as hard as we worked constantly. And there were a lot of drugs, I was doing a lot of drugs. . . . I would have had to walk away," she told the *Guardian*. "And I knew that the music we were going to bring to the world was going to heal so many people's hearts and make people so happy. And I thought: You know what? That's really important. There's not another band in the world that has two lead women singers, two lead women writers. That was my world's mission."

During live shows, Nicks would intro "Rhiannon" by saying, "This is a song about a witch." Details like these would help make her early onstage performances so iconic, even if it landed her in a bubbling cauldron of hot water. Music journalists described witnessing her talking in spooky, ancient-sounding language and entering trancelike states. Nicks told the *Los Angeles Times* in 2013: "In the beginning of my career, the whole idea that some wacky, creepy people were writing, 'You're a witch, you're a witch!' was so arresting. And there I am like, 'No, I'm not! I just wear black because it makes me look thinner, you idiots.'" (Before you cancel Stevie for fat-shaming, remember that diet culture was very different in the '70s and '80s than it is now.)

She at one point stopped wearing black (famously trying, and hating, the color apricot) because of the harassment, but eventually returned to her signature palette. "I do not believe in witchcraft as a natural philosophy at all. I just think it's fun. And I love black clothes and I love moons and stars and Merlin hats and Mickey Mouse. But no, I do not believe in that side of it at all," Nicks told *ET* in 1983, referring to the "evil" Satanic associations. However, she played a witch (and the song "Rhiannon" was used) in 2013's *American Horror Story: Coven*, demonstrating how, now that people think she's cool for being a witch (or at least dressing like one, living like one, and singing about them), she's not afraid to wear the label proudly.

3

If wearing black in the '80s might get you labeled a witch, not con-forming to traditional gender norms could ruin your life in an epic witch hunt even more absurd than Salem.

The 1980s in America was an era obsessed with the occult and children, as demonstrated by the emerging belief that kids were regularly victims of Satanic Ritual Abuse. The starkest example was the McMartin preschool trial, a day-care sexual abuse case that began in 1983 and lasted through 1990. This trial demon-strates the visceral fear that could be sparked by perceived attacks on the nuclear family, whether in the form of abortion, AIDS, or commie atheists.

The main individuals implicated were Ray Buckey, a teacher, along with his grandmother Virginia McMartin, the founder of the school, and his mother, Peggy McMartin Buckey, who was both an administrator and the owner of the school. The three family mem-bers and other staff were accused of hundreds of acts of sexual abuse—as well as exposing children to "flying witches" and doz-ens of other bizarre occult allegations, some apparently involving Chuck Norris and what sound like pentagram-shaped butt plugs. Although there was never enough evidence to make a single con-viction, the trial remains the longest and most expensive series of criminal trials in American history. Taxpayers footed the bill of $15 million spent on the word of children, influenced by adults, given life in a culture of fear . . . just like Salem. As reported by Richard Beck in *We Believe the Children: A Moral Panic in the 1980s*, during the hysteria of the trial, supporters of the defendants even ran newspaper ads reading "SALEM MASSACHUSETTS, 1692. MANHATTAN BEACH CALIFORNIA, 1985."

It all started when a mother, Judy Johnson, thought she saw redness around her two-year-old son's anus while giv-ing him a bath. She became suspicious of Raymond Buckley, a twenty-five-year-old man (who had previously been in legal trouble for cannabis and drunk driving) and possibly due to stereotypes about male childcare workers and preconceived notions of what type of work is suitable for a man. Raymond also volunteered at a nursing home, and between his caretaker and child-watching duties, this may have come off as a little too feminine; these were roles traditionally reserved for the midwife, for women. "In an era of fashion and booming wealth, where twenty-something men cruised around in sports cars trying to score women, a guy like Raymond was an anomaly—a soft spoken man still living under the wing of his mother, spending his days with little children," Matthew LeRoy and Deric Haddad write in *They Must Be Monsters: A Modern-Day Witch Hunt—the Untold Story of the McMartin Phenomenon, the Longest, Most Expensive Criminal Case in U.S. History*. While he wasn't gay, and he certainly wasn't a Satanic child molester, Buckley had a criminal past with cannabis at a bad time—coinciding with the heightened scrutiny of the nation's ongoing War on Drugs.

Johnson made her report to Detective Jane Hoag, a detective with the Manhattan Beach Police who was eager to make a name for herself and had just worked on a case involving a father who had been accused of molesting his daughters, which was still on her mind. The first doctor who did the physical exam on the Johnson child decided that it was "inconclusive," and the second had never previously made a diagnosis of sodomy, but this is what she reported. Later reassessments of the case identified immediate red flags here; at the risk of being graphic, if a child had actually been sodomized, there would have been far graver physical signs than redness.

Playing a horrid game of telephone, Peggy told parent after parent what she thought went down before any arrest had been issued against Buckley. When Buckley was arrested, police found nothing related to pedophilia; the most salacious piece found appears to have been an issue of *Playboy*. (Buckley may not have been super ambitious or eager to lock down a wife right away, but he was a regular straight dude, after all.) He was initially released due to lack of evidence. They couldn't prosecute him, and they knew it. So they found another way to hang him out to dry.

Shortly after releasing him, the Manhattan Beach Police sent out a letter to more than two hundred parents who currently had kids at the preschool, and plenty who had children that graduated, which opened with, "This department is conducting a criminal investigation involving child molestation (288 P.C.). Ray Buckley, an employee of Virginia McMartin's preschool, was arrested September 7, 1983, by this Department."

His life was over.

The townspeople once again went into a panic. Hundreds of children were questioned by their parents, but it didn't matter what they said: Buckley had to be guilty; in their parents' minds, these children had all been raped and they were bad parents for failing to notice it. Retribution was needed.

The hysteria spread from the parents to the students, who were eventually taken to be interviewed by the Children's Institute International. CII's pediatrician, Dr. Astrid Heger, reported over 90 percent of the children had genital scarring "consistent with a history of sexual abuse," LeRoy and Haddad report. Never mind that this is extremely unlikely—let's talk about how what's actually scarring is two hundred children being exposed to unnecessary rectal, vaginal, and complete examinations in the process. The CII's questioning methods included leading questions, in addition to the use of anatomically correct dolls. The taped "confessions" often began with the kid saying that nothing happened and ended with them basically saying, *Fine, it all happened. We killed babies, did sexy stuff, and the stoner and his hag of a grandmother were naked and worshipping Satan. If you say so, Doctor.* During the trial, the defense debunked the CII's methods of questioning as New Age techniques that lacked clinical validation—quite ironic for a case based on accusations of partying with Satan and witches.

And the charges from the parents, relayed through an increasingly hysterical Judy Johnson, grew weirder and weirder. "He said Ray chopped up rabbits, and that Peggy put some kind of a star in his bottom," Johnson told Detective Hoag, who knew about pentagrams and their association with the Church of Satan. Johnson, who kept detailed handwritten accounts in journals and her calendar, wrote: "Lots of candles . . . Ray pricked his pointed finger. It bled. Ray put it on the goat's anus . . . Old grandma played the piano . . . a real baby . . . the head was chopped off . . . brains were burned . . . Peggy killed the baby . . . Mitchell had to drink the baby's blood . . . on the altar . . . Mitchell's bottom was bleeding . . . Ray put a Tampax up his bottom to stop the bleeding . . . then he took it out." (The only thing that makes this different from Salem is that, back in 1692, Tampax hadn't been invented yet. The menstruating Puritans had to rely on rags, although in the days before birth control, excluding coitus interruptus, they actually had fewer periods than the women in the 1980s, as they were pregnant most of the time.)

While Ray was subjected to the worst of the accusations, the ideas swirling about Peggy's involvement, not just from Judy but from the entire community, relied on played-out fears of elderly women. Some of the interviews with children eventually included claims that Peggy danced about naked while all this ritualized Satanic sexual abuse and baby-killing was going down. The accused became known as the McMartin Seven, which included Ray, Peggy, and other teachers. "On a trip to a farm," one boy testified on the stand, "Ray chopped a pony to death with a long knife." And all of this allegedly went down during the preschool's limited morning school hours of operation without anyone noticing. One child even claimed that action star Chuck Norris was in on the satanic abuse after picking him out of a photo lineup.

There are some things you should know about Judy Johnson. She was a survivor of multiple childhood traumas. Her husband had just left her for a younger woman. And to top it all off, their older son was dying of cancer. There's a chance that her paranoia about sex abuse, the devil, and her younger son was just a lot of misplaced fear and anger. Judy self-medicated with alcohol, sinking deeper into addiction and becoming a danger to herself and those around her. During the trial, she was admitted to a psychiatric clinic and diagnosed as an acute paranoid schizophrenic. As word of her condition spread and she showed up to events drunk, parents distanced themselves from her and she was ostracized from the community, which continued its witch hunt based on her claims—even as they thought she was too "crazy" to say hello to at a PTA meeting.

And, of course, while the parents screeched accusations of the school using Satanic witchcraft to torture their children, plenty of them had their own relationship with the occult. One of the school mothers, Jackie, told her reporter boyfriend that she went to see what we can assume is a tarot reader, a woman who freely used the "witch" label, while pregnant with her daughter Julie. "The witch told me, 'Your daughter is going to be famous one day,'" she said, and asked her boyfriend to help find the witch so that they could find out if it was indeed the McMartin trials that she had predicted would make her baby famous. It wasn't just hysteria; in a very Los Angeles twist on Salem, being involved in a televised witch hunt was also a chance to get famous.

After seven years and costing the taxpayers of California over $15 million, Ray Buckley, who ended up spending five years in jail, having been denied bail, was a free man. (During his time locked up, the man in the cell next to him was none other than the actually evil Richard Ramirez, the serial killer known as the Night Stalker, who did rape, kill, and worship Satan.) Everyone walked away; the trial resulted in zero convictions. Peggy Ann Buckley's final statement was a dire warning. "I think people in the world need to know this was a witch-hunt; that nothing happened at this school. And this could happen to *anyone*."

Judy Johnson was found dead at the age of forty-two, in 1986, one hand clutching her phone, with a trail of blood behind her. She died of extreme alcohol poisoning, which caused internal hemorrhaging and vomiting.

4

While the Christian Right used Satanism to demonize any movement toward reproductive rights, such as Pat Robertson claiming feminism made women practice witchcraft, destroy capitalism, and become lesbians (some readers might be thinking he was correct in this assessment and it sounds pretty good), many of the actual devil-worshipping occultists of the time, like Crowley before them, actually harbored anti-abortion viewpoints themselves.

The infamous Anton LaVey (1930–1997), the founder of the Church of Satan, which saw its cultural height in the '80s, wrote against abortion. Note that his organization, the Church of Satan, has since made their stance clearer. Magus Peter H. Gilmore, high priest of the Church of Satan, told CNN in 2013, "We generally consider the use of abortion to be the purview of the woman whose body is carrying the child." When I reached out to the Church of Satan for comment on their current abortion stance, they directed me to their website, which, in a lengthy post, states that abortion is not a Satanic sacrament, but "an optional medical procedure which should be within the rights of the pregnant person to choose if they so desire, since being pregnant or not should be their decision."

While LaVey supported birth control—even if his preferred family planning method seems to be having sex with robots, as they can't get pregnant—he wrote, as detailed in the collection of essays by LaVey published in 1998, titled *Satan Speaks*:

> *Satanically speaking, I am against abortion. Yet I do consider a problem of overpopulation. Therefore, I advocate compulsory birth control. Unborn babies did not ask to be conceived. Once conceived, they should have loving, responsible parents, even if adoptive. A stupid, irresponsible woman should not have the right to "decide" what she does with her own body when in all other things, her mind is being controlled by impersonal vested interests. An unborn child's father should influence the outcome of a pregnancy if it can be determined that he is more responsible than the mother. If he is stupid, insensitive and irresponsible, he should be sterilized. Irresponsible parents, male or female, should simply be kept from having children.*

He once again describes his views against abortion in a letter, writing, as published in the 2010 *Letters from the Devil: The Lost Writing of Anton Szandor LaVey*, which includes copies of his newspaper advice column of the same name: "Abortion is unnatural and unnecessary. Man is the only animal who practices such wanton killing of its young. And yet man considers himself emancipated and more highly evolved than any other species. Legalized abortion would have a disastrously demoralizing effect on our society, for it would further instill the notion that human life is one of the cheapest commodities in the world." While there are plenty of reasons not to listen to this guy, it's important to note that none of that is true. Plenty of other animals abort, such as mongoose, cows, sharks, and rays.

LaVey was utterly obsessed with "humanoids," spending much time tinkering with life-size dolls. Though he never succeeded in engineering his dream girl, he did believe that his early-model off-brand Real Dolls could reduce unwanted pregnancies. "Unfortunately, many humans' sole contribution to the world—if it can be considered as such—is the ability to produce another human being," he wrote, showing that when it comes to reproductive justice, many Americans, including Satanic leaders, have complicated, changing, and often incongruous opinions.

Despite their founder's position, today, and even back then, many Satanists are vehemently pro-choice. Their system of beliefs looks to Lucifer as the ultimate individual, therefore making any personal choice regarding reproductive rights or health care valid. Satanists are even known for protesting (as the modern-day Satanic Temple often does) the government's infringement on these rights. The views of Satanists, much like Americans in general, do not always reflect the views of their often-problematic forebears. And, even LaVey, ever a man of contradictions, did once recommend therapeutic abortion rather than a nonexistent "spell to make her unpregnant" in response to a reader writing him for advice about such a spell, also included in *Letters from the Devil*.

Anton LaVey was often called Tony when he was younger. And like Tony Soprano, a fictional mobster whose New Jersey McMansion pool housed ducks, and whose (also fictional) shrink read about how sociopaths sometimes have no empathy for humans but go nuts for animals, LaVey, too, held a candle for animals while also allegedly being okay with human cannibalism. "There was, at times, an almost unbearable oppressiveness to his intolerance and anger. Here was a man who could spend hours delighting in playing forgotten songs, or playing with an animal, yet could become monstrously callous when he felt the need. LaVey was idealistically against hunting and would be the first person to stop to help an injured animal along the road, yet put a nickel in him and he would enthusiastically advocate putting a bounty on selected humans," writes Blanche Barton, the authorized biographer and former High Priestess, who was also LaVey's partner, and the mother of LaVey's son, Satan Xerxes Carnacki LaVey. Like most of his favored women, Barton is a bodacious blonde.

The Church of Satan, despite having absolutely nothing to do with the case, was name-dropped *a lot* during the McMartin trial and its related press. In 1985, the *Chicago Tribune* covered the trial, writing,

> *The Satanic Bible, written and published by LaVey in 1969, approves of the use of human sacrifice but only "to dispose of a totally obnoxious and deserving individual." It adds, however, that "under no circumstances would a Satanist sacrifice any animal or baby" and also forbids "rape, child molesting or the sexual defilement of animals."*
>
> *But Pat Metoyer, an intelligence officer with the Los Angeles Police Department, said in an interview: "People can interpret The Satanic Bible to mean just about anything. The true Satanist would offer the Devil the most appealing of sacrifices, something which is innocent. To most people the symbol of innocence is an infant."*

Despite how much attention the frenzied parents and cops who worked the case gave LaVey, he didn't seem to pay them the time of day. His authorized biography penned by Barton mainly focuses on questionable personal propaganda. One illustrative quote: "As with many young men who find themselves unusually well-endowed, Tony felt self-conscious undressing in front of other boys." The book further insisted that he had had a relationship with Marilyn

Monroe before her career took off, while they both worked at the Mayan Burlesque Theater in Los Angeles in 1948 (questionable) and that Hollywood blonde bombshell Jayne Mansfield was a student of his at one point (true).

LaVey infamously put a curse on Mansfield's boyfriend Sam Brody (who was first her divorce lawyer) as part of a jealous spat over the actress. When her son was mauled by a tiger at a private zoo and the couple died in a car accident, plenty of people blamed her bloody demise on her dark affiliations; it was helpful for gossip journalists that LaVey got his start as a big-cat trainer and kept a pet lion after he gave up the circus for Satan. Rumors circulated that Mansfield was decapitated, and LaVey even seemingly tries to take credit for that in his biography by claiming that around the time of Mansfield's death, he accidentally snipped her head off in a photo with a pair of scissors. (Mansfield's head was intact after her death. Mariska Hargitay, who would become iconic for her portrayal of Olivia Benson on *Law & Order: Special Victims Unit*, is Mansfield's daughter. She was in the car at the time, three and a half years old, and survived with a zigzag scar. Very Harry Potter–esque.)

While LaVey wrote advocating against abortion, he was sex positive for his time. In an interview with Carl Abrahamsson in *Anton LaVey and the Church of Satan*, Peggy Nadramia says: "He was very pro-woman and always thought they were his best allies and often the power behind many thrones. That's why it always brought me up short that he was antiabortion." His sex positivity apparently appealed to Mansfield, a woman not afraid to luxuriate in her high femme sex appeal when doing so could still be risky business. She lived in a Los Angeles pink palace; LaVey famously resided in an all-black Victorian house in San Francisco. The controversial sometimes-couple were both eccentric in their own ways.

If he were alive today to read this, it would make his blood boil, but, simply put, Tony LaVey was not actually all that scary. But

Satan scares people. Invoking Satan to scare people is the oldest trick in the book (at least in the AD era). And by using Satan to shock while simultaneously denouncing the Christian notion of the devil and using Lucifer as a model of the individual, he tapped into the same type of shock imagery combined with pseudophilosophy that the anti-choice crowd was using to deliver their message.

Some of LaVey's most interesting teachings stem from his time working as a musician and in the circus and have nothing to do with the devil at all. LaVey gives great advice on cat training. "You never teach cats 'tricks.' You just find out what they like to do and build an act around that." He eventually left the circus and founded the Church of Satan in 1966.

Outside of his Satanist duties, LaVey claimed to work as a photographer for the San Francisco Police Department, often taking on odd and illicit jobs, such as UFO sightings and suicides. While the ACAB (all cops are bastards) camp might have some jokes to make about that, the real dirt is that he was inspired by Nazi propaganda films and got into Satanism in part because he had heard whispers of a Black Order of Satan worshippers within the Third Reich. For all those out there using Lucifer to fight for justice, there is plenty of Satan and Nazi overlap. For instance, the Order of Nine Angles is a Satanic, left-handed path, occultist UK-based group that allegedly seeks to establish a militaristic new social order for a galactic civilization—so Aryan society can colonize the Milky Way galaxy, *of course*. The Order of Nine Angles also allegedly endorses human sacrifice using an odd reverse eugenics-like method of deciding who is the perfect sacrificial human—their ideal candidate being a "fake" Satanist, such as a member of the Church of Satan, whom they consider poseurs and pussies. These guys would laugh at LaVey's alleged Nazi inspiration, correctly asserting *they* are the real deal.

But left-handed-path leaders rarely seem to wish to unite; it can't be a unified movement because they all want their own religions and eventually just end up in dick-measuring con-tests. LaVey understood that he shared similarities with Crowley beyond their bald heads, so he did his research, but when he vis-ited Thelema in Berkeley, California, he was disgusted, as he found them to be a bunch of dirty hippies still stuck in the veins of tra-ditional Western and Eastern religious philosophy. "Anton con-cluded that the Thelemites' founder was a druggy poseur whose greatest achievements were as a poet and mountain climber," his biographer wrote.

He's not wrong.

Despite LaVey believing that he was much scarier than Crowley, the two of them at least overlapped on eugenics and sex with their female followers. And LaVey had thoughts about those female fol-lowers: his book *The Satanic Witch*, edited by LaVey's partner for twenty-four years, Diane Hegarty, mother to his daughter Zeena (who the internet has noted bears a shocking resemblance to Taylor Swift), hotly debates stockings versus panty hose. He loathed panty hose, which cover one's midsection, and therefore vagina, whereas, he argued, thigh-high stockings held up with a garter belt offered easier sexual access. He wrote: "Throw away your panty hose and forget about them! They are a curse perpetuated on women by people who would rather you weren't women."

While the scaredy-cats of society thought the Satanists were chopping up babies, they were actually giving fashion advice.

The text, complete with a bright-pink cover that would make Mansfield proud, includes a rather odd section on his self-created brand of eugenics, dividing men and women into various body types that he associated with different inherent behaviors. Using a circle divided into twelve sections, like a clock or the twelve houses in astrology, and classified by the four elements also found in astrology (fire, air, water, and earth), he splits men and women into twelve types, offering nuggets of wisdom so nutty it's hard to take them seriously enough to be offended. Here's an example: "The woman most prone to stereotyped lesbian activities is the twelve o'clock. The man most likely to fit the established image of the homosexual is the six o'clock." This system is a bizarre mix of spiritual eugenics and astrology, complete with advice on why dating based on your category is so important. "Because of forced egalitarianism, the lost science of eugenics, the art of typing people, has been all but outlawed, and the Darwinian process of natural selection has been virtually reversed," LaVey bemoaned.

Despite modern-day Satanists' efforts to establish a figure like LaVey as the icon of the individual rather than as anyone who actually *believed* in magic, LaVey did believe that he was channeling Satanic forces to manifest and inflict his will on the world . . . hence his concern that he himself decapitated Mansfield with a photo and some scissors. When asked, LaVey would likely say all his dark arts were aimed at ruining Christianity, but, not unlike some anti-abortion radicals, it seems mostly about making himself a rock star.

And, every now and then, he did some hard-core stuff. Hosting a chic cannibalism-themed dinner party is easy in California when you have the right connections.

You see, like anyone who finds themselves along the left-handed path, LaVey too hosted Black Masses, perversions of the Catholic Mass. His followers called him "the Black Pope," drawing on centuries of associating Satan with all that is scary and dark, whether wishing to invoke the fear of being alone in the woods at night or their Black neighbors.

LaVey's ceremonies were not always orchestrated rituals, but more like the type of elite dinner club one could imagine a billionaire tech bro getting hard for today. For instance, LaVey once held a seminar called "Cannibalism and Human Sacrifices," wherein guests were allegedly invited to partake the cooked thigh of a young white woman. The thigh was procured by a Berkeley physician who had attended LaVey's lectures. Hegarty, according to *The Secret Life of a Satanist*, basted the thigh with Triple Sec, fruit juices, and grenadine until it was sweet and ready to eat. At least the dinner party sounds like a level up in street cred from a Victorian-era spiritualist party invoking Indigenous ghosts with a proto-Ouija board, don't you think?

If one is to look at LaVey's life, and words, as with the big cats, he gives the most interesting cultural insight when speaking of the carnival. "Freaks were the royalty of the carny world—they got validation they never would have gotten on the outside," LaVey shares. "The human oddities, natural freaks, were in a much more esteemed position than sword-walkers or fire-eaters, or even tattooed people, who all had to learn their freakish talents or, in the case of tattoos, modify their bodies to make themselves distinguished. The natural freaks literally had a special birthright."

But while LaVey did offer solace for the freaks of the world, one can't call him the inclusive and rebellious officer of Lucifer modern left-handed-path followers are hungry for, and while he played a fabulous devil in Black Masses and on TV, there's no evidence to support he was involved in the abuse of any children, as the fabulists of the McMartin trial graspingly tried to suggest.

5

So, if the Church of Satan was led by an actor, and Los Angeles County blew $15 million on charges cooked up by coerced children that turned out to be baseless, who were the *real* witches of the time?

As Stevie Nicks quickly figured out by daring to live an adventurous life and pen a song about a witch, any friendly, peaceful pagans in the '80s were immediately associated with Christian interpretations of the devil. Social media wouldn't normalize (and profit) off occult-inspired outfits and rose-quartz beauty products by playing to the vanity of the self-described witch for several decades.

Laurie Cabot is an American high priestess who launched the Witches' League for Public Awareness (WLPA) in the 1980s to try to change the surrounding narrative of witches to better match the cultural picture with reality. Cabot quite successfully rocked the big '80s hair, which she has since let grow from an OG goth black to gray, gracefully aging from maiden to crone over the past few decades.

Cabot was inspired to create the WLPA after another negative media depiction of witches in *The Witches of Eastwick*, a 1987 film based on John Updike's novel. The so-called three Witches of Eastwick are in cahoots with the devil, basically living with him like Crowley's Scarlet Women or LaVey's Satanic Witches, which didn't sit well with Cabot, a woman who authored friendly books such as *Celebrate the Earth: A Year of Holidays in the Pagan Tradition*. "Here are three women who have nothing better to do, because they are so frustrated sexually, than to get involved with witchcraft," Cabot observed of the film in a 1992 interview with the *Washington Post*. "They are not witches. If they are anything, they are weekend Satanists. They don't do one witchy thing in the whole film."

Cabot ran the WLPA from Salem, where she still resides today. She has an online business and sells her handcrafted magic products at Enchanted, a witch shop on Pickering Wharf, a harborside shopping center in Salem, where you can buy crystals, candles, and potions. "When people ask me how to worship the devil, I say, 'You're in the wrong place,'" Cabot told *People* in 1987. "I've had to explain that I don't kill babies and drink blood." She describes her brand of witchcraft as "pre-Christian, an Earth religion," proving the ancient ways of merging rational thought and magic still exist millennia later.

The WLPA also works with Falwell's dreaded ACLU regarding freedom-of-religion issues, like when police departments erroneously label certain crimes "occult," which out-and-proud witches like Cabot then have to deal with. In a badass move, during the 1980s, the WLPA exposed *File 18*. This secret newsletter compiled by a cop contained an "occult hit list" for police to reference when they think they smell witchcraft or folks associated with pagan religions, like an *X-Files* rerun where Scully and Mulder spot a pentagram spray-painted on a building and erupt into a panic. The WLPA also acts as an information hub where folks can learn about the realities of witchcraft, which, in Cabot's case, is more about environmentalism than cannibalism and ritual orgies with Hollywood starlets.

While Cabot gives us an example of an actual self-described witch, proving the true practitioners at the time were a far cry from baby-killing, child-molesting monsters, there were also the activists working as midwives to secure reproductive rights.

In *Mrs. America*, the FX miniseries about Phyllis Schlafly (played by Cate Blanchett), Betty Friedan says, "Is that what everyone thinks? That I'm the Wicked Witch of the West and Gloria is Glinda?" Even Friedan perhaps had some internal misogyny to work through; beyond throwing the witch label on Schlafly, she was deliberate in excluding lesbians, calling gays the "lavender menace" for what she saw as slowing down the women's liberation movement. The *New York Times* describes her as "famously abrasive," and she was loud and unapologetic. While Friedan was of stouter build and older, she was the Big-*O* Original OG of the women's liberation movement. Meanwhile, the younger feminist activist Gloria Steinem, founder of *Ms. Magazine*, was skinny and classically beautiful. Her pretty privilege helped people take the movement more seriously because she was a traditionally desirable woman who truly didn't want to get married and, crucially, a woman whom douchebags couldn't accuse of being a feminist simply because she "couldn't land a husband." However, she was also hated for looking nice, because conservatives loathe secretly being attracted to a woman who stands for everything they're against. Friedan was on to something. In second-wave feminism, she was cast as the mean old hag, and Steinem was the young, beautiful, seductive maiden who put naughty thoughts about living life on one's own accord into the minds of otherwise well-behaved women.

In her memoir, *My Life on the Road*, Steinem dedicated it to

> *Dr. John Sharpe of London, who in 1957, a decade before*
> *physicians in England could legally perform an abortion*
> *for any reason other than the health of the woman, took*
> *the considerable risk of referring for an abortion a twenty-*
> *two-year-old American on her way to India. Knowing only*
> *that she had broken an engagement at home to seek an*
> *unknown fate, he said, "You must promise me two things.*
> *First, you will not tell anyone my name. Second, you*
> *will do what you want to do with your life." . . . Dear*
> *Dr. Sharpe, I believe you, who knew the law was unjust,*
> *would not mind if I say this so long after your death. I've*
> *done the best I could with my life. This book is for you.*

Steinem was then a twenty-two-year old American and one of the first second-wave feminists to talk about and report on abortion, unafraid of the ongoing bigotry. She was at the front lines, whether she was crusading for the Equal Rights Amendment or knowing from the get-go that *Roe v. Wade* wasn't secure enough. When it was overturned with *Dobbs v. Jackson Women's Health Organization* in 2022, Steinem told the press that she'd give the guest room of her famous Upper East Side Manhattan apartment to women traveling to the city to have the procedure safely.

Pat Maginnis (1928–2021), who, as *Slate* reports, was described by alt-weeklies as the "Che Guevara" of abortion reformers, doesn't have a touching tale about a British abortionist with a heart of gold. She performed two out of her three abortions herself. Of her second abortion, Maginnis told *Slate* staff reporter Lili Loofbourow that she had to "squat down and take my clean, scrubbed fingers and manipulate until I could get it to rebel and kick the fetus out. . . . I manipulated, I worked on it, and finally, at five months, the fetus went into—I went into labor. It took a long time and a lot of work." She along with friends and cofounders Lana Phelan and Rowena Gurner became known as the Army of Three, forming the Society for Humane Abortion's central trio, in 1962. If you prefer your activists a bit more punk, the Army of Three fitted the bill. Lana reportedly had an abortion on the outskirts of Tampa, Florida, in which the midwife used slippery elm bark, as utilized by Indigenous people. While it worked, it wasn't the most pleasant experience, and the Army of Three thought people deserved better reproductive health options. In the years leading up to *Roe*, when abortion was still illegal, the Society for Humane Abortion taught classes on female anatomy, how to find abortion doctors, and how to protect yourself if the police try to get involved.

The SHA and the Jane Collective, an underground abortion service in Chicago, helped people obtain abortions. "I am attempting to show women an alternative to knitting needles, coat hangers, and household cleaning agents," Maginnis said. While the SHA was a referral network, the Jane Collective taught people how to perform abortions themselves.

Before *Roe*, many states allowed one to obtain an abortion if they had a letter from a psychiatrist stating they were too "unsound" to have a child—a card plenty of people played. (Maginnis was also a political cartoonist and drew one depicting a woman begging her doctor, "How much for a psychosis?") Alive in a time when most women would have to persuade a doctor that she deserved an abortion for some moralized reason, whether it was being "too crazy" to be a mother or the usual approved reasons of rape or incest, the Che Guevara of abortion reformers proposed a radical idea: one should be allowed to have an abortion simply because they want one.

The 1980s and the years bookending it already have an over-the-top reputation, from the shoulder pads to cult-classic horror films such as *Nightmare on Elm Street*. Another movie, *The Witches of Eastwick*, inspired Laurie Cabot to create an organization debunking misleading stereotypes about practicing witches. Anton LaVey is rumored to have both consulted and played the devil in 1968's *Rosemary's Baby*, in which a pregnant young woman is warned about cannibals and Satanists. And, if we are to believe his biography, he even enjoyed cannibalism for shock value, but most of his theatrics were just that. While his organization, the Church of Satan, has evolved its views on abortion since its founder's heyday, one of the scariest things about LaVey isn't his nonexistent penchant for sacrificing babies, but the cruelty revealed in his writings against abortion.

Words have power, as does their repetition of them. It's why people have faith in prayer and spells. So, at the risk of sounding like a broken record (if those terrified of witch imagery at the time could pick one to visualize here, let's say it's Fleetwood Mac), once again, remember that the reproductive rights feminist heroes are always flawed, despite their epic contributions. This is demonstrated again by women like Betty Friedan, who may have given the world *The Feminine Mystique* and jump-started second-wave feminism, but did so under the haze of the lavender menace. Smoke and mirrors decorate this era as much as any other, and hypocrisy continues to linger like cigarette smoke in a carpet, as demonstrated by the Reagans' ability to court the Moral Majority even when their own views didn't perfectly align or consult an astrologer for Air Force One departure times at the height of the Satanic Panic. But while Reagan had the most power, and LaVey perhaps the most street cred, in the history of abortion rights, the scariest villains of the time were those who, because they answered to their own violent god, cared not for repercussions, even if it came with prison sentences, such as Shelley Shannon, convicted of the attempted murder of George Tiller, and Michael Griffin, convicted of the murder of David Gunn.

Now brace yourself, because we're going to meet more like them in the modern era. And this time, there's pizza.

CHAPTER 6

BLOOD-DRINKING PIZZA PARTIES AND GOING GAY FOR ABORTION RIGHTS

1

The year is 2023. I'm sitting at a Midtown Manhattan steakhouse, two blocks away from where Madame Restell's mansion stood, with Marisol Vibración, my dear friend and a practicing witch. Over the chatter, a pianist pours out "My Way" by Frank Sinatra, the son of an abortionist and midwife. Purple lights fall across Marisol's face as I ask her what she, as a trans woman, thinks about reproductive rights. She pauses and takes a sip from her martini. "I think . . . they're not even thinking about us. People are thinking about how cishet couples can keep having babies or plan their families in their purviews. Those who we deem worthy of passing on their bloodlines."

Another sip from her glass.

"With my Black-brown trans body . . . you weren't even thinking about me in this conversation. Even Black cis women just got invited. We're still playing catch-up."

In 1916, Margaret Sanger pioneered the opening of the first Planned Parenthood clinic. Fast-forward more than six decades, and in 1978, a monumental shift occurred with Faye Wattleton's appointment. She not only became the second woman to steer the organization but also made history as the first Black woman to do so.

Growing up as a cis woman, I learned all about my period and how I could get pregnant if I had sex. I didn't learn these things only from my mother, but also in an awkward middle school sex ed talk.

"I think the thing that would distinguish me from my cis woman peers is that they've had people to talk to this whole time about it. I had to do a lot of this by myself for the first twenty-something years," Marisol says. We pause to listen to the music and enjoy our medium-rare steaks with an ample side of fries. The piano player takes requests, and he's now on to Marisol's pick: "Never Too Much" by Luther Vandross. She is wearing an asymmetrical black dress accented with a blue fishnet bodysuit and matching blue heels. She describes her own witchcraft practice as "very astrologically synced. And it's very artistic as well. For me everything is an offering, from my tears, to my orgasms, to the makeup that I put on my face, to the glass I enjoy with dinner. All of it is an offering if I want it to be, and if I remember to let it be."

Reproductive justice, compared to the historical reproductive rights movement she was talking about, *does* consider trans people. The movement isn't merely about the mechanics of reproduction. It's a union of the personal and the political in which one's reproductive choices are intertwined with elements as broad as racial landscapes, the economy, and even environmentalism. It calls for a revolution demanding that reproductive rights include sex ed, birth mortality, maternal well-being, family planning, sexual health care for the disabled, and queer activism. Elevated by the passionate advocacy of organizations like the SisterSong Women of Color Reproductive Justice Collective and key figures such as Loretta Ross, who originated the phrase, this is more than mere terminology. It's not just a phrase; it's an invocation and battle cry.

When asked about what she sees as the first steps toward reproductive justice, Marisol says, "Educating people on the fact that trans people can lactate and trans men can give birth," adding, "I'm still learning stuff every day, and I'm part of the demographic."

Because it's not just something public schools skip teaching. In states such as Florida, it is in many instances illegal for school staff and educators to even talk about queerness or gender identity. In early 2022, Florida's governor, Ron DeSantis, enacted the "Don't Say Gay" bill (HB 1557), effective from July 1, 2022. This law aimed to restrict classroom discussions on sexual orientation and gender identity, originally from kindergarten through the third grade. As of the time of this writing, two federal lawsuits are contesting the law. This law was then expanded in May 2023, prohibiting sexual orientation or gender identity be taught in prekindergarten through *eighth grade*, limiting sex ed in sixth through twelfth grades, and requiring that any reproductive health that is taught "be age-appropriate or developmentally appropriate for students in accordance with state standards." It's applicable to both public and charter schools. And books in school libraries across the country, largely those from Black and queer authors or featuring any mention of sex, reproduction, or nontraditional families, have been banned in this decade at a rate higher than ever.

As Marisol points out, trans women often have to think about reproductive health in ways that most cis women don't. "All trans people have to have this conversation internally before we start our transitions medically, because a lot of medical transitions and hormone therapy can render a person infertile regardless of where they're started or where they're headed," she explains.

Transgender women now have the option to freeze their sperm for future use when and if they decide to have children. Fertility centers offer sperm-freezing services within their advanced on-site laboratories. In these facilities, sperm can be preserved safely for an indefinite period, ensuring it's available when (and if) the moment is right. Transgender women with a female partner can use the cryopreserved sperm for insemination. For male-to-female individuals without a female partner, the option of working with a gestational carrier is available. This approach involves procuring eggs from a carefully selected donor, which are then inseminated with frozen sperm to create embryos that are transferred to the gestational carrier, per Yale Medicine.

"I had to have that conversation when I decided to start my hormones, and we're, what, a year and eight months into my hormonal journey?" she says. "My doctor was like, 'If you have even a sliver of a chance of wanting your own biological kids, you should freeze stuff now, because you don't know if you'll be able to in the future.'"

At the risk of losing the Women's March pussyhat knitters: This chapter isn't about you. This is a book about witch hunts. I am aware that as a cis white lady living in New York City who doesn't want children, if I get pregnant, abortion will likely always be available for me, as it was both before and after *Roe*, whether I had gone to Madame Restell or Planned Parenthood. (Although I should emphasize again that 60 percent of abortions are performed elsewhere than Planned Parenthood. One of the dangers of giving Planned Parenthood so much attention is that pregnant people don't know that there are other places they can go!)

As much as some want to keep the narrative the same as it's been since the sexual revolution, while sexism still exists—despite the "lavender menace" Betty Friedan feared—second-wave feminists succeeded. Well, in some ways. Abortion is still illegal in some states, although as some followers of the left-handed path will tell you, looking to the government for answers is not the solution. But it is no longer that weird to be a woman who, like me, decides to prioritize her career over having children. My wants and desires are no longer radical.

Neither is being a witch. Hell, today identifying as a witch can be a way to get followers. Instead, it's the women and witches like

Marisol who are being hunted. "The witch hunt against trans femmes is the worst one of them all," she says. She was threatened with gun violence at the Atlantic Avenue station on the L subway line in East New York, shortly before we met up. "I've lived in New York City my whole life, and I've dealt with threats my whole life. And people think, like, no harm comes to queer people in this city, like it's a gay holy land." At least thirty-three transgender and gender-nonconforming people were killed in the United States in 2023. That's almost twice as many as Salem.

"I think a lot of it is because, on a national level, we're normalizing dehumanizing trans women. Like, portraying us as these ignorant, sex-crazed nothings. Not even people. This is where language really matters, because the whole 'I'm a real woman' or 'I'm a biological woman' argument that TERFs [trans-exclusionary radical feminists] like to make is 'I'm also a real woman.' The last time I checked, I'm still carbon-based life," Marisol quips, reminding me of Heka's and society's desire to force people into neat little boxes that don't exist.

Marisol's trans identity is intertwined with the question of having children. "I will also say, you know, this is my personal experience with trans womanhood: I spent my whole childhood and adolescence mourning the fact that I couldn't carry a baby to term. And that was what grounded me in my certainty of who I am. At fourteen, fifteen, sixteen, I was hearing my cis femme peers talking about how babies are the last thing they would ever want, and I'm sitting there thinking I would give anything to have the opportunity."

The Supreme Court, including Justices Kagan and Sotomayor, two more women nominated by Obama, made it federally legal for same-sex couples to marry through their 5–4 decision in *Obergefell v. Hodges* during Pride month, June 2015. But Obama didn't magically fix the conditions for queer love in America. "There's a witch hunt on people who are attracted to trans people as well," Marisol says. It's not lost on her that, while the anti-trans narrative typically falls back on "traditional values" rhetoric, the two-spirits were here first. "Going back to 'traditional' values cheapens that term, because it's like, I'm more traditional than you are, baby. My people have been around way longer than you have. Tradition? Go suck a bag of dicks with your tradition."

Even though the occult is now past the point of cool—it's basically basic—she isn't counting on self-proclaimed witches to help her secure a place at the table. "We're experiencing witchcraft being openly practiced like never before," she says. "Witchcraft has a lot of power to it, and collective magic can definitely effect massive change, like the kind that we need to see. But I do not have the faith that the current witch community will be capable of combating this with this flawed perception of womanhood, menstruation, and moon cycles in general."

Ironically, since the word "occult" refers to what is hidden, one of the reasons witchcraft has spread so virulently is the visibility made possible on social media. Political witch hunts have also gone cyber. In 2015, an anti-choice hacker got into Planned Parenthood's website and stole employee data. Just like medicine and magic, the internet can be used for good (telemedicine and mail-to-home access to the abortion pill) and evil (anti-abortion hackers and harassment). And modern-day witches, who can now not only put the word "witch" in their social media bios, but also make money through online consultations, tarot, astrology, and more, can use their platforms to share information on how to safely access abortion in a post-*Dobbs* world. If witchcraft can become mainstream, and witches can use their power for change, there's no reason not to have hope that a country with safe access to abortion could also become a reality.

Perhaps bringing pagan practices out of the shadows made them less powerful. Are all the wild baby-eating parties happening only on QAnon message boards? Are we left with nothing but rose-quartz face rollers? Maybe. But in many ways, the witch's use of social media makes sense because of these platforms' sense of community. This holds true for accessing abortions online, too. On the one hand, the internet makes it easier to learn about reproductive health, obtain the abortion pill, and talk to others who've been through the same experience. On the other, smartphones allow big companies and the government to monitor us more closely. While sharing data is against some company's privacy policies, there's growing concern that period-tracking apps could even share their data with the government.

If you're worried about online privacy, consider the Tor browser a modern-day protection spell. Tor, an acronym for "The Onion Router," is a free tool championing online privacy. By routing user data through a global network of volunteer-run relays, it obscures (how occult) users' locations and usage from network surveillance or traffic analysis. This process masks users' identities, ensuring their online actions remain anonymous.

In today's world where anyone can be a content creator, people turn to their phones rather than tune in to regularly scheduled programs. The average person is on their phone for almost seven hours a day. That's a lot of screen time. According to Nielsen, linear TV, or just turning on the television to watch regularly scheduled content, rather than using a streaming service such as Netflix, now makes up less than 50 percent of all TV usage.

The devil may still be scary to some, but thanks to social media, it's also become generally mainstream. Just ask rapper Lil Nas X, who pole-dances into hell and gives Lucifer a lap dance before taking his horns for himself in his 2021 "Montero (Call Me by Your Name)" music video, which he announced through Instagram to his nearly eleven million Instagram followers, expertly pissing off the Right with his unabashedly gay, tongue-in-cheek display. Then, of course, there was the infamous Grammy performance by Sam Smith and Kim Petras, who invoked the devil and danced in a cage to "Unholy," for which they won the award for Best Pop Duo/ Group Performance at the 2023 Grammys. Petras, the first openly trans person to win in the category, accepted the award wearing a red dress and veil, as everyone saw on IG, looking like Winona Ryder about to get married in *Beetlejuice.*

By now, most people know that witches and the devil are not something to fear, so those who are brave enough can use such imagery for political change (or just awesome pop music) without fear of torture or being burned at the stake. But not without fear of backlash. Ted Cruz called the "Unholy" performance "evil," and while it absolutely slapped, even the Church of Satan didn't like it. In an interview with TMZ, David Harris, a magister of the Church of Satan, said he thought the performance was "alright" although "nothing particularly special."

Oppression is nothing new or original, but there does seem to have been a fiery resurgence that's holding hands with the movement to reverse reproductive rights. It's reminiscent of the conservative convergence that succeeded in uniting Catholics with Evangelicals to elect Reagan in part as a reaction to the free-love and feminist movements of the 1960s and '70s. Thanks to pre-exposure prophylactics, plenty of gay men can now enjoy condomless sex like they did in the days before AIDS. PrEP refers to medications that reduce the risk of contracting HIV if taken before exposure to the virus occurs. PrEP reduces the risk of getting HIV from sex by about 99 percent when taken as prescribed.

Zachary Zane, author of *Boyslut: A Memoir and Manifesto,* which focuses on how to overcome sexual shame and find queer community, tells me that PrEP's impact on gay and bi men over the past fifteen years has been bigger than the major hookup app Grindr's. "HIV is very manageable now, and you can live a full life as an

HIV-positive person; but this obviously wasn't always the case. We also lost so many loved ones. So to have a pill and all you have to do is take it daily, and you won't contract HIV? It was huge—a game changer. Queer men could have sex without fear. We could love and date without fear," Zane, a thirty-three-year-old bisexual icon—a bicon, if you will—tells me.

PrEP isn't the only medical intervention that has changed Zane's (extremely active, with a body count of more than three thousand at time of reporting) sex life. As someone who sleeps with all genders and genitals, he's also now the proud recipient of a vasectomy. "I know with certainty that I do not want children. As such, I never want to be put in a situation where I am forced to have a child that I do not want. And after *Roe v. Wade* got over-turned, the odds of that happening increased," he says. Zane was given nitrous oxide and put in a twilight state (which is about what one can expect for a surgical abortion; pain relief for patients taking the abortion pill is another story) and listened to Fleet-wood Mac (shout-out to Stevie) on his AirPods during the proce-dure. He says other than mild pain—comparable to being "gently punched" in the testicles—during the first forty-eight hours, the recovery wasn't bad at all. He couldn't work out or have sex for a week, although he managed, and six weeks later, tests confirmed that he was shooting blanks. "Women are so appreciative when I say I've had a vasectomy. They really appreciate that I'm also tak-ing responsibility and removing some of the burden from them," he says.

Zach's vasectomy was covered by insurance. Most insurers will also cover a hysterectomy—*if* it's medically necessary and your doctor recommends it. While some job-based health plans cover abortion, generally, most do not. Plus, even if you manage to get an abortion covered by insurance (which is unlikely), you must live in a state where it's legal for it to do you any good.

For cis men who don't want kids, a vasectomy is the way to go. The alternatives are still evolving. A "paper abortion" is a (currently hypothetical) legal concept that would give a man the right to terminate his legal and financial responsibilities for a child during pregnancy. It follows the old joke: your body, your choice; my money, my choice. It's a concept that, outside of some libertarian types and bold intersectional feminists, is still considered pretty problematic and is not legal anywhere in the United States. But it's an interesting thought experiment for people with vaginas who don't want kids to imagine how they would feel if roles were reversed. In the landmark 1993 Kansas case *Hermesmann v. Seyer*, Colleen Hermesmann established a precedent by successfully contending that a woman has the legal right to seek child support from the father of her child, regardless of whether the conception resulted from a criminal act perpetrated by the woman. The case involved a sixteen-year-old babysitter having sex with the twelve-year-old she looked after, getting pregnant, when she was seventeen and he was thirteen, and then successfully suing him for child support.

While the main issue people take with a paper abortion is that child-support laws are meant to protect the child, not the parent, currently, no lawmaker really wants to touch the subject, in part because of the assumption that men could use paper abortions to pressure their sexual partners into obtaining a real one. Some of this relies on admittedly outdated stereotypes of manipulative women (or their angry pistol-wielding fathers) pressuring a young man into marriage for knocking her up.

You might remember that in his *Dobbs* opinion, Justice Alito cited Sir Matthew Hale, a figure known for his belief in witches, leading to the execution of some by burning. Additionally, in his notable common-law treatise, Hale asserted that marital rape could not constitute a crime, arguing that marriage implied an irreversible consent to sexual relations, a stipulation that applied solely to the wife. "For by their mutual matrimonial consent and contract," he wrote, "the wife hath given herself up in this kind unto the husband which she cannot retract." In 1662, during the Bury St. Edmunds witch trials that took place in Suffolk, England, Hale presided over a trial in which two women, Amy Duny and Rose Cullender, were charged with "bewitching" seven other people (in particular, children). Both Duny and Cullender were hanged.

When *Roe* was overturned, the streets pulsated with both protests and celebrations. While the laws will likely have gotten stricter since this sentence was typed, as of May 1, 2024, twenty-one states currently ban or restrict abortion earlier in pregnancy than the standard *Roe* set, primarily in the South. Other states, such as Kansas, Montana, California, Vermont, Michigan, and Kentucky, saw resounding support for a woman's right to choose through voter referendums or new legislation. Meanwhile, harrowing maternal deaths rose, especially for Black women, even as the overall impact of the ruling on abortion rates has remained veiled in ambiguity.

But even as we mourned the loss of *Roe*, a question lingered in the minds of many: What if we used this as an opportunity to craft better laws than *Roe*, which was always flimsy AF and everyone should have known it? "The real threat of losing *Roe* offers an opportunity for us to start again, and this time with women and queer people of color in every aspect of leadership, including in philanthropy, research, strategy, and movement building," said Cherisse Scott, CEO and founder of SisterReach, a reproductive justice nonprofit based in Tennessee, as Robin Marty's *New Handbook for a Post-Roe America* reports.

And not everyone who was pissed about *Roe*'s reversal cared only about the right to choose. *Dobbs* also put doctors at risk. With their own necks to protect, and varied personal attitudes on the subject, medical professionals may not be friends to people seeking abortion care in a post-*Roe* world. Two dozen esteemed medical collectives, such as the American Medical Association and the American College of Obstetricians and Gynecologists, were pretty honest about the apparent quandary physicians grapple with. In their poetic plea to the Supreme Court regarding *Dobbs v. Jackson*, they articulated: "The ban forces clinicians to make an impossible choice between upholding their ethical obligations and following the law."

Plenty of folks were surprised when Alito's infamous draft leaked. Just like they were surprised when Hillary lost to Trump despite failing to campaign in all the important places and calling potential future constituents a "basket of deplorables." Witches and activists like Becky Bullard, founder and CEO of Democrasexy, who is from Texas and also known as the "Civic Witch," told me that she was not surprised at all. Nor did she clutch her pearls—or her statement star earrings, as her style is more David Bowie than Audrey Hepburn—when she read Alito's citation of Hale. "Hale's misogynistic tendrils extend well into today's conservative legislative and legal thinking. This is especially true here in Texas, where patriarchy reigns and women are not entitled to their own bodies," Bullard tells me. She pointed to Texas state representative Jonathan Stickland's comments in an online forum in 2008: "Rape is nonexistent in marriage, take what you want my friend!" One of the rituals Bullard offers as a Civic Witch is a "Texorcism," a service that aims to cast the evil out of Texas.

Although Obama tried to save the fate of *Roe* by nominating Attorney General Merrick Garland to the Supreme Court after Scalia's death, the Republicans' commitment to reversing reproductive rights—and doing absolutely nothing in an effort to make sure the Obama administration could be derided as a wholesale failure in future campaigns—paid off. Garland's appointment to the Court was ignored by Republican-led

Judiciary Committees until it expired nearly a year later, and the seat was given to conservative darling Neil Gorsuch, appointed by President Donald Trump.

Conservatives demonstrate that playing dirty can be effective. While Michelle Obama's words "When they go low, we go high" are admirable, perhaps the Democrats need a plan stronger than marches accented with pink pussyhats, one that better acknowledges trans women, to start. Of course Trump did damage and played a significant role in the makeup of the Supreme Court that overturned *Roe*, including appointing Neil Gorsuch, Brett Kavanaugh, and Amy Coney Barrett. (Witches hexed his appointees, to no avail.) But the Republicans, and before them other religious conservatives abusing the names of Jesus and Satan, have been plotting this forever, and we were all silly to be surprised when they succeeded.

In November 2020, a group of LGBTQIA+ couples gathered in Tyler, Texas, for a "marriage-a-thon." Their purpose: to protest the appointment of Amy Coney Barrett to the Supreme Court. Thirty members of the local queer community participated, with five couples officially tying the knot. Conducting these unions was Raynie Castañeda, a nonbinary individual with long brown hair, a lip piercing, super-cute glasses, and the type of tarot skills people go wild about. Castañeda is recognized by their Instagram followers as @thatficklewitch.

And then there's Catland Books, a Brooklyn occult store that hosted a "Ritual to Hex Brett Kavanaugh" in October 2018, spooky season, shortly after Kavanaugh's confirmation. Dakota Bracciale, the event's organizer and a queer, nonbinary witch, explained that it served as an "act of resistance." The event included a second ritual called "The Rites of the Scorned One" to offer a safe space for survivors to get angry. "We're raising visibility and letting people know they're not alone with the monsters. Even the witches are coming out of the woodwork to stop this," Bracciale told *Time*. Catland Books closed its brick-and-mortar location in 2023 after ten years of operation.

But get ready to clutch those pearls. The pro-abortion crowd isn't the only side with seemingly cool Gen Z leaders. The pro-life (actually, these activists prefer "life-affirming") have some, too. Abortion views aside, they're seemingly leftists, a term these leaders say rightly belongs to their movement. As profiled by the *New York Times*, there's Kristin Turner, just twenty-two years old, who serves as the communications director for the Progressive Anti-Abortion Uprising. The organization is focused on educating the public about "the exploitative influence of the Abortion Industrial Complex through an anti-capitalist lens."

While the *New York Times* describes Turner as using "she/they" in their bio in their article from July 2022 by Ruth Graham, at the time of this writing, Turner uses "she/her." Turner protests abortions, but also supports Black Lives Matter and uses #ACAB in her Instagram bio. "My anti-abortion activism is in total alignment with my anarchist framework. I believe systems of harm perpetuated by capitalism, white supremacy, the prison industrial complex, and other apparatuses of oppression are largely the motivating factor for elective abortion in the US," Turner told me.

Accompanying a mug shot of herself from the Alexandria's Sheriff's Office that Turner posted to her Instagram account, she asks, "What are you willing to do?"—words that sound familiar after studying the anti-abortion activism of the 1980s and '90s. But not only does Turner not advocate violence, she also questions private property, writing, "Rescue entails disregarding property lines, and connected laws," and even acknowledges her own "MASSIVE privilege as a white woman" when describing her experience with the police. "The Right-To-Life movement was never about birthing more white babies for the workforce," she tells me, which is indeed a common misassumption the pro-choice camp makes about those who protest abortion. "The heritage of the anti-abortion movement belongs to leftists. It belongs to the anti-war, anti-death penalty activists who first began taking nonviolent direct action and Rescuing at abortion centers in the 70s. Putting their bodies between the butchers and the babies, as they did in other leftist movements then, and as modern-day Rescuers do now." Those on the Left who support abortion are doing themselves a disservice (*Roe* was overturned, remember) by ignoring or remaining unaware of this faction of the movement or insisting that those who oppose abortion do so solely for the creation of creating more workers.

She also plays punk rock. Turner and a San Francisco–based friend launched a band, aptly named the EmbryHoez. Within their burgeoning playlist, a song titled "The Hotties Will Dismantle Roe" stands out:

> *They say it's empowerment*
> *They say it's women's rights*
> *But all I see's oppression*
> *And might makes right.*

While the band is currently on pause as its members are scattered across the country, Turner notes that she has plans for it in the future.

Just like gender isn't binary, even if Turner has updated her pronouns since being featured in the *New York Times*, Americans can't be put into two boxes labeled "deplorables" and "nasty women." The latter category, whose spokeswoman ran on a pro-choice platform, has a personal set of abortion opinions as complicated as Reagan's. Hillary Clinton, who identifies as an "old-fashioned Methodist," disclosed in a 1994 interview with

Newsweek that she believed abortion is morally wrong. This offers insight into Clinton's 2016 remarks on NBC's *Meet the Press*, in which she referred to the fetus as an "unborn person," causing consternation among many pro-choice advocates. Despite all this, in a 2016 presidential debate, Trump said that Clinton would allow abortions so late that doctors could "rip the baby out of the womb of the mother just prior to the birth of the baby."

"Now, you can say that that's okay, and Hillary can say that that's okay, but it's not okay with me," Trump blabbered in their third and last presidential debate. "Because based on what she is saying, and based on where she's going and where she's been, you can take a baby and rip the baby out of the womb. In the ninth month, on the final day, and that's not acceptable."

In reality, 2016 Hillary Clinton was pro-choice and, regarding late-term abortions, while careful to paint them as heartbreaking, explained that if a mother's life was at risk, the government should not get involved. Granted, a lot has changed since the '90s, and Hillary is allowed to have viewpoints that evolve. It appears Trump's views have changed as well.

Back in 1999, Trump said, "I am very pro-choice." Today, he's a lot of things, though "pro-choice" is likely not among them. In statements relatable to some of the pharaohs, he's also made a few too many comments implying he might be into his daughter Ivanka.

But he won.

And appointed the justices who overturned *Roe*.

And helped succeed in convincing people that Hillary Clinton ate babies.

2

On a chilly day in Washington, DC, January 6, 2021, America, and the world, sat stunned and watched as a swarm of Trump supporters stormed the US Capitol. The insurrection was mounting as a joint session of Congress was certifying the Electoral College votes from the 2020 presidential election, which confirmed Joe Biden as the president-elect.

Five people died on or immediately following the day, including one cop. Within the following seven months, four more officers who had been on the scene died by suicide. The financial damages resulting from the breach surpassed $2.7 million. And followers of QAnon, the conspiracy theory that originated on Far Right message boards and still alleges that Donald Trump is battling a deep-state conspiracy of Satanic pedophiles, were involved in every stage from inception to insurrection. At the time of reporting, many QAnon adherents have been convicted or are awaiting trial for their roles in the infamous event that revealed our country is not the fortress one would like to think—metaphorically or literally, as the Capitol's walls were scaled and doors were breached.

The QAnon conspiracy theory revolves around the existence of an anonymous military intelligence group, known collectively as Q. Followers believe Q is at the center of an epic covert war of biblical proportions between good and evil. The Democrats are the devil, obviously, and Donald Trump is a holy savior, fighting "the rising tide of socialism and Satanism," as Mike Rothschild writes in *The Storm Is Upon Us: How QAnon Became a Movement, Cult, and Conspiracy Theory of Everything*, with one hand, while the other grabs their assumed "enemies" by the pussy.

Believers in QAnon are an Inquisition of the internet; they call themselves "digital soldiers." QAnon perpetuates, among others, dangerous myths that Barack Obama is "secretly a gay Muslim usurper" and Hillary Clinton is a "blood-drinking ghoul who murders everyone in her way," as Rothschild writes. He notes how they consider their "drops," or pieces of "intel" revealed on message boards, holy text.

But they're effective.

Jake Angeli, originally Jacob Anthony Chansley, born circa 1988, is known as the "QAnon Shaman." With a face painted in American-flag colors, shirtless, donning a horned headpiece made with coyote skin (co-opting Native traditions), he became the face of the cult when he was photographed inside the Capitol on that infamous January 6. Along with animal hides, he's also decked out in tattoos, including the Valknot, an ancient Norse symbol frequently depicted in carvings and designs to symbolize the afterlife associated with the god Odin. Once upon a time, when Vikings roamed, Odin was a wise old man who ruled war and death, but also wisdom. But just like the Sanskrit svastika, which means "good fortune" or "well-being," became the swastika, his symbol was repurposed by white supremacists.

Chansley was arrested on January 9, 2021, on federal charges of "knowingly entering or remaining in any restricted building or grounds without lawful authority, and with violent entry and disorderly conduct on Capitol grounds," according to the US Attorney's Office. In November 2021, he entered a guilty plea to a solitary charge, resulting in a sentence of 41 months, equivalent to 3.4 years, in prison. He completed only a portion of this sentence before being moved to a halfway house on March 28, 2023, and subsequently released from there on May 25, 2023. Chansley has been called an ecofascist who weaponized his religious position as a "shaman" to get out of getting a COVID vaccine while in prison. The attorney claimed his client's "longstanding status as a practicing Shaman precludes him from feeding into his body any vaccination." Chansley was kicked out of the US Navy in 2007 for refusing an anthrax vaccine. And, while it was later revoked, for at least a week he milked his self-adopted status as a religious figure to enjoy an all-organic diet in jail.

The word "shaman" can be traced back to the language of the

Jurchen people of ancient China. The word comes from the Manchu-Tungus language family, with its root, "sar," meaning knowledge or understanding.

It's used rampantly in the psychedelic community.

And QAnon.

And, despite many self-described witches piping up that using the word "shaman" is for culture vultures, the IG witch and New Age community greatly overlaps with QAnon on this front. Scrolling through #witchesofIG during the pandemic, one could find New Age and wellness influencers—the type, as Rothschild reports, QAnon researcher Marc-André Argentino calls "Pastel QAnon"—rocking a pair of millennial pink yoga pants with "World Hellth Organisation" printed on the ass.

While some followers don't believe that COVID-19 exists at all, QAnon groups have propagated several bogus claims regarding the disease, such as suggesting it was intentionally created and released by the deep state. They see vaccines as tools for government control and surveillance and post misogynistic and nutty memes about how having sex with a woman who's gotten "the jab" (or getting it yourself) will make you sterile. But despite the sexism, anti-Semitism, and basically everything one would expect from a hate group, QAnon is not just for basement-dwelling outcasts from society. A poll conducted by NPR/Ipsos in December 2020 revealed that more than a third of Americans believe in a deep state, which is a cloaked backstage crew of the government of unelected officials, bureaucrats, and sometimes even intelligence agencies that secretly pull the strings behind the scenes. And during the pandemic, these conspiracies spread far and wide—your friend from high school with whom you text only once a year might have gotten into it or your mom's coworker who used to just post salad pics.

It was these followers who boosted slogans like "Save the Children," not referring to the charity org but weaponized to propagate the claim that Hillary and her friends sold children for sex (but kept a few around for themselves to drink their blood, of course). The accusations are rampant, usually nonsensical, and take aim at various agencies and organizations in what appears random to most outside the core believers. In 2020, QAnon adherents showed up at a Chicago rally to protest Pizzagate and somehow got to chanting "ICE loves our children."

In reality, they were experiencing both psychological and physical harm resulting from "inadequate and inappropriate medical care," according to a report conducted by the FXB Center for Health and Human Rights at Harvard University. The US Immigration and Customs Enforcement has been accused of reproductive violence against adult detainees.

In 2020, ICE detainees in a Georgia facility told the *New York Times* they were sterilized without their consent. The Irwin County Detention Center in Ocilla, Georgia, made headlines after a nurse, Dawn Wooten, filed a whistleblower complaint alleging that detainees confided in her they had had their uteruses removed without being fully told what was happening and without their consent. Investigators stated that they did not find evidence to support the "mass hysterectomies" allegations, but admitted to "serious issues" related to medical procedures and policies.

There were also claims that ICE detainees weren't adequately vaccinated for COVID-19. The pandemic meant that health facilities and hospitals had to shut down or at least put reproductive health on the backburner. It opened a door for many states to start implementing stricter abortion laws, even before *Dobbs*. Did the fear of mass death, recalling the Black Plague, play a role? Maybe. For millions of people, the definition of life changed. With loved ones dying behind plastic sheets, the failure of our medical system revealed, and kissing rendered deadly, the rights to life and to live one's desired life became more important than ever. While simply not wanting children is a valid reason alone, the pandemic gave many people more reasons than ever to choose not to have a child, or to postpone doing so, from the horrifying health care revealed during the pandemic to the shortage of baby food to sweeping economic fallout. Helpfully, COVID-19 also brought the rise of telemedicine, through which people can now obtain safe and effective medical abortion pills at home (between Zoom coven meetings).

Regarding abortion, the QAnon crowd is generally against it, and they use the "Save the Children" narrative to tell their ghoulish tale that the liberal folks of Washington are all killing babies, drinking their blood, and sometimes fucking them along the way. The idea that Jews drank the blood of children for virility was also a popular conspiracy theory during the Dark Ages. This "secretive cabal" narrative has been anti-Semitic since, well, probably at least Jesus's time. One of QAnon's core beliefs is that there are high-level child-trafficking rings who drain and drink the blood of children, or create a very powerful and potent drug called adrenochrome extracted from live kids' adrenal glands, or both. According to Q, the likes of Hillary Clinton and George Soros, a billionaire Democratic philanthropist, enjoy partaking.

In a since-deleted YouTube video, prominent QAnon believer Liz Crokin stated: "It comes from children. The drug is extracted from the pituitary glands of tortured children. It's sold on the black market. It's the drug of the elites. It is their favorite drug. It is beyond evil. It is demonic. It is so sick," Rothschild reports. It almost sounds like a potion La Voisin would create—and Anton LaVey would pretend that he could.

Adrenochrome does exist. It's a compound naturally occurring in the body, yet it remains relatively underexplored in scientific research, with only a few studies from the mid-twentieth century examining its potential role in conditions like schizophrenia. This substance, which is a bright-violet color, captivated the minds of writers like Aldous Huxley, author of the 1954 book *The Doors of Perception*, who likened it to the psychedelic substance mescaline—although he never tried it (adrenochrome, that is). Hunter S. Thompson also mentioned adrenochrome in his writing, and there's a famous scene in Terry Gilliam's 1998 film adaptation *Fear and Loathing in Las Vegas* in which Thompson, played by fallen icon Johnny Depp, takes it, stating, "There's only one source for this stuff... the adrenaline glands from a living human body. It's no good if you get it out of a corpse."

But perhaps QAnon's most famous theory is Pizzagate, which combines Satanism, pizza, and baby-blood drinking elites. The Satanic Panic didn't die. It just evolved and started serving pizza to enjoy with your baby blood.

Pizzagate is a conspiracy theory that Hillary and Bill Clinton and other "liberal elites" are or were part of a child sex-trafficking ring operated out of the restaurant Comet Ping Pong in DC, where in the basement they engage in occult rituals and have a "pedo code" that refers to young girls as "pizza" and young boys as "hot dogs," Rothschild describes. In reality, Comet Ping Pong *is* owned by a rich, elite guy. James Alefantis is a chef and restaurateur who founded two restaurants, Comet Ping Pong and the American rustic restaurant Buck's Fishing & Camping. In 2012, *GQ* crowned him one of the fifty most powerful people in Washington, DC. He's also openly gay and has received hundreds of death threats.

The Pizzagate conspiracy theory emerged following the release of John Podesta's emails by WikiLeaks. Podesta is currently the senior adviser to the president for clean energy innovation and implementation and previously served as counselor to President Barack Obama and White House chief of staff to Bill Clinton. He chaired Hillary Clinton's campaign for president in 2016. One of the leaked emails was from the Serbian performance artist Marina Abramović, inviting Mr. Podesta to a "Spirit Cooking" dinner at her place. This dragged Abramović into #PizzaGate, where Mr. Podesta was rumored to be part of the supposed child-trafficking operation. (Coincidentally, the artist herself has a history of speaking out about reproductive health care, too. In 2016, Abramović gave an interview, stating, "I had three abortions because I was certain that it would be a disaster for my work. One only has limited energy in the body, and I would have had to divide it.")

Just about everyone who believed in Pizzagate assumed "Spirit Cooking" involved cannibalism, as the event shared its name with Abramović's book and performance, where she showcased on the walls of an Italian gallery whimsical recipes using blood. In reality, she simply prepared basic meals for around twenty patrons of her art institution. Lady Gaga was even pulled into the "Satanic spirit cooking hunt and party" after QAnon shared photos of her with Abramović. "These demonic spirits of witchcraft, sexual perversion, and child sacrifice are seducing too many Christians at an alarming rate," Jeremiah Johnson Ministries posted on Facebook about Biden and Gaga in November 2020, with another user calling Gaga "a high-ranking witch in the music industry." Gaga sang the national anthem at Biden's inauguration.

Years later, in 2020, Abramović reflected on the event, saying, "We had lots of fun. There was no human blood, or baby serving, or sex orgies." She expressed disbelief about the conspiracy narratives that had emerged, commenting that it was "just insane." If I have to hand it to LaVey for something, it's that at least he *actually* spread the joy of cannibalism (even if he never really partook) and hosted rituals that definitely sound like orgies, rather than merely being accused of doing both by a bunch of people who think vaccines can turn us into Wi-Fi hot spots.

Things came to a head in December 2016 when Edgar Maddison Welch of North Carolina took it upon himself to travel to DC and "investigate" Pizzagate himself, firing an AR-15 rifle inside the pizzeria and leaving after finding no evidence of sex trafficking. He pleaded guilty to federal charges of assault with a dangerous weapon and moving a firearm across state lines and was handed a four-year prison sentence.

Comet Ping Pong *has* hosted naughty gatherings—concerts in their back room. Perhaps the most hard-core thing to ever really go down there was metal band Municipal Waste's show in 2011.

3

Organizations such as the controversial Satanic Temple took the devil back from Republicans, turning their own weapon against them, through political campaigns such as *The Statue of Baphomet*. This bronze sculpture of a goat-headed, angel-winged occult figure, crowdfunded in 2014 and unveiled in 2015, symbolizes the use of devil imagery for political advocacy. The Satanic Temple proposed donating it for display on the Oklahoma Capitol grounds in an effort to get the state supreme court to remove the Ten Commandments monument, and, once this actually worked, the Satanic Temple retracted their request to place *Baphomet* on Oklahoma public property. Depending on whom you ask, the Satanic Temple is made up either of trolls known for using the image of Satan to agitate for causes such as freedom of speech or organized Satanists effecting real political change. Within the occult world and internet communities who pay attention to such things, some love them, while others loathe them.

"Satan is a symbol of the Eternal Rebel in opposition to arbitrary authority, forever defending personal sovereignty even in the face of insurmountable odds. Satan is an icon for the unbowed will of the unsilenced inquirer—the heretic who questions sacred laws and rejects all tyrannical impositions," their website reads, where I am directed to during an interview with Satanic priestess, ordained minister within the Satanic Temple, and death doula

Shiva Honey. "Like Anatole France and William Blake, we view this literary Satan as a symbolic liberator that fights against oppression. The Church of Satan and LaVey promoted a sort of authoritarian philosophy rooted in social Darwinism. Our philosophies differ significantly. We strive to effect real cultural and policy change that reflects our values," Shiva tells me.

The Satanic Temple's third tenet is "One's body is inviolable, subject to one's own will alone." In 2023, the Satanic Temple established TST Health, which provides free religious telehealth medication abortion care. When *Roe* was overturned, TST founded the Samuel Alito's Mom's Satanic Abortion Clinic, an online abortion clinic that sends the abortion pill via mail to those in New Mexico who wish to perform the Satanic Temple's Religious Abortion Ritual. The "ritual" involves the recitation of two of their tenets with a personal affirmation that is intertwined with rites associated with the abortion. "Because prerequisite procedures such as waiting periods, mandatory viewing of sonograms, and compulsory counseling contravene Satanists' religious convictions, those who perform the religious abortion ritual are exempt from these requirements and can receive first-trimester abortions on demand in states that have enacted the Religious Freedom Restoration Act," the group's website reads.

On April 23, 2016, members of the Detroit chapter of the TST, then directed by Jex Blackmore, counterprotested the Citizens for a Pro-Life Society's protest of Planned Parenthood. Temple members dressed in BDSM gear, wearing baby masks and diapers while engaging in flagellation, to "expose the anti-choice protest as an act of fetal idolatry, highlighting the fetishization and abstraction of the 'baby.'" Remember the Army of God protesters in the early 1990s in Wichita who crawled like babies outside of clinics in a manner of protest? TST's use of theatrics is inspired by those they wish to challenge.

Jex Blackmore, who uses "they/them" pronouns, is an inter-disciplinary artist, organizer, and activist whose work takes aim at institutions of social and sexual oppression. Raven-haired, with black nail polish and an upside-down pentagram tattooed on their left palm, they have continued their work as a Satanist abortion activist since stepping aside from the Satanic Temple due to ideo-logical differences; as detailed in the 2019 documentary about the group *Hail Satan?* TST maintains that Blackmore made a death threat toward Trump at a nonsanctioned Detroit rally. "The reality is that during a Satanic ritual, billed under my own name and very intentionally unrelated to TST, I said 'Execute the Presidents' as part of a long list of suggested inflammatory direct actions (other proposals included 'release snakes in the Governor's mansion,' and 'storm press conferences')," Jex told me. "They took this to be a sincere threat to the President at the time, who was Trump. What they misunderstood is that I meant ALL presidents. The thought that I would narrow my vision on just one splotch in the rotten glob offends me, as if I would be so naive as to believe that the removal of one President would absolve the system of its sins."

Regardless, Blackmore wins the horned crown for being too hard-core even for Satanists. But don't worry. They have contin-ued their work as a Satanist and abortion activist and are still piss-ing off the anti-choice crowd, too.

Blackmore enraged conservatives and broke the internet when they took the abortion pill live on FOX in January 2022 to termi-nate a pregnancy in an effort to demonstrate how safe medical abortions are and, as their enemies did for centuries, use their Satanist cred to bring attention to the issue. "It was a wild ride, in part because I had no idea it was going to get as much attention as it did," Blackmore tells me. Before the FOX interview, they had just been collaborating on a guerrilla poster campaign in Detroit with the national organization Shout Your Abortion. Members from that organization took mifepristone outside of the Supreme Court a few years earlier, which Blackmore found inspiring. "When I was invited onto the television debate to discuss the availability of mail-order abortion pills, I thought that it would be an opportunity to demonstrate the ease and effectiveness of the medication," they continued. "Taking the medication on live TV, especially a FOX affiliate, allowed the message to reach folks who normally would not be exposed to information about medical mail-order abortion. I think this action was tremendously successful given that goal."

The rules around who can obtain mifepristone, and how, are in a whirlwind of change across the United States, moving too quickly to keep up with from the time of reporting to when this text finds its way into readers' hands. As of August 2023, a federal appeals court panel said that the abortion pill should remain legal in the United States but recommended significant restrictions on patients' access to it, gearing up for a blowout before the Supreme Court. Thankfully, in June 2024, the Supreme Court threw out the lawsuit attempting to restrict access to mifepristone, protecting the abortion pill.

Medical abortions have been on the scene in the United States since 2000. You can do it from the comfort of your own home (or live on FOX). By 2020, more than half of all abortions in the United States, rising from 39 percent in 2017, were nonsurgical, medication abortions. The biggest risk surrounding the abortion pill is that, with increased regulation and scrutiny, people are scared to seek this safe, proven, and effective treatment and instead seek out unsafe alternatives. (Misoprostol can be purchased from veterinarian and pet pharmacy stores online, as it also can treat arthritis and ulcers in dogs.) And after taking mifepristone and misoprostol, should you experience a side effect such as prolonged bleeding and want to see a doctor, here's an important fact: the medication won't show up on any tests (hail Satan). You don't have to tell them you have induced a miscarriage; any blood-work results will be the same as if one just happened on its own.

If you do get a medication abortion, ideally, you shouldn't be alone when you take it. Drink plenty of water, take pain relievers as needed, and if possible have someone around to assist you while the process is ongoing. While some places offer sedation such as nitrous oxide during surgical abortions, medical abortions typically continue the theme of Eve's curse, and no additional painkillers are prescribed, leading many people to seek out relief for the considerable pain through backchannels or simply grin and bear it.

Blackmore is also an abortion doula. While they can confidently say that the abortion pills are both safe and effective, they note that experiences with pain vary from those similar to intense period cramps to acute, grueling pain. "For the latter, I would describe it as a deep throbbing punctuated by a prolonged, searing wrenching in the uterus," Blackmore says. "Everyone should take painkillers of some kind if they are able. It's challenging to fight for pain management when we are barely holding on to access to medication to begin with, and I think that points to the project of punishing pregnant people. Pain and suffering are part of the design to control our bodies."

Herbal abortions can still be found within the witch and pagan communities, including through Sister Zeus, an information hub that highlights our old friends cotton root bark and pennyroyal (one of the more toxic choices available). And the controversial herbalist Susun Weed, a high priestess of Dianic Wicca and a known name to most modern pagans, writes about using jack-in-the-pulpit root as a sterility promoter, while also noting that one must be careful, as it can be toxic and even lethal. *Vice* reports that Weed allows only women (by her definition) to come study with her, but many people in the herbalist and witch communities have turned against her due to abuse allegations. (In 2018 she was charged with criminal obstruction of breathing and blood circulation when she was accused of choking a student for incorrectly tying a bag of lettuce.) Weed seems proud of her anger, telling *Vice*, "It's not for everyone to be a shaman."

Many people understandably are concerned about how to obtain a surgical abortion in the post-*Roe* world. While medical abortions put the procedure in your hands, that also means that you have to go through painful cramping and heavy bleeding at home, as opposed to a visit to a doctor's office. Surgical abortions can take a shorter amount of time and be more effective. As these are the forms that are most on the table, there are those following in Pat Maginnis's footsteps and teaching civilians to perform them themselves. (You should know by now that, historically, doctors were far from the only ones to perform abortions.)

Papaya workshops, created by the Bixby Center for Global Reproductive Health, of the University of California, San Francisco, are events where people can practice nonmedication-based abortions outside a medical setting. Instructors use papayas to teach you how to perform your own medical abortion. (Although please, please, *please* just get one from a medical professional if you can.) The fruit makes an excellent learning tool, as the papaya is about the same shape and size as the uterus and is filled with seeds. And it's not an arbitrary choice of fruit: in witchcraft, the papaya is often used in cleansing and banishing spells. But papayas are used for more than just practicing abortions. They are considered one of the safest herbal emmenagogues, used by folks all over the world, including India, South America, and Africa. The seeds and unripe fruit are thought to reinstate menstruation, according to Sam Wise's *Sacred Choice: Paganism, Witchcraft, and Reproductive Justice*, which advises eating one unripe papaya every day of the week leading up to your period or consuming one to two tablespoons of fresh seeds or one to two teaspoons of dried seeds three times a day for six days.

To regain and preserve reproductive rights and body autonomy, we must keep voting for pro-choice candidates—with the understanding that it might be time to turn to your community rather than federal legislators. Arguing that people can "vote with their feet," or simply relocate to states with more favorable policies, is absurd. Teenagers without money can't. Poor trans people can't. Moving is expensive, and let's not forget April Matson, the two-spirit who had to sleep in a tent in 2016 to cross state lines from South Dakota to Colorado to obtain an abortion.

When asked what the most efficient form of abortion activism is, Blackmore responds:

> Abortion is a community responsibility and we need to build autonomous, locally organized networks of support. Yes, we need the big dogs to fight against anti-abortion legislation in the courts, but as far as I can see, the political movement has the resources it needs. It has millions of dollars at its disposal, and a population that's in favor of abortion access; and they've still failed to protect access. We are figuring out how to get abortion through the mail, legal or not. We are stocking up on birth control and Plan B. We are finding ways of having safe abortions, no need for the coat hanger, self-managed, and at home. The movement is learning how to care for itself, how to innovate, and how to focus on the people who matter most. This is how we meet needs as quickly as possible.

It's what makes them a proud member of the left-handed path. "Thelema, The Church of Satan, and The Satanic Temple have each posited their organization as law-abiding and supportive of the established order, transgressive only in their limited perception of personal sexual expression and celebration of minor profanities," Blackmore laments. "Each of these groups have advocated for members to support and respect the laws of the state, despite often being laws which perpetuate tyranny and inequality, and point to the justice system as the appropriate avenue for political dissent—which is a corrupt, failed institution which has historically supported religious despotism, Christian privilege, racism, homophobia, and state violence—demonstrating their inability to recognize how they uphold and maintain oppressive social structures that benefit the institution of the church and the tyranny of the state."

We need a radically different approach to reproductive rights than the one we've been coasting on. To get there, people who identify as witches and are seriously interested in changing the world must reckon with the fact that we can't blame it all on Trump or anyone in the government. Hillary Clinton isn't a devil worshiper who sells sex with children out of DC pizza shops and owes her continued existence to their adrenal glands, but she's not necessarily our friend, either. Going forward, we need a plan that calls back to the outcasts: the community of the witch, the coven; the knowledge and care of the midwife; and a narrative free from heaven and hell so we can empower everyone to enjoy life on earth.

CONCLUSION

W e've journeyed through the vast expanse of human history, so what's next? Jex is spot-on: Many politicians really suck at their jobs, and a return to community organizing on a local level, outside of the government, is a must. But if we don't get active and consistently vote, too—especially in local elections—the anti-choice movement will keep gaining ground. As states methodically curtail abortion access, masterminded by Republican lawmakers and their fervently religious backers, we're left to wonder about the road ahead.

From Ramses the Great, who fathered more than one hundred children and donned eye shadow made of gemstones, to out-of-touch Supreme Court justices making critical decisions based on an Anglophile who burned witches and advocated for rape within marriage, it's evident some leaders lack insight. And while throwing around insults like "baskets of deplorables" might be momentarily satisfying, history shows it can cost votes. It's crucial to engage directly with our communities, overcome divisions, and rally our allies.

"Recognizing your privilege" might sound trite, but it is vital to be aware of our rights and responsibilities within this movement. Even pro-life activists are doing it. Familiarize yourself with your state laws, engage with your community, and understand who's most affected by legal changes so you can direct your mutual aid there. From Cleopatra's costumes to QAnon's online forums, our tales and experiences are interconnected, whether we're learning that tenets of the reproductive justice movement, such as believing in the rights both to have children and to prevent or end a pregnancy, are ancient concepts, not new ones, or we're reflecting on how Elon Musk's twelve kids and counting make him powerful, while a poor Black family who wanted the same number of off-spring would be frowned upon and stop receiving the aid required to care for them. It would be naive to assume that issues like trans women's rights or the forced sterilization of immigrant women in ICE facilities won't impact those of us who don't belong to those identities. Consider your privilege as a form of power: What can you achieve from where you are?

Recall the Salem resident who claimed to see a dozen "radiant jellyfish," likely due to poor eyesight and possibly influenced by hallucinogens. Today, we have optometrists, so the same ignorance isn't excusable. While challenges like anti-abortion and anti-drag laws and educational restrictions persist, we're also witnessing a normalization of psychedelics, which are evolving from a fringe drug to almost mainstream. If LSD can rebrand itself from hippie hogwash to basically a form of elitist performance enhancer, maybe we can change some narratives too and one day win the fight for reproductive justice.

Eve's curse is real only because the people in charge said it was. Society's norms and dictates are often set by those in power, but the tides are shifting. Now, one can proudly identify as a witch or Satanist and capitalize on it. No one's going to burn you. However, they might team up and get politically organized with others who share their viewpoints on abortion and take down *Roe*, which we should have realized was flimsy AF, while you're busy knitting a millennial pink pussyhat.

Reproductive oppression and witch hunts have always been intertwined. In antiquity, the 1 percent wanted lower classes to reproduce to ensure there were plenty of soldiers. We relate to this today, as many folks feel that the government wants to control the population to ensure there are plenty of workers (although the nation's leading economists insist that criminalizing abortion is terrible for the workforce). While a higher-up like Ramses the

Great likely had help with child care for his hundred kids, other classes found a way to invoke religious rites through life forces such as the Nile to plan their families on their own terms, long before the birth of religions that split family planning into two solid camps: anti-choice or pro-choice. As antiquity bled into the Middle Ages and even the so-called Enlightenment, perhaps out of fear of death that stemmed from the plague and (in a story that's getting really old) joined with misogyny and anti-Semitism, oppressors like the inquisitors found an outlet for their hatred in the concept of witches.

By the time Europeans began to colonize North America, such hatred, which was rooted in fear, didn't die out. It transformed like a cruel spell and played out in the atrocities committed against enslaved and Indigenous people. One doesn't need to do much research on the persecution of such communities, their conjuring traditions, and the reproductive violence inflicted on them to realize that while what happened in Salem was over-the-top and tragic, it almost starts to feel like a red herring for the *really* scary witch hunts of the era.

Despite their legacies, the men often enshrined in occult history as the scariest of scaries, such as Crowley and LaVey, frankly don't always deserve the pearl-clutching reputation that conservatives give them. They, themselves, penned writing that, at least by today's standards, is conservative when it comes to abortion rather than the pro-baby-eating spell books the Right would have you believe. They say the greatest trick the devil ever played was convincing the world that he did not exist. Evil is very real, but its hiding place is not with those who proclaim the left-handed path. That is *far* too obvious. This is why this book exists: to draw attention to Ray Buckey, unfairly persecuted, and Madame Restell, a badass until recently almost as lost to history as the true authorship behind the works of Trota of Salerno.

Words have power. Spells can work. Education is the first step to enlightenment.

In the spirit of the reproductive justice movement, this book aims to stir you into action. But amid the work and activism, don't forget to find joy. If Nancy Reagan could rely on astrology for presidential flight schedules, you're allowed to indulge in your horoscope.

And we really, really need to bring back dancing naked in the woods.

SOURCES

CHAPTER 1

Armstrong, Kate J. "Blood Magic: A History of Menstruation." *The Exploress*, June 8, 2022. www.theexploresspodcast.com/episodes/2021/7/28 /blood-magic-a-brief-history-of-menstruation.

Baker, Patty. "Abortion." In *Oxford Classical Dictionary*, December 22, 2015. https://oxfordre.com/classics/display/10.1093/acrefore/9780199381135.001 .0001/acrefore-9780199381135-e-4;jsessionid=A4D6D1E2E30C7B7777FA 55047A8FCCDE.

The Book of the Dead. London: Department of Egyptian and Assyrian Antiquities, British Museum, 1920.

Brazan, Madison. "Controlling Their Bodies: Ancient Roman Women and Contraceptives." *Journal of Undergraduate Research & Scholarly Work*. Accessed October 20, 2023. https://provost.utsa.edu/undergraduate -research/journal/files/vol4/JURSW.Brazan.COLFA.revised.pdf.

Brown, Eric. *Ancient History: A Concise Overview of Ancient Egypt, Ancient Greece, and Ancient Rome—Including the Egyptian Mythology, the Byzantine Empire and the Roman Republic*. North Haven, CT: Guy Saloniki, 2019.

Callan, Maeve B. "Of Vanishing Fetuses and Maidens Made-Again: Abortion, Restored Virginity, and Similar Scenarios in Medieval Irish Hagiography and Penitentials." *Journal of the History of Sexuality* 21, no. 2 (2012): 282–296. https://doi.org/10.1353/sex.2012.0031.

"Christian Living." For Christian Eyes Only, March 26, 2019. www.forchristianeyesonly.com/christian-living/.

Conaboy, Chelsea. "She Started Selling Abortion Pills Online. Then the Feds Showed Up." *Mother Jones*, February 11, 2019. www.motherjones.com /politics/2019/02/she-started-selling-abortion-pills-online-then-the-feds -showed-up/.

Davis, Henry. *Creating Christianity: A Weapon of Ancient Rome*. London: Independent Publishing Network, 2020.

De Witte, Melissa. "Using Economics to Understand the Wide-Reaching Impacts of Overturning *Roe v. Wade*." *Stanford News*, July 18, 2022. https://news.stanford.edu/2022/07/18/using-economics-understand-wide -reaching-impacts-overturning-roe-v-wade/.

Gannon, Mega. "King Tut's Parents Were Cousins, Not Siblings: Researcher." Live Science, October 24, 2022. www.livescience.com/27106-king-tut -parents-were-cousins.html.

Habiger, Petra. "Menstruation, Menstrual Hygiene and Woman's Health in Ancient Egypt." Museum of Menstruation and Women's Health, 1998. www.mum.org/germnt5.htm.

Hamm, Andrew. "*Dobbs v. Jackson Women's Health Organization*." SCOTUSblog. Accessed April 23, 2023. www.scotusblog.com/case-files/cases /dobbs-v-jackson-womens-health-organization/.

Herman, Eleanor. "A Brief History of Calling Women Witches: Eleanor Herman on the Patriarchy's Timeless Demonization of Powerful Women." Literary Hub, September 19, 2022. https://lithub.com/a-brief-history-of -calling-women-witches/.

Hippocrates. *Generation; Nature of the Child; Diseases 4; Nature of Women and Barrenness*. Translated by Paul Potter. Cambridge, MA: Harvard University Press, 2012.

"Hippocratic Oath." In *Encyclopædia Britannica*. Accessed April 23, 2023. www.britannica.com/topic/Hippocratic-oath.

"Jul 16, 1054 CE: Great Schism." National Geographic Society, May 20, 2022. https://education.nationalgeographic.org/resource/great-schism/.

King, Arienne. "Family Planning in Greco-Roman Antiquity." In *World History Encyclopedia*, September 27, 2022. www.worldhistory.org/article/2024 /family-planning-in-greco-roman-antiquity/.

Major, Ralph H. "The Papyrus Ebers." In *Annals of Medical History*, 1930. www.ncbi.nlm.nih.gov/pmc/articles/PMC7945839/.

Mark, Joshua J. "Orosius." In *World History Encyclopedia*, April 3, 2019. www.worldhistory.org/Orosius/.

Marty, Robin. *New Handbook for a Post-*Roe *America: The Complete Guide to Abortion Legality, Access, and Practical Support*. New York: Seven Stories Press, 2021.

Matt, Daniel Chanan, trans. *The Zohar: Pritzker Edition*. Stanford, CA: Stanford University Press, 2004.

Muramoto, Osamu. "Solving the Socratic Problem: A Contribution from Medicine." *Mouseion: Journal of the Classical Association of Canada* 15, no. 3 (2018): 445–473. muse.jhu.edu/article/717955.

"On Midwifery and the Diseases of Women." In *Encyclopædia Britannica*. Accessed April 23, 2023. www.britannica.com/topic/On-Midwifery-and -the-Diseases-of-Women.

Oria, Shelly. Essay in *I Know What's Best for You: Stories on Reproductive Freedom*. San Francisco: McSweeney's, 2022.

Orosius, Paulus. *The Seven Books of History Against the Pagans*. Translated by Roy Joseph Deferrari. Washington, DC: Catholic University of America Press, 2001.

Packman, Zola M. "Rape and Consequences in the Latin Declamations." *Studies in Classical Antiquity* 8, no. 1 (1999). https://journals.co.za/doi/abs/10.10520/EJC100435.

Planned Parenthood. "What Is the Effectiveness of the Pull Out Method?" Accessed October 20, 2023. www.plannedparenthood.org/learn/birth-control/withdrawal-pull-out-method/how-effective-is-withdrawal-method-pulling-out.

Plato. *Charmides.* Translated by Thomas G. West and Grace Starry West. Indianapolis: Hackett, 1986.

Plutarch. *Life of Antony.* Edited by C. B. R. Pelling. Cambridge: Cambridge University Press, 1988.

Pollack, Rachel. *Seventy-Eight Degrees of Wisdom: A Book of Tarot.* San Francisco: Red Wheel/Weiser, 2007.

Potts, Malcolm. "History of Birth Control." In *Encyclopædia Britannica.* Accessed October 20, 2023. www.britannica.com/science/birth-control/History-of-birth-control.

Riddle, John M. *Eve's Herbs: A History of Contraception and Abortion in the West.* Cambridge, MA: Harvard University Press, 1997.

"*Roe v. Wade* (1973)." Legal Information Institute. Accessed April 23, 2023. www.law.cornell.edu/wex/roe_v_wade_%281973%29.

"The Septuagint: LXX." Home—The Septuagint: LXX. Accessed April 24, 2023. www.septuagint.bible/home#.

Shakespeare, William. *The Tragedy of Julius Caesar.* Edited by Barbara A. Mowat and Paul Werstine. New York: Simon & Schuster Paperbacks, 2011.

Smith, Lesley. "The Kahun Gynaecological Papyrus: Ancient Egyptian Medicine." *BMJ Sexual & Reproductive Health* 37, no. 1 (2011). https://srh.bmj.com/content/37/1/54.

"Socrates." In *Stanford Encyclopedia of Philosophy,* May 26, 2002. https://plato.stanford.edu/entries/socrates/#SocStr.

Stensvold, Anne. *A History of Pregnancy in Christianity: From Original Sin to Contemporary Abortion Debates.* New York: Routledge, Taylor & Francis Group, 2015.

This Day in History. "The Battle of Actium." History.com. Accessed March 6, 2024. www.history.com/this-day-in-history/the-battle-of-actium.

Wasson, Donald L. "Constantine I." In *World History Encyclopedia,* April 19, 2013. www.worldhistory.org/Constantine_I/.

Wise, Sam. *Sacred Choice: Paganism, Witchcraft, and Reproductive Justice.* Independently published, 2022.

CHAPTER 2

Barrett, Thomas M., ed. "Pope Sixtus V." In *Catholic Encyclopedia*, 2021. www.newadvent.org/cathen/14033a.htm.

Bell, Keaton. "Paris Hilton on Her Revealing New Documentary: 'I'm Not a Dumb Blonde. I'm Just Really Good at Pretending to Be One.'" *Vogue*, September 15, 2020. www.vogue.com/article/paris-hilton-talks-about -her-new-documentary.

"Birth Control and Abortion in the Middle Ages." Medievalists.net, June 24, 2022. www.medievalists.net/2013/12/birth-control-and-abortion-in-the -middle-ages/.

Boguet, Henry. *An Examen of Witches Drawn from Various Trials of Many of This Sect in the District of Saint Oyan de Joux Commonly Known as Saint Claude in the County of Burgundy Including the Procedure Necessary to a Judge in Trials for Witchcraft*. Edited by Montague Summers. 1929. Reprint, Mineola, NY: Dover, 2009.

Boon, Donald. "Apostolicae Sedis Moderationi." In *Catholic Encyclopedia*. Accessed May 29, 2023. www.newadvent.org/cathen/01645a.htm. The text is found in Acta Pii IX (Rome, 1871), I, V, 55–72, and frequently in manuals of moral theology and canon law.

Broedel, Hans Peter. *The "Malleus Maleficarum" and the Construction of Witchcraft Theology and Popular Belief*. Manchester: Manchester University Press, 2009.

Christian, Helen. "Plague and Persecution: The Black Death and Early Modern Witch-Hunts." American University Digital Research Archive, April 27, 2011. https://dra.american.edu/islandora/object/1011capstones%3A96 /datastream/PDF/view.

Costagliola, Michel. "Fires in History: The Cathar Heresy, the Inquisition and Brulology." Annals of Burns and Fire Disasters, September 30, 2015. www.ncbi.nlm.nih.gov/pmc/articles/PMC4883611/#:~:text=The%20 Cathars%20are%20among%20the,the%20stake%20on%20huge% 20pyres.

Damousi, Joy. "Fleas to Flu to Coronavirus: How 'Death Ships' Spread Disease Through the Ages." *Conversation*, May 15, 2023. https://theconversation.com/fleas-to-flu-to-coronavirus-how-death -ships-spread-disease-through-the-ages-137061.

Editors of Encyclopedia Britannica. "Cathari." In *Encyclopædia Britannica*, August 9, 2007. www.britannica.com/topic/Cathari.

Ehrenreich, Barbara, and Deidre English. *Witches, Midwives & Nurses: A History of Women Healers*. 1973. Reprint, New York: Feminist Press at the City University of New York, 2010.

Faust, Drew. "Statement on 'Black Mass.'" Harvard, Office of the President, May 12, 2014.

Federici, Silvia. *Witches, Witch-Hunting, and Women*. Oakland, CA: PM Press, 2018.

Franc, Martin Le. *Le champion des dames*. Edited by Robert Deschaux. 5 vols. Paris: H. Champion, 1999.

Frith, John. "Syphilis: Its Early History and Treatment Until Penicillin and the Debate on Its Origins." *Journal of Military and Veterans' Health* 20, no. 4 (2012). https://doi.org/https://doi-ds.org/doilink/11.2021-47955651 /JMVH Vol 20 No 4.

Green, Monica Helen, trans. *The Trotula: An English Translation of the Medieval Compendium of Women's Medicine*. Philadelphia: University of Pennsylvania Press, 2002.

History.com Editors. "Black Death: Causes, Symptoms & Impact." History.com, September 17, 2010. www.history.com/topics/middle-ages/black-death.

"The History of Romance." National Women's History Museum, February 13, 2017. www.womenshistory.org/articles/history-romance#:~:text= During%20the%2018th%20century,clans%20and%20to%20consolidate %20fortunes.

Institoris, Heinrich, Jakob Sprenger, and Montague Summers. *Malleus Maleficarum*. Lawrence, KS: Digireads, 2009.

Larner, Christina. *Witchcraft and Religion: The Politics of Popular Belief*. 1984. Reprint, Oxford: Blackwell, 1987.

Lemay, Helen Rodnite. *Women's Secrets: A Translation of Pseudo–Albertus Magnus's "De Secretis Mulierum" with Commentaries*. Albany: State University of New York, 1992.

Liu, Edward C., and Wen W. Shen. "Updated July 20, 2022: The Hyde Amendment, an Overview—CRS Reports." Congressional Research Service, July 20, 2022. https://crsreports.congress.gov/product/pdf/IF/IF12167.

Monet, Dolores. "History of the Mourning Dress: Black Clothing Worn During Bereavement." Bellatory, April 10, 2022. https://bellatory.com/fashion -industry/FashionHistoryMourningDressBlackClothingWornDuring Bereavement.

Müller, Wolfgang P. *The Criminalization of Abortion in the West: Its Origins in Medieval Law*. 2012. Reprint, Ithaca, NY: Cornell University Press, 2017.

Pruitt, Sarah. "Why Do Witches Ride Brooms? The History Behind the Legend." History.com, October 19, 2021. www.history.com/news/why-witches -fly-on-brooms.

Reagan, Leslie J. *When Abortion Was a Crime: Women, Medicine, and Law in the United States, 1867–1973*. Berkeley: University of California Press, 1997.

Reyes, Natalie. "Skeleton Key Shop—About." Skeleton Key Shop, 2023. https://skeletonkeyshop.com/pages/about-us.

Rodilla, Vincent, and Alicia López-Castellano. "Salernitan Women." *Hektoen International, an Online Medical Humanities Journal* (January 3, 2022). https://hekint.org/2020/10/14/salernitan-women/.

Stensvold, Anne. *A History of Pregnancy in Christianity: From Original Sin to Contemporary Abortion Debates*. London: Routledge, 2015.

Stork, Nancy P. "Inquisition Records of Jacques Fournier: An On-going English Translation of the Inquisition Records of Jacques Fournier, Bishop of Pamiers, France, 1318–1325." San Jose State University, February 22, 2023. www.sjsu.edu/people/nancy.stork/jacquesfournier/.

Toomer, Jessica. "La Voisin, France's Murderous Fortune Teller." SYFY Official Site, October 22, 2021. www.syfy.com/syfy-wire/la-voisin-frances-murderous-fortune-teller.

Zimmer, Carl. "Did the 'Black Death' Really Kill Half of Europe? New Research Says No." *New York Times*, February 10, 2022. www.nytimes.com/2022/02/10/science/black-death.html#:~:text=The%20%E2%80%9CBlack%20Death%E2%80%9D%20is%20one,of%20people%20across%20the%20continent.

CHAPTER 3

"Africans in America, Part 2: Religion and Slavery." PBS Resource Bank. Accessed August 2023. www.pbs.org/wgbh/aia/part2/2narr2.html.

Alexander, Kathy. "Reverend Samuel Parris of Salem Village, Massachusetts." Legends of America, December 2022. www.legendsofamerica.com/ma-samuelparris/.

Alvarado, Denise. *Witch Queens, Voodoo Spirits & Hoodoo Saints: A Guide to Magical New Orleans*. Newburyport, MA: Weiser Books, 2022.

"Ann Foster Home, Site Of." Salem Witch Museum. Accessed March 13, 2024. https://salemwitchmuseum.com/locations/ann-foster-home-site-of/.

Austin, Beth. "1619: Virginia's First Africans." Hampton History Museum, December 2018. https://hampton.gov/DocumentCenter/View/24075/1619-Virginias-First-Africans.

Beck, Abaki, and Rosalyn Lapier. "For Indigenous Peoples, Abortion Is a Religious Right." *Yes! Magazine*, June 30, 2022. www.yesmagazine.org/opinion/2022/06/30/abortion-indigenous-peoples-reproductive-health.

"Bible Gateway Passage: Exodus 22:18—King James Version." Bible Gateway. Accessed August 13, 2023. www.biblegateway.com/passage/?search=exodus+22%3A18&version=KJV.

SOURCES

Blakemore, Erin. "The Criminalization of Abortion Began as a Business Tactic." History.com, January 22, 2018. www.history.com/news/the-criminalization-of-abortion-began-as-a-business-tactic.

Boomer, Lee. "The Middle Passage." Women & the American Story, February 8, 2023. https://wams.nyhistory.org/early-encounters/spanish-colonies/the-middle-passage/.

"Brainerd Mission." University of Tennessee at Chattanooga Finding Aids. Accessed August 13, 2023. https://findingaids.utc.edu/agents/corporate_entities/17.

Chireau, Yvonne Patricia. *Black Magic: Religion and the African American Conjuring Tradition*. Berkeley: University of California Press, 2006.

Christiansen, Jill. "The Salem Witch Trials Memorial: Finding Humanity in Tragedy." Smithsonian Center for Folklife and Cultural Heritage, October 27, 2022. https://folklife.si.edu/magazine/salem-witch-trials-memorial.

Chuck, Elizabeth, and Haimy Assefa. "She Hoped to Shine a Light on Maternal Mortality Among Native Americans. Instead, She Became a Statistic of It." NBCNews.com, February 8, 2020. www.nbcnews.com/news/us-news/she-hoped-shine-light-maternal-mortality-among-native-americans-instead-n1131951.

"*Coffin v. United States*, 156 U.S. 432 (1895)." Justia Law. Accessed August 2023. https://supreme.justia.com/cases/federal/us/156/432/.

"Congressional Record: Indian Health Care Improvement Act Amendments of 2007; Congressional Record Vol. 154, No. 31." Congress.gov, 2008. www.congress.gov/congressional-record/volume-168/issue-154/senate-section.

Conway, George A., and John C. Slocumb. "Plants Used as Abortifacients and Emmenagogues by Spanish New Mexicans." *Journal of Ethnopharmacology* 1, no. 3 (1979): 241–261. https://doi.org/10.1016/s0378-8741(79)80014-8.

Corbett, Bob. "Re: 13115: Potteryrn Wondering About Abortion and Vodou (Fwd)." Bob Corbett's Haiti Page, September 14, 2002. http://faculty.webster.edu/corbetre/public_html/haiti-archive-new/msg13078.html.

Culpepper, Karen J. "*Gossypium spp.* (Cotton Root Bark): A Symbol of Herbal Resistance." American Herbalists Guild. Accessed August 2023. https://americanherbalistsguild.com/sites/americanherbalistsguild.com/files/jahg_autumn_2017_final_cotton_root_culpepper.pdf.

"Dawes Act (1887)." National Archives and Records Administration. Accessed August 11, 2023. www.archives.gov/milestone-documents/dawes-act.

Dayton, Cornelia Hughes. "Taking the Trade: Abortion and Gender Relations in an Eighteenth-Century New England Village." Omohundro Institute of

Early American History and Culture, January 1991. www.jstor.org/stable/2937996.

Dine, Ranana. "Scarlet Letters: Getting the History of Abortion and Contraception Right." Center for American Progress, October 31, 2022. www.americanprogress.org/article/scarlet-letters-getting-the-history-of-abortion-and-contraception-right/.

"Dorcas Hoar Home, Site Of." Salem Witch Museum. Accessed December 9, 2019. https://salemwitchmuseum.com/locations/dorcas-hoar-home-site-of/.

"Early Choctaw History." National Parks Service. Accessed August 8, 2023. www.nps.gov/natr/learn/historyculture/choctaw.htm.

Ehrenreich, Barbara, and Deidre English. *Witches, Midwives & Nurses: A History of Women Healers*. 1973. Reprint, New York: Feminist Press at the City University of New York, 2010.

Evans, Jules. "Occult Eugenics and the Hermetic Order of the Golden Dawn." *Medium*, December 10, 2021. https://julesevans.medium.com/6-dune-the-hermetic-order-of-the-golden-dawn-and-occult-eugenics-8a6f0d3e04e7.

Fandrich, Ina Johanna. *Mysterious Voodoo Queen Marie: A Study of Powerful Female Leadership in Nineteenth Century New Orleans*. London: Routledge, 2014.

"Federally Recognized Indian Tribes and Resources for Native Americans." USA.gov. Accessed August 13, 2023. www.usa.gov/tribes.

Federici, Silvia. *Witches, Witch-Hunting, and Women*. Oakland, CA: PM Press, 2018.

Fourmy, Signe Peterson. "'She Had Smothered Her Baby on Purpose': Enslaved Women and Maternal Resistance." Age of Revolutions, July 25, 2022. https://ageofrevolutions.com/2022/07/25/she-had-smothered-her-baby-on-purpose-enslaved-women-and-maternal-resistance/.

"Goldenrod." In *Encyclopædia Britannica*. Accessed August 12, 2023. www.britannica.com/plant/goldenrod.

Gonzales, Nicolle. "Placenta & Umbilical Cord Ceremonies: Ancestral Knowledge in a Contemporary World." Indigenous Goddess Gang, January 10, 2019. www.indigenousgoddessgang.com/home-1/2018/12/9/placenta-amp-umbilical-cord-ceremonies-ancestral-knowledge-in-a-contemporary- world.

Grantham, Bill. *Creation Myths and Legends of the Creek Indians*. Gainesville: University Press of Florida, 2002.

Greenberg, Jon. "Politifact—Jon Stewart: Slave Trade Caused 5 Million Deaths." Politifact, March 18, 2014. www.politifact.com/factchecks/2014/mar/18/jon-stewart/jon-stewart-slave-trade-caused-5-million-deaths/.

Guns, Germs & Steel. "The Story of . . . Smallpox—and Other Deadly Eurasian Germs." PBS, 2005. www.pbs.org/gunsgermssteel/variables/smallpox .html.

Gurr, Barbara. Essay in *Reproductive Justice: The Politics of Health Care for Native American Women*. New Brunswick, NJ: Rutgers University Press, 2015.

Haile, Nardos. "Why You Should Rethink Burning Sage and Smudging in the New Year." Salon, January 1, 2024. www.salon.com/2024/01/01 /burning-sage-smudging-alternatives/.

Hand, Greg. "The Story of Cincinnati's Very Own Voodoo Doctor," *Cincinnati Magazine*, December 8, 2022. www.cincinnatimagazine.com/article /the-story-of-cincinnatis-very-own-voodoo-doctor/.

Harvard University. "History." Harvard University, July 19, 2023. www.harvard.edu/about/history/.

Hutcheson, Cory Thomas. *Llewellyn's Complete Book of North American Folk Magic: A Landscape of Magic, Mystery, and Tradition*. Woodbury, MN: Llewellyn, 2023.

Jezerniczky, Luca. "Prostitution, Social Class and Legal Regulation in the History of Makeup." *Oxford Student*, June 7, 2017. www.oxfordstudent.com /2017/06/07/prostitution-social-class-legal-regulation-history-makeup/.

"John Smith." Jamestown Rediscovery: Historic Jamestowne. Accessed March 18, 2024. https://historicjamestowne.org/history/pocahontas/ john-smith/.

Johnson, Michael P. "Runaway Slaves and the Slave Communities in South Carolina, 1799 to 1830." *William and Mary Quarterly* 38, no. 3 (1981): 418. https://doi.org/10.2307/1921955.

Keckeisen, Katie. *Beyond the Veil: Spiritualism in the 19th Century*. Edited by Karlena Barbosa. CAPRA, O. Henry Museum, Brush Square Museums, Austin Parks & Recreation, City of Austin, 2018. Online exhibit, October 2018.

Kilpatrick, Alan. *The Night Has a Naked Soul: Witchcraft and Sorcery Among the Western Cherokee*. Syracuse, NY: Syracuse University Press, 1997.

Kimama, Hakidonmuya. *13 in 1: The Authentic Native American Herbalist's Bible*. Independently published, 2023.

Knox, Howard A. "Measuring Human Intelligence." *Scientific American*, January 9, 1915. www.scientificamerican.com/article/measuring -human-intelligence/.

Kozhimannil, Katy B., Julia D. Interrante, Alena N. Tofte, and Lindsay K. Admon. "Severe Maternal Morbidity and Mortality Among Indigenous Women in the United States." *Obstetrics & Gynecology* 135, no. 2 (2020): 294–300. https://doi.org/10.1097/aog.0000000000003647.

Law Students for Reproductive Justice. "If You Really Care About Reproductive Justice, You Should Care About Transgender Rights." Law Students for Reproductive Justice, September 2015. https://nwlc.org/wp-content /uploads/2015/08/rj_and_transgender_fact_sheet.pdf.

Lewis, Thomas. "Transatlantic Slave Trade." In *Encyclopædia Britannica*, July 7, 2023. www.britannica.com/money/topic/transatlantic-slave-trade.

Linder, Douglas O. "Cotton Mather." Famous Trials. Accessed August 2023. https://famous-trials.com/salem/2037-sal-bmat.

Marty, Robin. *New Handbook for a Post-Roe America: The Complete Guide to Abortion Legality, Access, and Practical Support*. New York: Seven Stories Press, 2021.

Mather, Cotton. *Memorable Providences, Relating to Witchcrafts and Possessions*. Accessed August 2023. http://law2.umkc.edu/faculty/projects /ftrials/salem/ASA_MATH.HTM.

Mills, Richard. "Remarks at a UN General Assembly Commemorative Meeting for the Intl Day of Remembrance of the Victims of Slavery and Transatlantic Slave Trade." United States Mission to the United Nations, March 25, 2021. https://usun.usmission.gov/remarks-at-a-un-general-assembly -commemorative-meeting-for-the-intl-day-of-remembrance-of-the -victims-of-slavery-and-transatlantic-slave-trade/.

Nowak, Donna M. "Women, the Church and Equality: The Religious Paradox." Master's thesis, State University of New York, Buffalo State College, 2016.

O'Brien, Sam. "Remembering 'Witch Cakes,' the Evil-Fighting Baked Goods of the 1600s." *Atlas Obscura*, September 30, 2022. www.atlasobscura.com /articles/what-are-witch-cakes.

Offences Against the Person Act. 2010. www.law.cornell.edu/women-and -justice/resource/offences_against_the_person_act.

OnHisOwnTrip. "Ten Interesting Facts About Angola." On His Own Trip, March 27, 2023. https://onhisowntrip.com/ten-interesting-facts-about -angola/.

Phillips, Kimberly. "Abortion in Colonial America: A Time of Herbal Remedies and Accepted Actions." UConn Today, August 22, 2022. https://today .uconn.edu/2022/08/abortion-in-colonial-america-a-time-of-herbal -remedies-and-accepted-actions/.

The Pluralism Project. "Vodou, Serving the Spirits." Harvard University, 2020. https://hwpi.harvard.edu/files/pluralism/files/vodou-serving_the _spirits_0.pdf.

"Research Guides: Indian Removal Act: Primary Documents in American History." Library of Congress. Accessed August 9, 2023. https://guides.loc .gov/indian-removal-act.

Riddle, John M. *Eve's Herbs: A History of Contraception and Abortion in the West*. Cambridge, MA: Harvard University Press, 1997.

Roberts, Alaina E. *I've Been Here All the While: Black Freedom on Native Land*. America in the Nineteenth Century. Philadelphia: University of Pennsylvania Press, 2021.

———. "Tulsa Massacre and Native History." CNN, May 9, 2021. www.cnn.com/2021/05/09/us/tulsa-massacre-native-history-alaina -roberts/index.html.

Roberts, Dorothy E. *Killing the Black Body: Race, Reproduction, and the Meaning of Liberty*. New York: Vintage, 1999.

"*Roe v. Wade* (1973)." Legal Information Institute. Accessed April 23, 2023. www.law.cornell.edu/wex/roe_v_wade_%281973%29.

"Roger, Mary, and Margaret Toothaker Home, Site Of." Salem Witch Museum. Accessed March 13, 2024. https://salemwitchmuseum.com/locations /roger-mary-margaret-toothaker-home-site-of/.

Rust, Randal. "The New York Slave Revolt of 1712." American History Central, October 12, 2022. www.americanhistorycentral.com/entries/new-york -slave-revolt-of-1712/.

Sager, Rebekah. "Alabama Artist's Monument to 'Mothers of Gynecology' Stands as a Symbol of Body Autonomy." *American Independent*, May 11, 2023. https://americanjournalnews.com/montgomery-alabama -mothers-gynecology-racism-art-michelle-browder/.

Schiff, Stacy. "Unraveling the Many Mysteries of Tituba, the Star Witness of the Salem Witch Trials." *Smithsonian Magazine*, November 2015. www.smithsonianmag.com/history/unraveling-mysteries-tituba -salem-witch-trials-180956960/.

———. *The Witches: Salem, 1692*. New York: Little, Brown, 2015.

Smithers, Gregory D. "Cherokee 'Two Spirits': Gender, Ritual, and Spirituality in the Native South." *Early American Studies* 12, no. 3 (2014): 626–651. www.jstor.org/stable/24474873.

"Smoking During Pregnancy." Centers for Disease Control and Prevention, April 28, 2020. www.cdc.gov/tobacco/basic_information/health_effects /pregnancy/index.htm.

Stafford, Kat. "Why Do So Many Black Women Die in Pregnancy? One Reason: Doctors Don't Take Them Seriously." AP News, May 23, 2023. https://projects.apnews.com/features/2023/from-birth-to-death /black-women-maternal-mortality-rate.html.

Stebbins, Sarah J. "Pocahontas: Her Life and Legend." National Parks Service. Accessed August 2023. www.nps.gov/jame/learn/historyculture /pocahontas-her-life-and-legend.htm.

Steiger, Brad. *American Indian Magic: Sacred Pow Wows & Hopi Prophecies.* New Brunswick, NJ: Inner Light, 1986.

"The Story of . . . Smallpox—and Other Deadly Eurasian Germs." PBS. Accessed March 7, 2024. www.pbs.org/gunsgermssteel/variables/smallpox.html.

Suarez, Fatima. "Poisoning as Revenge for Intimate Violence Against Enslaved Women." Clayman Institute for Gender Research, June 1, 2022. https://gender.stanford.edu/news/poisoning-revenge-intimate -violence-against-enslaved-women.

Taylor, Marygrace. "Placenta Encapsulation: Is It Safe to Take Pills Made from Your Own Placenta?" What to Expect, March 23, 2022. www.whattoexpect.com/first-year/postpartum-health-and-care /placenta-encapsulation.

"10 Facts about Thomas Jefferson for His Birthday." National Constitution Center. Accessed August 10, 2023. https://constitutioncenter.org/blog /10-facts-about-thomas-jefferson-for-his-birthday#.

Tippet, Krista, and Patrick Bellegarde-Smith. "Speaking of Faith: Living Vodou." *Journal of Haitian Studies* 14, no. 2 (2008): 144–156. www.jstor.org/stable/41715194.

"Two-Spirit: Health Resources." Lesbian, Gay, Bisexual, and Transgender Health. Accessed August 4, 2023. www.ihs.gov/lgbt/health/twospirit/.

Ungar, Laura, and Heather Hollingsworth. "Post-*Roe*, Native Americans Face Even More Abortion Hurdles." AP News, February 15, 2023. https://apnews.com/article/abortion-us-supreme-court-oklahoma -sd-state-wire-south-dakota-24541ed0e66b5e1e1cd8b84e7e2e3159.

"The United States and the Haitian Revolution, 1791–1804." Office of the Historian, Foreign Service Institute. Accessed August 2023. https://history.state.gov/milestones/1784-1800/haitian-rev.

"Wabanaki Fashion." Maine Memory Network. Accessed August 4, 2023. www.mainememory.net/sitebuilder/site/2976/slideshow/1728/display ?format=list&prev_object_id=4665&prev_object=page.

Warner, Kelsey. "Hands-On Learning Activities: Children's Life in the Seventeenth-Century." Salem Witch Museum, May 28, 2020. https://salemwitchmuseum.com/2020/05/24/hands-on-learning -activities/.

Waxman, Olivia B. "Slavery in America Didn't Start in Jamestown in 1619." *Time*, August 20, 2019. https://time.com/5653369/august-1619 -jamestown-history/.

Weigel, David. "Took Away Our Way of Life/Vacuum, Misoprostol and Knife." Reason.com, March 6, 2008. https://reason.com/2008/03/06/took-away -our-way-of-life-vacu/.

"Where Can I Get an Abortion?" US Abortion Clinic Locator. Accessed August 12, 2023. www.abortionfinder.org/abortion-guides-by-state.

Williams, Daniel K. *Defenders of the Unborn: The Pro-life Movement Before* Roe v. Wade. New York: Oxford University Press, 2016.

Williams, Heather Andrea. "How Slavery Affected African American Families." TeacherServe. Accessed August 2023. https://nationalhumanitiescenter .org/tserve/freedom/1609-1865/essays/aafamilies.htm.

Wise, Sam. *Sacred Choice: Paganism, Witchcraft, and Reproductive Justice.* Independently published, 2022.

"Witchcraft." History Matters. Accessed August 2023. https://historymatters .gmu.edu/d/6763/.

Wolchover, Natalie. "Did Cold Weather Cause the Salem Witch Trials?" NBC News, April 20, 2012. www.nbcnews.com/id/wbna47117880.

Worcester, Donald E., and Thomas F. Schilz. "The Spread of Firearms Among the Indians on the Anglo-French Frontiers." *American Indian Quarterly* 8, no. 2 (1984): 103–115. https://doi.org/10.2307/1184207.

Zhang, Sarah. "The Surgeon Who Experimented on Slaves." *Atlantic*, April 18, 2018. www.theatlantic.com/health/archive/2018/04/j-marion -sims/558248/.

CHAPTER 4

Bartley, Lisa. "Scientology Settles 'Forced Abortion' Lawsuit Out of Court." ABC 7, July 24, 2018. https://abc7.com/scientology-forced-abortion -lawsuit-settlement-david-miscavige/3812446/.

Beyer, Catherine. "Why Is Scientology So Expensive?" Learn Religions, February 11, 2019. www.learnreligions.com/how-much-does-scientology -cost-95805.

Cabot, Laurie. "Laurie Cabot Official Website." Laurie Cabot, 2022. www.lauriecabot.com/.

"Church of Scientology Settles LA Suit with Ex-Member Claiming Coerced Abortion and That She Had to Work as a Pre-Teen." *Los Angeles Daily News*, July 24, 2018. www.dailynews.com/2018/07/24/church-of -scientology-settles-la-suit-with-ex-member-claiming-coerced-abortion -and-that-she-had-to-work-as-a-pre-teen/.

Churton, Tobias. *Aleister Crowley: The Biography: Spiritual Revolutionary, Romantic Explorer, Occult Master and Spy.* London: Watkins, 2011.

Cogan, Marin. "Not All Religions Oppose Abortion." *Vox*, July 3, 2022. www.vox.com/2022/7/3/23190408/judaism-rabbi-abortion-religion -reproductive-rights.

Crowley, Aleister. *The Book of Lies.* Independently published, 2021.

———. *The Book of the Law.* 1976. Reprint, York Beach, ME: Weiser Books, 1987.

———. *The Confessions of Aleister Crowley: An Autohagiography.* 1969. Reprint, New York: Penguin, 1989.

———. *The Equinox of the Gods.* 1936. Reprint, London: New Falcon, 1991.

Editors of Encyclopedia Britannica. "Star of David." In *Encyclopædia Britannica*, August 25, 2023. www.britannica.com/topic/Star-of-David.

———. "Wicca." In *Encyclopædia Britannica*. Accessed August 23, 2023. www.britannica.com/topic/Wicca.

"Fitter Family Contests." Eugenics Archive. Accessed August 24, 2023. www.eugenicsarchive.org/eugenics/topics_fs.pl?theme=8#:~:text=At%20most%20contests%2C%20competitors%20submitted,was%20awarded%20a%20silver%20trophy.

Foley, Ryan. "List: Churches, Pro-life Offices Torched, Vandalized by Abortion Activists Since Supreme Court Leak." *Christian Post*, June 24, 2022. www.christianpost.com/news/churches-pro-life-offices-burned-vandalized-since-supreme-court-leak-list.html.

George, Cindy. "How Much Does an Abortion Cost Without Insurance?" GoodRx, May 16, 2022. www.goodrx.com/conditions/abortion/how-much-does-an-abortion-cost-without-insurance.

Gibbs, Nancy. "The Pill at 50: Sex, Freedom and Paradox." *Time*, April 22, 2010. https://content.time.com/time/magazine/article/0,9171,1983884-1,00.html.

Gross, Jenny, and Aimee Ortiz. "*Roe v. Wade* Plaintiff Was Paid to Switch Sides, Documentary Says." *New York Times*, May 19, 2020. www.nytimes.com/2020/05/19/us/roe-v-wade-mccorvey-documentary.html.

"Heroin, Morphine and Opiates—Definition, Examples & Effects." History.com. Accessed August 19, 2023. www.history.com/topics/crime/history-of-heroin-morphine-and-opiates#section_6.

"The Holocaust." National WWII Museum, June 22, 2017. www.nationalww2museum.org/war/articles/holocaust.

Hubbard, L. Ron. *Dianetics: The Modern Science of Mental Health.* 1950. Reprint, Los Angeles: Bridge, 2007.

Kaczynski, Richard. *Perdurabo: The Life of Aleister Crowley.* 2002. Reprint, Berkeley: North Atlantic Books, 2010.

Lachman, Gary. *Aleister Crowley: Magick, Rock and Roll, and the Wickedest Man in the World.* New York: Tarcher/Penguin, 2014.

Leon, Sharon M., and Randall Hansen. "An Image of God: The Catholic Struggle with Eugenics." *Journal of American History* 103, no. 2 (2016). https://doi.org/10.1093/jahist/jaw254.

McDonald, Hannah. "14 Facts About Margaret Sanger." Mental Floss, July 20, 2018. https://www.mentalfloss.com/article/549270/facts-about-margaret-sanger.

McManus, Tracey. "3 Former Scientology Workers Sue, Saying They Were Trafficked as Children." *Tampa Bay Times*, April 28, 2022. www.tampabay.com/news/clearwater/2022/04/28/3-former-scientology-workers-sue-saying-they-were-trafficked-as-children/.

Nash, Nathaniel C. "Mengele an Abortionist, Argentine Files Suggest." *New York Times*, February 11, 1992. www.nytimes.com/1992/02/11/world/mengele-an-abortionist-argentine-files-suggest.html.

Oria, Shelly. *I Know What's Best for You: Stories on Reproductive Freedom.* San Francisco: McSweeney's, 2022.

Planned Parenthood. "The History & Impact of Planned Parenthood." Accessed September 15, 2023. www.plannedparenthood.org/about-us/who-we-are/our-history.

Reagan, Leslie J. *When Abortion Was a Crime: Women, Medicine, and Law in the United States, 1867–1973.* Berkeley: University of California Press, 1997.

Riddle, John M. *Eve's Herbs: A History of Contraception and Abortion in the West.* Cambridge, MA: Harvard University Press, 1997.

Risen, James, and Judy L. Thomas. *Wrath of Angels: The American Abortion War.* New York: Basic Books, 1998.

Roberts, Dorothy E. *Killing the Black Body: Race, Reproduction, and the Meaning of Liberty.* New York: Vintage, 1999.

Rutherford, Adam. *Control: The Dark History and Troubling Present of Eugenics.* New York: W. W. Norton, 2022.

Saint Thomas, Sophie. *Glamour Witch: Conjuring Style and Grace to Get What You Want.* Newburyport, MA: Weiser Books, 2023.

Stensvold, Anne. *A History of Pregnancy in Christianity: From Original Sin to Contemporary Abortion Debates.* New York: Routledge, Taylor & Francis Group, 2015.

Stern, Alexandra Minna. "Forced Sterilization Policies in the US Targeted Minorities and Those with Disabilities—and Lasted into the 21st Century." Conversation, August 26, 2020. https://theconversation.com/forced-sterilization-policies-in-the-us-targeted-minorities-and-those-with-disabilities-and-lasted-into-the-21st-century-143144.

Uenuma, Francine. "'Better Babies' Contests Pushed for Much-Needed Infant Health but Also Played into the Eugenics Movement." *Smithsonian Magazine*, January 17, 2019. www.smithsonianmag.com/history/better-babies-contests-pushed-infant-health-also-played-eugenics-movement-180971288/.

United States Holocaust Memorial Museum. "Jewish Badge: During the Nazi Era." Accessed September 17, 2023. https://encyclopedia.ushmm.org /content/en/article/jewish-badge-during-the-nazi-era.

Williams, Daniel K. *Defenders of the Unborn: The Pro-life Movement Before Roe v. Wade.* New York: Oxford University Press, 2019.

Wise, Sam. *Sacred Choice: Paganism, Witchcraft, and Reproductive Justice.* Independently published, 2022.

Wright, Jennifer. *Madame Restell: The Life, Death, and Resurrection of Old New York's Most Fabulous, Fearless, and Infamous Abortionist.* New York: Hachette Books, 2023.

Ye Hee Lee, Michelle. "For Planned Parenthood Abortion Stats, '3 Percent' and '94 Percent' Are Both Misleading." *Washington Post*, December 7, 2021. www.washingtonpost.com/news/fact-checker/wp/2015/08/12/for -planned-parenthood-abortion-stats-3-percent-and-94-percent-are-both -misleading/.

Zeidman, Lawrence A. "Forced Sterilization Under the Nazis: Preventing People with Neuropsychiatric Disorders from Polluting the German Gene Pool." In *Brain Science Under the Swastika: Ethical Violations, Resistance, and Victimization of Neuroscientists in Nazi Europe.* Oxford: Oxford University Press, 2020.

CHAPTER 5

Abrahamsson, Carl. *Anton LaVey and the Church of Satan.* Rochester, VT: Inner Traditions, 2022.

Alsharif, Mirna, and Ray Sanchez. "Bodies of Covid-19 Victims Are Still Stored in Refrigerated Trucks in NYC." CNN, May 7, 2021. www.cnn.com /2021/05/07/us/new-york-coronavirus-victims-refrigerated-trucks /index.html.

Annas, George J. "Medical Judgment in Court and in Congress: Abortion, Refusing Treatment, and Drug Regulation." American Bar Association. Accessed October 10, 2023. www.americanbar.org/groups/crsj/publications / human_rights_magazine_home/human_rights_vol34_2007/fall2007 /hr_fall07_annas/.

Associated Press. "Robertson Letter Attacks Feminists." *New York Times*, August 26, 1992. www.nytimes.com/1992/08/26/us/robertson-letter -attacks-feminists.html.

Barbuti, Angela. "Gloria Steinem Says She Will Put Up Abortion-Seekers in NYC Home." *New York Post*, June 27, 2022. https://nypost.com /2022/06/25/gloria-steinem-says-she-will-put-up-nyc-abortion -seekers/.

Barton, Blanche. *The Secret Life of a Satanist: The Authorized Biography of Anton Szandor LaVey*. Port Townsend, WA: Feral House, 2014.

Beck, Richard. *We Believe the Children: A Moral Panic in the 1980s*. New York: PublicAffairs, 2015.

Bennington-Castro, Joseph. "How AIDS Remained an Unspoken—but Deadly—Epidemic for Years." History.com, June 1, 2020. www.history.com/news /aids-epidemic-ronald-reagan.

Bergren, Joe. "Stevie Nicks' Long History with Witchcraft." *Entertainment Tonight*, October 10, 2018. www.etonline.com/stevie-nicks-history -with-witchcraft-rhiannon-to-ahs-apocalypse-110434.

Blumenthal, Max. "Agent of Intolerance." *Nation*, June 29, 2015. www.thenation.com/article/archive/agent-intolerance/.

Boehm, Jessica. "Sandra Day O'Connor, the Mom: How She Raised 3 Boys and Broke the Glass Ceiling." *Arizona Republic*, March 15, 2019. www.azcentral .com/story/news/local/phoenix/2019/03/15/us-supreme-court-justice -sandra-day-oconnor-mom-raised-3-boys-arizona/2681012002/.

Brown, Bruce D. "A Cauldron of Controversy." *Washington Post*, September 13, 1992. www.washingtonpost.com/archive/lifestyle/1992/09/13/a-cauldron -of-controversy/1bd6dd24-602c-4f20-b273-4a9a0acb2cb9/.

Carlton, Genevieve. "How Jayne Mansfield's Gruesome Death Sparked Rumors About Decapitation and Satanic Curses." All That's Interesting, July 16, 2022. https://allthatsinteresting.com/jayne-mansfield-death.

Casta, Nicole. "Falwell Called NOW 'the National Order of Witches.'" Media Matters for America, November 23, 2004. www.mediamatters.org /jerry-falwell/falwell-called-now-national-order-witches.

Chambers, Marcia. "Sex Case Accuser Is Discovered Dead." *New York Times*, December 21, 1986. www.nytimes.com/1986/12/21/us/sex-case-accuser -is-discovered-dead.html.

Church of Satan. "Is Abortion a Satanic Sacrament?" Church of Satan, August 5, 2020. www.churchofsatan.com/is-abortion-a-satanic-sacrament/.

Colker, Ruth. "Homophobia, AIDS Hysteria, and the Americans with Disabilities Act." HeinOnline. Accessed October 11, 2023. https://heinonline.org/HOL/LandingPage?handle=hein.journals/jgrj8.

Conlon, Rose. "Abortion Rights Opponents Across the Country Want to Charge Women with Murder." NPR, July 13, 2023. www.npr.org /2023/07/13/1187435403/abortion-abolitionists-across-the-country -want-to-charge-women-with-murder.

Duncan, Lauren E. "Gloria Steinem: The Childhood Foundations of a Feminist." *Journal of Personality* 91, no. 1 (2022): 193–206. https://doi.org/10.1111/jopy.12732.

Eberle, Paul, and Shirley Eberle. *The Abuse of Innocence: The McMartin Preschool Trial.* Amherst, NY: Prometheus Books, 2007.

Eldridge, Alison. "Yule." In *Encyclopædia Britannica.* Accessed October 20, 2023. www.britannica.com/topic/Yule-festival.

Falwell, Jerry. "1984-05-09 Memo from Jerry Falwell 1." Jerry Falwell Library. Accessed October 10, 2023. https://cdm17184.contentdm.oclc.org/digital /collection/p17184coll12/id/76246.

Flanagan, Caitlin. "Losing the 'Rare' in 'Safe, Legal, and Rare.'" *Atlantic*, December 6, 2019. www.theatlantic.com/ideas/archive/2019/12/the -brilliance-of-safe-legal-and-rare/603151/.

Fox, Margalit. "Betty Friedan, Who Ignited Cause in 'Feminine Mystique,' Dies at 85." *New York Times*, February 5, 2006. www.nytimes.com/2006 /02/05/us/betty-friedan-who-ignited-cause-in-feminine-mystique-dies -at-85.html.

Franklin, Ben A. "Shot Fired Through Window of Blackmun Home." *New York Times*, March 5, 1985. www.nytimes.com/1985/03/05/nyregion/shot-fired -through-window-of-blackmun-home.html.

Friedan, Betty, and Anna Quindlen. *The Feminine Mystique.* New York: W. W. Norton, 2001.

Gallup. "Abortion Trends by Gender." Gallup.com, June 23, 2023. https://news.gallup.com/poll/245618/abortion-trends-gender.aspx.

Gamarekian, Barbara. "Ginsburg: A Quiet Life Turns Public." *New York Times*, November 3, 1987. www.nytimes.com/1987/11/03/us/ginsburg-a-quiet-life -turns-public.html.

Goodman, Ellen. "'Voodoo Biology.'" *Washington Post*, November 1, 1985. www.washingtonpost.com/archive/politics/1985/11/02/voodoo -biology/29b80644-027b-4466-900b-cd8e214f96ab/.

Goodstein, Laurie. "Falwell: Blame Abortionists, Feminists and Gays." *New York Times*, September 19, 2011. www.theguardian.com/world/2001 /sep/19/september11.usa9.

Greenhouse, Linda. "Sandra Day O'Connor and the Reconsideration of *Roe v. Wade.*" PBS, September 10, 2021. www.pbs.org/wgbh/americanexperience /features/sandra-day-oconnor-and-reconsideration-roe-v-wade/.

Guiley, Rosemary Ellen. *The Encyclopedia of Witches, Witchcraft and Wicca.* New York: Checkmark Books, 2008.

Hevesi, Dennis. "Mildred Jefferson, 84, Anti-abortion Activist, Is Dead." *New York Times*, October 18, 2010. www.nytimes.com/2010/10/19/us /19jefferson.html.

History.com Editors. "History of AIDS." History.com, July 13, 2017. www.history.com/topics/1980s/history-of-aids.

———. "Saturnalia: Meaning, Festival & Christmas." History.com. Accessed October 10, 2023. www.history.com/topics /ancient-rome/saturnalia.

Inzani, E., H. H. Marshall, F. J. Thompson, G. Kalema-Zikusoka, M. A. Cant, and E. I. Vitikainen. "Spontaneous Abortion as a Response to Reproductive Conflict in the Banded Mongoose." *Biology Letters* 15, no. 12 (2019). https://doi.org/10.1098/rsbl.2019.0529.

"Joan Andrews the Woman Who Would Be a Martyr." *South Florida Sun Sentinel*, October 2, 1988. www.sun-sentinel.com/1988/10/02/joan -andrews-the-woman-who-would-be-a-martyr/.

Kaczor, Bill. "Abortion Issue Pulled 2 Parallel Lives to Fatal Meeting—Griffin, Gunn: Men Were More than Symbols." *Seattle Times*, March 14, 1993. https://archive.seattletimes.com/archive/?date=19930314&slug=1690413.

Koch, Ariel. "The ONA Network and the Transnationalization of Neo-Nazi-Satanism." *Studies in Conflict & Terrorism* (2022): 1–28. https://doi.org /10.1080/1057610x.2021.2024944.

Langford, Terri, and Jordan Rudner. "Supreme Court Justice Antonin Scalia Found Dead in West Texas." *Texas Tribune*, February 13, 2016. www.texastribune.org/2016/02/13/us-supreme-court-justice-antonin -scalia-found-dead/.

LaVey, Anton Szandor, and Kevin I. Slaughter. *Letters from the Devil: The Lost Writings of Anton Szandor LaVey*. Underworld Amusements. 2010.

———. *Satan Speaks*. 1998. Reprint, Los Angeles: Feral House, 2003.

LaVey, Anton Szandor. *The Satanic Witch*. Los Angeles: Feral House, 2003.

Lee, Nora Kelly. "Why Wasn't Antonin Scalia Autopsied?" *Atlantic*, March 17, 2016. www.theatlantic.com/politics/archive/2016/02/antonin-scalia -autopsy/463251/.

Leon, Harmon. "Listen to the Reagan Administration Laughing at the AIDS Epidemic." *Vice*, December 1, 2015. www.vice.com/en/article/yvx4zy /listen-to-the-reagan-administration-laughing-at-the-aids-epidemic-511.

LeRoy, Matthew, and Deric Haddad. *They Must Be Monsters: A Modern-Day Witch Hunt—the Untold Story of the McMartin Phenomenon, the Longest, Most Expensive Criminal Case in U.S. History*. San Diego: Manor, 2018.

Lewin, Tamar. "Abortion Foe Sued in Killing of Doctor at a Clinic." *New York Times*, March 10, 2995. www.nytimes.com/1995/03/10/us/abortion-foe -sued-in-killing-of-doctor-at-a-clinic.html.

Little, Jim. "Pensacola Was Once the Anti-abortion Battleground as Bombings and Murders Rocked Nation." *Pensacola News Journal*, June 25, 2022. www.pnj.com/story/news/2022/06/24/abortion-pensacola-has-long -complex-role-roe-vs-wade-debate/9648854002/.

Liptak, Adam. "What Did *Roe v. Wade* Say?" *New York Times*, December 1, 2021. www.nytimes.com/2021/12/01/us/politics/roe-wade-supreme -court.html.

Loofbourow, Lili. "The Forgotten Abortion-Rights Activist Who Forever Changed the Abortion Debate with a Single Idea." *Slate*, December 4, 2018. https://slate.com/human-interest/2018/12/pat-maginnis -abortion-rights-pro-choice-activist.html.

Maginnis, Pat. "Lana's Story." Pat Maginnis. Accessed February 7, 2023. www.patmaginnis.org/index.php/lanas-story-2/.

"Man Who Killed Late-Term Abortion Doctor Gets Lighter Sentence." CBS News, November 23, 2016. www.cbsnews.com/news/scott-roeder-man -who-killed-george-tiller-late-term-abortion-doctor-gets-new-lenient -sentence/.

Marty, Robin. *New Handbook for a Post-Roe America: The Complete Guide to Abortion Legality, Access, and Practical Support.* New York: Seven Stories Press, 2021.

McDowell, Jeanne Dorin. "The True Story of 'Mrs. America.'" Smithsonian .com, April 15, 2020. www.smithsonianmag.com/history/true-story -mrs-america-180974675/.

McLaughlin, Eliott C. "Longshot Presidential Candidate to Put Abortion in Your Face During Super Bowl." CNN, January 23, 2012. www.cnn.com/2012/01/22/us/super-bowl-abortion-ads/index.html.

Merelli, Annalisa. "A Brief History of a Marketing Masterpiece: Branding the Anti-abortion Movement 'Pro-Life.'" *Quartz*, January 28, 2017. https://qz.com/896566/where-does-the-term-pro-life-come-from.

"Michael Griffin, Murderer of Pensacola Abortion Doctor David Gunn, Is Denied Parole." *Pensacola News Journal*, October 31, 2017. www.pnj.com /story/news/2017/10/31/parole-hearing-set-today-convicted-murderer -pensacola-abortion-doctor/819716001/.

Miller, Mac. "Political Economics in Brief: 'Reaganomics.'" Northeastern University Economics Society, March 28, 2016. https://web.northeastern .edu/econsociety/political-economics-in-brief-reaganomics/.

National Abortion Federation. "Shelley Shannon." National Abortion Federation, September 16, 1992. https://prochoice.org/wp-content /uploads/Shelley-Shannon-.pdf.

Neill, A. S. *Summerhill: A Radical Approach to Child Rearing.* New York: Hart, 1960.

Neuhaus, Cable. "Salem's Official Witch, Laurie Cabot, Finds Grave Errors in Eastwick." People.com, June 29, 1987. https://people.com/archive /salems-official-witch-laurie-cabot-finds-grave-errors-in-eastwick-vol -27-no-26/.

Niskanen, William A. "Reaganomics." In *The Concise Encyclopedia of Economics*. Accessed October 11, 2023. www.econlib.org/library/Encl /Reaganomics.html.

Occult World. "Witches League of Public Awareness." Occult World. Accessed March 27, 2024. https://occult-world.com/witches-league -public-awareness/.

Ozug, Matt, Sarah Handel, Alisa Chang, and Patrick Jarenwattananon. "Inside Pat Maginnis' Radical (and Underground) Tactics on Abortion Rights in the '60s." NPR, May 5, 2022. www.npr.org/2021/10/29/1047068724/pat -was-an-early-radical-abortion-rights-activist-her-positions-are-now -common.

Planned Parenthood. "What Are Disadvantages to Breastfeeding as Birth Control?" Planned Parenthood. Accessed October 11, 2023. www.plannedparenthood.org/learn/birth-control/breastfeeding /what-are-disadvantages-using-breastfeeding-birth-control#:~: text=But%20breastfeeding%20isn't%20a,another%20kind%20of%20 birth%20control.

Powell, Michael. "Randall Terry Fights Gay Unions. His Son No Longer Will." *Washington Post*, April 22, 2004. www.washingtonpost.com/ac2/wp-dyn /A32934-2004Apr21?language=printer.

Prager, Joshua. "Opinion: The Groundbreaking and Complicated Life of Mildred Fay Jefferson." CNN, May 10, 2022. www.cnn.com/2022/05/10 /opinions/abortion-pro-life-hero-mildred-fay-jefferson-prager/index.html.

Quigley, Joan. *What Does Joan Say? My Seven Years as White House Astrologer to Nancy and Ronald Reagan*. Secaucus, NJ: Birch Lane Press, 1990.

Reagan, Leslie J. *When Abortion Was a Crime: Women, Medicine, and Law in the United States, 1867–1973*. Berkeley: University of California Press, 1997.

Reed, Jack. "Friends Say Griffin's Violence Unexpected." *Tampa Bay Times*, March 12, 1993. www.tampabay.com/archive/1993/03/12/friends-say -griffin-s-violence-unexpected/.

Reveal, Judith C. "Wattleton, Faye (1943–)." In Encyclopedia.com, October 22, 2023. www.encyclopedia.com/women/encyclopedias -almanacs-transcripts-and-maps/wattleton-faye-1943.

Risen, James, and Judy L. Thomas. *Wrath of Angels: The American Abortion War*. New York: Basic Books, 1998.

"Satanism Haunts Tales of Child Sex Abuse." *Chicago Tribune*, July 29, 1985. www.chicagotribune.com/1985/07/29/satanism-haunts-tales-of-child -sex-abuse/.

Satel, Sally L. "The 'Open Secret' on Getting a Safe Abortion Before *Roe v. Wade*." *New York Times*, June 4, 2022. www.nytimes.com/2022/06/04 /opinion/sunday/psychiatrists-abortion-roe.html.

Sheppard, Nathaniel Jr. "Doctor's Abduction Stuns Steel Town." *New York Times*, August 23, 1982. www.nytimes.com/1982/08/23/us/doctor-s-abduction-stuns-steel-town.html.

Southern Poverty Law Center. "Florida Abortion Foe Charged in Molestation." Southern Poverty Law Center Intelligence Report, November 12, 2003. www.splcenter.org/fighting-hate/intelligence-report/2003/florida-abortion-foe-charged-molestation.

Specter, Michael. "Shot Fired Through Blackmun's Window." *Washington Post*, March 4, 1985. www.washingtonpost.com/archive/politics/1985/03/05/shot-fired-through-blackmuns-window/270a0516-2c7f-4c5e-9002-d017515a5131/.

Steinem, Gloria. *My Life on the Road*. New York: Random House, 2016.

Stengel, Richard. "Nothing Less than Perfect: Faye Wattleton." *Time*, December 11, 1989. https://content.time.com/time/magazine/article/0,9171,959328,00.html.

Stensvold, Anne. *A History of Pregnancy in Christianity: From Original Sin to Contemporary Abortion Debates*. New York: Routledge, Taylor & Francis, 2015.

Stevens, Jenny. "Stevie Nicks on Art, Ageing and Attraction: 'Botox Makes It Look Like You're in a Satanic Cult!'" *Guardian*, October 14, 2020. www.theguardian.com/music/2020/oct/14/stevie-nicks-on-art-ageing-and-attraction-botox-makes-it-look-like-youre-in-a-satanic-cult.

Szal, Roxy. "U.S. Department of Justice Indicts Nine Anti-abortion Extremists for Clinic Invasion." *Ms. Magazine*, April 8, 2022. https://msmagazine.com/2022/04/07/lauren-handy-fetus-fetal-remains-justice-department-anti-abortion-dc-clinic-invasion/.

Tibary, Ahmed. "Abortion in Cattle—Reproductive System." *Merck Veterinary Manual* (October 5, 2022). www.merckvetmanual.com/reproductive-system/abortion-in-large-animals/abortion-in-cattle.

Troy, Gil. "Why Ronald Reagan Picked Sandra Day O'Connor—and Why George W. Bush Might Want to Follow His Example." History News Network. Accessed October 11, 2023. https://historynewsnetwork.org/article/12821.

Valenti, Lauren. "Stevie Nicks Opens Up About Her Abortion and What's at Stake in the 2020 Election." *Vogue*, October 15, 2020. www.vogue.com/article/stevie-nicks-abortion-fleetwood-mac-2020-election-reproductive-rights#:~:text=She%20spoke%20about%20the%20impact,Fleetwood%20Mac%2C%E2%80%9D%20she%20explains.

Villarreal, Yvonne. "Stevie Nicks Talks 'American Horror Story': 'I Was Scared to Go There.'" *Los Angeles Times*, January 8, 2014. www.latimes.com/entertainment/tv/showtracker/la-et-st-stevie-nicks-american-horror-story-20140107-story.html.

Volandes, Stellene. "Why Nancy Reagan Loved Red." *Town & Country*, March 6, 2016. www.townandcountrymag.com/society/news/a5295 /nancy-reagan-style-icon/.

Westenfeld, Adrienne. "Mrs. America Navigates Betty Friedan's Titanic Influence on Feminism." Esquire.com, April 22, 2020. www.esquire.com /entertainment/tv/a32225378/betty-friedan-mrs-america-true-story/.

Williams, Daniel K. *Defenders of the Unborn: The Pro-life Movement Before* Roe v. Wade. New York: Oxford University Press, 2019.

Woolf, Chris. "Scalia's Ties with Secretive Aristocratic Hunting Society." *The World from PRX*, February 26, 2016. https://theworld.org /stories/2016-02-26/scalia-s-ties-secretive-aristocratic-hunting-society.

Young, Cathy. "Jerry Falwell's Paradoxical Legacy." *Reason*, August–September 2007. https://reason.com/2007/07/31/jerry-falwells-paradoxical-leg/.

CHAPTER 6

Appleby, Julie. "Three Things to Know About Health Insurance Coverage for Abortion." NPR, July 13, 2022. www.npr.org/sections/health -shots/2022/07/13/1111078951/health-insurance-abortion.

"Arizona Man Sentenced to 41 Months in Prison on Felony Charge in Jan. 6 Capitol Breach." US Department of Justice, November 17, 2021. www.justice.gov/usao-dc/pr/arizona-man-sentenced-41-months-prison -felony-charge-jan-6-capitol-breach.

Belluck, Pam, and Adam Liptak. "Appeals Court Upholds Legality of Abortion Pill but with Significant Restrictions." *New York Times*, August 16, 2023. www.nytimes.com/2023/08/16/health/abortion-pill-ruling.html.

Bettelheim, Adriel. "Abortions Surged in States near Those with New Bans: Study—Axios." Axios, September 7, 2023. www.axios.com/2023/09/07 /abortions-surged-state-bans.

Burke, Minyvonne. "Texas Pastor Says Gay People Should Be 'Shot in the Back of the Head' in Shocking Sermon." NBCNews.com, June 9, 2022. www.nbcnews.com/nbc-out/out-news/texas-pastor-says-gay-people -shot-back-head-shocking-sermon-rcna32748.

Cauterucci, Christina, and Jonathan L. Fisher. "Comet Is D.C.'s Weirdo Pizza Place. Maybe That's Why It's a Target." *Slate*, December 6, 2016. https://slate.com/human-interest/2016/12/comet-ping-pong-is-a-haven -for-weirdos-and-now-a-target.html.

Contributors, Rewire News Group. "Tennessee Lawmakers Cut Off My Mic, but I Won't Be Silenced." Rewire News Group, September 17, 2019. https://rewirenewsgroup.com/2019/09/11/tennessee-lawmakers-cut-off -my-mic-but-i-wont-be-silenced/.

Davis, Wes, and Alex Cranz. "It's Official, People Aren't Watching TV as Much as They Used To." *Verge*, August 15, 2023. www.theverge.com /2023/8/15/23833516/nielsen-tv-cable-50-percent-decline-viewership -bum-bums.

Daw, Stephen. "Church of Satan Says Sam Smith & Kim Petras' 'Unholy' Performance Was More 'Meh' than Satanic." *Billboard*, February 8, 2023. www.billboard.com/culture/pride/sam-smith-kim-petras-unholy -grammys-church-of-satan-reacts-1235250622/#!

De Witte, Melissa. "Using Economics to Understand the Wide-Reaching Impacts of Overturning *Roe v. Wade*." *Stanford News*, July 18, 2022. https://news.stanford.edu/2022/07/18/using-economics -understand-wide-reaching-impacts-overturning-roe-v-wade/.

Dickerson, Caitlin, Seth Freed Wessler, and Miriam Jordan. "Immigrants Say They Were Pressured into Unneeded Surgeries." *New York Times*, September 29, 2020. www.nytimes.com/2020/09/29/us/ice -hysterectomies-surgeries-georgia.html.

Dickson, E. J. "We Asked Satanists What They Think of the New Lil Nas X Video." *Rolling Stone*, March 29, 2021. www.rollingstone.com/culture /culture-news/lil-nas-x-montero-call-me-by-your-name-video-church -of-satan-1147634/.

Elving, Ron. "What Happened with Merrick Garland in 2016 and Why It Matters Now." NPR, June 29, 2018. www.npr.org/2018/06/29/624467256 /what-happened-with-merrick-garland-in-2016-and-why-it-matters-now.

Fischer, Rob, Reid Cherlin, Jason Zingerle, and Jason Horowitz. "The 50 Most Powerful People in Washington." *GQ*, January 18, 2012. www.gq.com /gallery/50-most-powerful-people-in-washington-dc.

Friedberg, Brian. "The Dark Virality of a Hollywood Blood-Harvesting Conspiracy." *Wired*, July 31, 2020. www.wired.com/story/opinion-the -dark-virality-of-a-hollywood-blood-harvesting-conspiracy/.

Galston, William A. "*Roe v. Wade* Overturned Despite Public Opinion." Brookings, June 24, 2023. www.brookings.edu/articles/roe-v-wade -overturned-despite-public-opinion/.

Giardina, Henry. "This Nonbinary Witch Threw a Mass Marriage to Protest Amy Coney Barrett." *Them*, November 17, 2020. www.them.us/story /nonbinary-witch-mass-marriage-texas-protest-amy-coney-barrett.

Graham, Ruth. "'The Pro-Life Generation': Young Women Fight Against Abortion Rights." *New York Times*, July 3, 2022. www.nytimes.com /2022/07/03/us/pro-life-young-women-roe-abortion.html.

Grimes, Andrea. "Who Cares About Pot? Stickland's Rape Views Are Horrifying." *Texas Observer*, April 20, 2019. www.texasobserver.org /jonathan-stickland-rape-post/.

Guo, Shuyun, and Yanjun Liang. "An Investigation into the Origin of the Term 'Shaman.'" *Sibirica* 14, no. 3 (2015). https://doi.org/10.3167 /sib.2015.140303.

Harkins, Gina. "Navy Career of 'QAnon Shaman' Ended After He Refused Anthrax Vaccine." Military.com, January 12, 2021. www.military.com /daily-news/2021/01/12/navy-career-of-qanon-shaman-ended-after -he-refused-anthrax-vaccine.html.

Henigsman, DO, Stacy A., and Caitlin Geng. "Hysterectomy Cost: Insurance, Type, and Method." *Medical News Today*, January 26, 2023. www.medicalnewstoday.com/articles/how-much-does-a -hysterectomy-cost.

"The Herbalism Community Is at War with Itself over Abuse Allegations." *Vice*, April 7, 2022. www.vice.com/en/article/m7vnxv/the-herbalism -community-is-at-war-with-itself-over-abuse-allegations.

"Identifying Far-Right Symbols That Appeared at the U.S. Capitol Riot." *Washington Post*, January 15, 2022. www.washingtonpost.com/nation /interactive/2021/far-right-symbols-capitol-riot/.

"John Podesta." Center for American Progress, September 14, 2022. www.americanprogress.org/people/podesta-john/.

Katella, Kathy. "Maternal Mortality Is on the Rise: 8 Things to Know." *Yale Medicine* (May 22, 2023). www.yalemedicine.org/news/maternal -mortality-on-the-rise.

Kekatos, Mary. "Majority of OB-GYNs believe overturning *Roe* led to more maternal deaths: Survey." ABC News, June 21, 2023. https://abcnews .go.com/Health/majority-obgyns-overturning-roe-ledmaternal-deaths -survey/story?id=100241112.

Kennedy, Merrit. "'Pizzagate' Gunman Sentenced to 4 Years in Prison." NPR, June 22, 2017. www.npr.org/sections/thetwo-way/2017/06/22/533941689 /pizzagate-gunman-sentenced-to-4-years-in-prison.

Kristen Turner (@kristinturnerlife). Instagram photo, www.instagram.com /p/CbFvn37LKJM/?hl=en.

Langone, Alix. "Brooklyn Witches Plan to Put a Hex on Brett Kavanaugh." *Time*, October 14, 2018. https://time.com/5424289/brooklyn-witches -hex-supreme-court-brett-kavanaugh/.

Legare, Robert. "'QAnon Shaman' Jacob Chansley Sentenced to 41 Months in Prison for Role in January 6 Attack." CBS News, November 17, 2021.

www.cbsnews.com/news/jacob-chansley-qanon-shaman-sentenced
-january-6-attack-capitol/.

Lenharo, Mariana. "After *Roe v. Wade*: US Researchers Warn of What's to Come." *Nature News*, June 24, 2022. www.nature.com/articles /d41586-022-01775-z.

Levenson, Michael. "Planned Parenthood Says Hacker Compromised Information for 400,000 Patients." *New York Times*, December 2, 2021. www.nytimes .com/2021/12/01/us/planned-parenthood-data-breach-los-angeles.html.

Link, Devon. "Fact Check: There Is No Evidence to Support Claims That Lady Gaga Is a Witch." *USA Today*, November 4, 2020. www.usatoday.com /story/news/factcheck/2020/11/03/fact-check-there-no-evidence-lady -gaga-witch/6147108002/.

Littlefield, Amy. "The Christian Legal Army Behind the Ban on Abortion in Mississippi." *Nation*, November 30, 2021. www.thenation.com/article /politics/alliance-defending-freedom-dobbs/.

Mandler, C. "Teaching About Sexuality and Gender Identity Is Now Banned in Florida Public Schools." CBS News, April 20, 2023. www.cbsnews.com /news/florida-public-schools-ban-teach-gender-identity-sexuality/.

Marty, Robin. *New Handbook for a Post-Roe America: The Complete Guide to Abortion Legality, Access, and Practical Support*. New York: Seven Stories Press, 2021.

Meltzer, Marisa. "How New Age Spirituality and Sensitive Masculinity Led to QAnon." *Washington Post*, March 29, 2021. www.washingtonpost.com /magazine/2021/03/29/qanon-new-age-spirituality/.

Merlan, Anna. "The Herbalism Community Is at War with Itself over Abuse Allegations." *Vice*, April 7, 2022. www.vice.com/en/article/m7vnxv/the -herbalism-community-is-at-war-with-itself-over-abuse-allegations.

Meuller, Eleanor, and Nick Niedzwiadek. "Unions Wade Gingerly into Abortion After SCOTUS Ruling." *Politico*, June 27, 2022. www.politico.com /newsletters/weekly-shift/2022/06/27/unions-wade-gingerly-into -abortion-after-scotus-ruling-00042485.

"Migrant Children in U.S. Detention Face Physical, Mental Harms: Report." Harvard T. G. Chan School of Public Health, January 22, 2024. www.hsph.harvard.edu/news/hsph-in-the-news/migrant-children-in-u-s -detention-face-physical-mental-harms-report/.

Montoya-Galvez, Camilo. "Investigation Finds Women Detained by ICE Underwent 'Unnecessary Gynecological Procedures' at Georgia Facility." CBS News, November 15, 2022. www.cbsnews.com/news/women -detained- ice-unnecessary-gynecological-procedures-georgia-facility -investigation/.

Mukpo, Ashoka. "The 'ICE Kids': ACLU." American Civil Liberties Union, February 24, 2023. www.aclu.org/news/immigrants-rights/the-ice-kids.

Neuman, Scott. "Obama: Supreme Court Same-Sex Marriage Ruling 'a Victory for America.'" NPR, June 26, 2015. www.npr.org/sections/thetwo-way/2015/06/26/417731614/obama-supreme-court-ruling-on-gay-marriage-a-victory-for-america.

Oria, Shelly. *I Know What's Best for You: Stories on Reproductive Freedom.* San Francisco: McSweeney's, 2022.

Paradis, Justine. "Outside/In: Ecofascism at the Capitol Riot." New Hampshire Public Radio, January 22, 2021. www.nhpr.org/environment/2021-01-22/outside-in-ecofascism-at-the-capitol-riot.

Planned Parenthood. "Is the Abortion Pill Safe? Read About Abortion Pill Safety." Planned Parenthood. Accessed October 23, 2023. www.plannedparenthood.org/learn/abortion/the-abortion-pill/how-safe-is-the-abortion-pill.

"Prep." Centers for Disease Control and Prevention, June 3, 2022. www.cdc.gov/hiv/basics/prep.html.

Puglise, Nicole. "Marina Abramović Says Having Children Would Have Been 'a Disaster for My Work.'" *Guardian*, July 26, 2016. www.theguardian.com/artanddesign/2016/jul/26/marina-abramovic-abortions-children-disaster-work.

Reilly, Katie. "Hillary Clinton Transcript: 'Basket of Deplorables' Comment." *Time*, April 29, 2021. https://time.com/4486502/hillary-clinton-basket-of-deplorables-transcript/.

Renaud, Myriam. "Why Hillary Clinton Is Morally Conflicted About Abortion." *Atlantic*, August 17, 2016. www.theatlantic.com/politics/archive/2016/08/hillary-clinton-abortion/494723/.

"Reproductive Options for Transgender Individuals." Yale Medicine (February 10, 2023). www.yalemedicine.org/conditions/transgender-reproductive-options.

Reuters Fact Check. "'QAnon Shaman' Was Not Freed Early Due to Footage Proving Jan. 6 Riot Was 'Hoax.'" Reuters, April 6, 2023.

"Revealing Average Screen Time Statistics." Banklinko, March 11, 2024. https://backlinko.com/screen-time-statistics.

https://backlinko.com/screen-time-statistics Riddle, John M. *Eve's Herbs: A History of Contraception and Abortion in the West.* Cambridge, MA: Harvard University Press, 1997.

Roberts, Catherine. "These Period Tracker Apps Say They Put Privacy First. Here's What We Found." *Consumer Reports*, May 25, 2022. www.consumerreports.org/health/health-privacy/period-tracker-apps

-privacy-a2278134145/.

Rosner, Elizabeth. "Arizona 'Karen' with '$40,000 Rolex' Trashes Face Mask Display in Target." *New York Post*, July 6, 2020. https://nypost.com /2020/07/06/arizona-karen-with-40000-rolex-trashes-face-mask -display-in-target/.

Rothschild, Mike. *The Storm Is upon Us: How QAnon Became a Movement, Cult, and Conspiracy Theory of Everything*. Brooklyn: Melville House, 2022.

Samuelson, Kate. "Pizzagate: What to Know About the Conspiracy Theory, the Fake News Story with Real Consequences." *Time*, December 5, 2016. https://time.com/4590255/pizzagate-fake-news-what-to-know/.

Schoenbaum, Hannah. "Report Says at Least 32 Transgender People Were Killed in the U.S. in 2022." PBS, November 16, 2022. www.pbs.org /newshour/nation/report-says-at-least-32-transgender-people-were -killed-in-the-u-s-in-2022.

Sellers, Jennifer. "Leading Medical Groups File Amicus Brief in *Dobbs v. Jackson*." American Medical Association, September 21, 2021. www.ama-assn.org/press-center/press-releases/leading-medical -groups-file-amicus-brief-dobbs-v-jackson.

Simmons-Duffin, Selena. "For Doctors, Abortion Restrictions Create an 'Impossible Choice' When Providing Care." NPR, June 24, 2022. www.npr.org/sections/health-shots/2022/06/24/1107316711/doctors -ethical- bind-abortion.

Staff, TMZ. "Sam Smith, Kim Petras' 'Unholy' Grammy Performance Underwhelms Church of Satan." TMZ, February 8, 2023. www.tmz.com /2023/02/08/sam-smith-kim-petras-unholy-grammy-performance -church-satan-underwhelmed/.

"*State Ex Rel. Hermesmann v. Seyer*." Justia Law. Accessed October 23, 2023. https://law.justia.com/cases/kansas/supreme-court/1993/67-978-3.html.

Stensvold, Anne. *A History of Pregnancy in Christianity: From Original Sin to Contemporary Abortion Debates*. New York: Routledge, Taylor & Francis, 2015.

Sung, Morgan. "Activist Jex Blackmore Took an Abortion Pill on Live TV. The Moment Went Viral." NBCNews.com, January 28, 2022. www.nbcnews .com/news/us-news/activist-jex-blackmore-took-abortion-pill-live-tv -moment-went-viral-rcna13851.

Taub, Amanda. "The 17th-Century Judge at the Heart of Today's Women's Rights Rulings." *New York Times*, May 19, 2022. www.nytimes.com /2022/05/19/world/asia/abortion-lord-matthew-hale.html.

"Texorcism Ritual." Democrasexy. Accessed October 23, 2023. www.democrasexy.com/texorcism.

"Three Men Charged in Connection with Events at U.S. Capitol." US Department of Justice. Last modified January 12, 2021. www.justice.gov /usao-dc/pr/three-men-charged-connection-events-us-capitol.

Tinker, Ben. "Reality Check: Trump on Clinton Allowing Abortions 'in the 9th Month, on the Final Day.'" CNN, October 20, 2016. www.cnn.com /2016/10/20/politics/donald-trump-hillary-clinton-abortion-fact-check /index.html.

"Tracking Abortion Bans Across the Country." *New York Times*, May 24, 2022. www.nytimes.com/interactive/2022/us/abortion-laws-roe-v-wade.html.

"Trump in 1999: 'I Am Very Pro-Choice.'" NBCNews.com, October 10, 2023. www.nbcnews.com/meet-the-press/video/trump-in-1999-i-am-very -pro-choice-480297539914.

TST. "About Us." TST. Accessed October 23, 2023. https://thesatanictemple .com/pages/about-us.

———. "Samuel Alito's Mom's Satanic Abortion Clinic." TST. Accessed October 23, 2023. https://thesatanictemple.com/pages/samuel-alitos-moms -satanic-abortion-clinic.

Walsh, Joe. "'Q Shaman' Jacob Chansley Won't Take a Covid Vaccine in Jail, Lawyer Says." *Forbes*, February 24, 2021. www.forbes.com/sites /joewalsh/2021/02/24/q-shaman-jacob-chansley-wont-take-a-covid -vaccine-in-jail-lawyer-says/?sh=7d68f0db49e7.

"Will Revitalizing Old Blood Slow Aging?" Columbia University Irving Medical Center, February 9, 2023. www.cuimc.columbia.edu/news/will -revitalizing-old-blood-slow-aging.

Wise, Sam. *Sacred Choice: Paganism, Witchcraft, and Reproductive Justice*. Independently published, 2022.

Wiseman, Eva. "The Dark Side of Wellness: The Overlap Between Spiritual Thinking and Far-Right Conspiracies." *Guardian*, October 17, 2021. www.theguardian.com/lifeandstyle/2021/oct/17/eva-wiseman -conspirituality-the-dark-side-of-wellness-how-it-all-got-so-toxic.

Yurcaba, Yo. "DeSantis Signs 'Don't Say Gay' Expansion and Gender-Affirming Care Ban." NBC News, May 17, 2023. www.nbcnews.com/nbc-out/out -politics-and-policy/desantis-signs-dont-say-gay-expansion-gender -affirming-care-ban-rcna84698.

Zane, Zachary. *Boyslut: A Memoir and Manifesto*. New York: Abrams, 2023.

ACKNOWLEDGMENTS

Thank you to my agent, Eric Smith, for always believing in me. Thank you to Shannon Kelly, Amber Morris, Carolyn Levin, and the whole Running Press team for understanding this work's importance and urgency. Thank you to my editor, Adrienne Crezo, who helped me navigate the absurd task of covering four thousand years of history (and its citations) with ease. A great thanks to Kindall Gant and Annette Wamsley for your extremely helpful insights and perspectives. My partner and my friends for supporting me throughout this process; I love you so much. And massive thanks to Marisol, Jex, Zach, and all my sources for trusting me. Perhaps most important, thank you to Loretta J. Ross, without whom we may not have reproductive justice; Madame Restell, the glamorous twentieth-century abortionist; and what the hex, I'll say it:

all the other witches who came before me whom they couldn't burn.

RESOURCES AND PLACES TO DONATE

Mention of specific organizations in this book does not imply endorsement by the author or publisher, nor does it imply that such organizations have endorsed the author or publisher.

Abortion Care Network: Two out of three abortions are obtained from independent clinics, yet a disproportionate number of these clinics have closed in the past decade. This organization supports these clinics, aiding their community and social media presence, while providing contraception and abortion education. Additionally, they work to counter harassment and anti-choice violence around clinics, ensuring dignified reproductive care for all.

Advocates for Youth: They champion contraceptives, racial justice, LGBTQ+ rights, sexual education, and more, focusing on adolescents and young adults. Their Abortion Out Loud campaign collaborates with educational institutions to aid young individuals needing contraception or abortion.

Afiya Center: Concentrating on the health-care needs of Black women, this group addresses areas from abortion access to HIV programming and reproductive justice.

American Civil Liberties Union: The ACLU is a leading civil rights organization in the United States, advocating for liberties and safety regardless of party affiliation. They're currently litigating in key states and lobbying nationwide for reproductive justice.

Bold Futures: Based in New Mexico, this women-of-color-led organization focuses on policy changes and community organizing around reproductive health, particularly for Black, Indigenous, and Latina women.

Gender Justice: Located in Minnesota, they strive to ensure reproductive health-care access for trans people and challenge transphobia.

Holler Health Justice: As West Virginia's premier nonprofit, they offer financial and practical abortion support, catering especially to at-risk populations.

National Black Women's Reproductive Agenda: They aid Black women, who face heightened poverty and wage disparities in the United States, in accessing abortion and reproductive care, in addition to lobbying, community outreach, and reproductive rights education.

National Council of Jewish Women: This organization works on various initiatives such as expanding US abortion access, aiding Ukrainian refugees, and combating human trafficking. In the arena of reproductive access, they've led protests, lobbied for reproductive equality—including backing the Black Maternal Health Momnibus Act—and engaged with political leaders to guarantee abortion access for all women, irrespective of income, religion, and race.

National Latina Institute for Reproductive Justice: Addressing the unique challenges facing people of color and immigrants, especially in border states like Texas, they educate Latinx communities about abortion access and reproductive justice.

New Voices for Reproductive Justice: Serving areas in Pennsylvania and Ohio, they are dedicated to advancing reproductive justice for Black communities, with an all-encompassing approach to health.

Planned Parenthood: With more than a century of history, they stand as the United States' largest provider of reproductive health services, including birth control and abortion.

SisterSong: The SisterSong Women of Color Reproductive Justice Collective, also known as SisterSong, is a national activist organization dedicated to reproductive justice for women of color.

Texas Equal Access Fund (TEA Fund): Reacting to Texas's restrictive abortion laws, this fund aids those seeking abortions outside the state, with a particular emphasis on assisting marginalized communities.

INDEX